A HISTORY OF MODERN BURMA

Burma has lived under military rule for nearly half a century. The results of its 1990 elections were never recognized by the ruling junta and Aung San Suu Kyi, leader of Burma's pro-democracy movement, was denied her victory. She has been under house-arrest ever since. Now increasingly an economic satellite and political dependent of the People's Republic of China, Burma is at a crossroads. Will it become another North Korea, will it succumb to China's political embrace or will the people prevail? Michael Charney's book – the first general history of modern Burma in over five decades – traces the highs and lows of Burma's history from its colonial past to the devastation of Cyclone Nargis in 2008. By exploring key themes such as the political division between lowland and highland Burma, monastic opposition to state control, the chronic failure to foster economic prosperity, and the ways in which the military has exerted its control over the country, the author explains the forces that have made the country what it is today.

MICHAEL W. CHARNEY is Senior Lecturer in the Department of History, School of Oriental and African Studies, University of London. His previous publications include *Powerful Learning: Buddhist Literati and the Throne in Burma's Last Dynasty, 1752–1885* (2006) and *Southeast Asian Warfare, 1300–1900* (2004).

A HISTORY OF MODERN BURMA

MICHAEL W. CHARNEY

School of Oriental and African Studies, University of London

CAMBRIDGE
UNIVERSITY PRESS

CAMBRIDGE UNIVERSITY PRESS
Cambridge, New York, Melbourne, Madrid, Cape Town, Singapore, São Paulo,
Delhi, Dubai, Tokyo, Mexico City

Cambridge University Press
The Edinburgh Building, Cambridge, CB2 8RU, UK

Published in the United States of America by Cambridge University Press, New York

www.cambridge.org
Information on this title: www.cambridge.org/9780521617581

First published 2009
Third printing 2010

Printed in the United Kingdom at the University Press, Cambridge

A catalogue record for this publication is available from the British Library

Library of Congress Cataloguing in Publication data
Charney, Michael W.
A history of modern Burma / Michael W. Charney.
p.   cm.
Includes bibliographical references and index.
ISBN 978-0-521-85211-1 (hardback) – ISBN 978-0-521-61758-1 (paperback)
1. Burma – Politics and government – 1948–   I. Title.
DS530.4.C45   2008
959.105 – dc22   2008037150

ISBN 978-0-521-85211-1 hardback
ISBN 978-0-521-61758-1 paperback

Contents

Figures

Maps

Chronology

1886	Upper Burma annexed by British
1886–1888	High point of pacification campaign in Upper Burma
1900	Gokteik Gorge Bridge completed
1906	Young Men's Buddhist Association founded
1910	Rangoon Police Amendment Act
1914–1918	World War I
1920	General Council of Buddhist (later Burmese) Associations founded; Rangoon Development Trust established; Universities Act; University boycott begins
1921	U Ottama imprisoned
1922	Whyte Committee visits Burma
1923	Diarchy established in Burma
1924	Ottama released from prison
1928–1929	Simon Commission visits Burma
1930	Impact of Great Depression hits Burma; outbreak of *Hsaya* San rebellion; Communal riots in Rangoon
1930–1931	First Indian Round Table Conference
1931	*Hsaya* San hung
1931–1932	Special Burma Round Table Conference
1935	Government of Burma Act
1936	Rangoon University Strike
1937	Burma gains limited self-government; separation from India; Ba Maw first Burmese Prime Minister
1938	Oilfield workers' strike
1939	World War II breaks out in Europe; U Pu becomes Prime Minister; Burma Freedom Bloc established
1940	Colonial arrests of Thakin leaders; Aung San goes to Japan; U Saw becomes Prime Minister
1941	World War II breaks out in Asia; Saw arrested
1942	Japanese armies occupy Burma

1943	Ba Maw regime granted independence by the Japanese
1944	The Anti-Fascist People's Freedom League established
1945	Burmese rebellion against Japanese; Japan defeated; end of World War II; British Military Administration; First Executive Council
1946	Labour forms government in Britain
1947	Second Executive Council; Panglong Conference; national elections; Aung San assassinated
1948	Burma becomes independent; U Nu is first Prime Minister
1949	Civil War breaks out; Guomindang in Shan State
1954	Burma rejects membership in South East Asia Treaty Organization; Sixth Great Buddhist Council held
1956	Second national elections since independence; U Ba Swe becomes Prime Minister
1958	AFPFL "split"
1958–1960	Caretaker Government
1960	Nu returns as Prime Minister
1961	Buddhism made the state religion
1962	Military coup; Revolutionary Council established under Ne Win
1963	Eradication of the private press begins; management of economy changes from Brigadier Aung Gyi to Brigadier Tin Pe
1964	Monastic riots; nationalization of private businesses
1965	Renewed monastic disturbances
1966–1967	Key civilian political leaders released from detention
1968	Internal Unity Advisory Board established
1969	Nu establishes the Parliamentary Democracy Party
1970	The United National Liberation Front established
1971	First BSPP Congress
1972	UNLF invasion
1973	Nu expelled from Thailand
1974	Burma's second Constitution; nominal civilian rule under BSPP; labour strikes; U Thant riots
1976	Military Coup plot foiled; World Bank Aid Consortium for Burma established
1977	Purge of BSPP leadership
1978	General election
1981	Ne Win formally steps down as President of the Union

1983	North Korean agents kill South Korean cabinet members visiting Rangoon
1987	Sale of land or businesses to foreigners banned; UN gives Burma Least Developed Country status; demonetization decree causes widespread hardship
1988	Popular revolution; Ne Win resigns from BSPP; fall of BSPP government; the State Law and Order Restoration Council seizes power under General Saw Maung; National League for Democracy established
1989	Communist Party of Burma dissolves
1990	National elections; National League for Democracy victory; results ignored by SLORC
1991	Aung San Suu Kyi awarded the Sakharov Prize for Human Rights and the Nobel Peace Prize
1992	Convening Commission for the National Convention established; Than Shwe replaces Saw Maung as SLORC Chairman
1993	Union Solidarity and Development Association established
1993–1995	Ceasefire negotiations with ethnic rebels
1997	SLORC replaced by the State Peace and Development Council; US sanctions declared by Clinton administration
2000	Improvement in Myanmar–Indian relations; state exerts control over Internet access
2002	Ne Win family arrested; Myanmar Consortium on HIV/AIDS established
2003	Dipeyin incident
2004	Purge of Khin Nyunt and associates
2005	Capital begins to shift from Rangoon to Naypyidaw Myodaw
2007	Monk-led demonstrations in Rangoon (Yangon) and other cities, suppressed by the Burmese security forces
2008	Constitutional referendum; Cyclone Nargis

Abbreviations

ABPO	All-Burma Peasants' Organization
ABSDF	All Burma Students' Democratic Front
AFPFL	Anti-Fascist People's Freedom League
APCLGB	Abstract of the Proceedings of the Council of the Lieutenant-Governor of Burma
ASEAN	Association of Southeast Asian Nations
BBAQB	*Burma British Association Quarterly Bulletin*
BBC	British Broadcasting Corporation
BBCN	BBC News
BBCSWB	BBC Summary of World Broadcasts
BCP	Burma Communist Party (the White Flags)
BDA	Burma Defence Army
BEDC	Burma Economic Development Corporation
BIA	Burma Independence Army
BNA	Burma National Army
BSC	Buddha Sasana Council
BSSO	Buddha Sasana Sangha Organisation
BSPP	Burma Socialist Program Party
BWB	*Burma Weekly Bulletin*
BWPP	Burma Workers' and Peasants' Party
CASB	Civil Affairs Service (Burma)
CCEI	Committee to Combat Economic Insurgency
CIA	Central Intelligence Agency
CPB	Communist Party of Burma (the Red Flags)
CSB	Civil Supplies Board
DSI	Defence Services' Institute
DVB	Democratic Voice of Burma News
FEER	*Far Eastern Economic Review*
FT	*Financial Times*
GCBA	General Council of Burmese/Buddhist Associations

GEACPS	Greater East Asia Co-Prosperity Sphere
GMD	Guomindang
GMR	*Guardian* magazine (Rangoon)
GNP	Gross National Product
GNR	*Guardian* newspaper (Rangoon)
GUK	*Guardian* (United Kingdom)
IBMND	Intelligence Bureau of the Ministry of National Defence
ICS	Indian Civil Service
IHT	*International Herald Tribune*
ISI	Import Substitution Industrialization
IUAB	Internal Unity Advisory Board
JMA	Japanese Military Administration
JVC	joint venture corporation(s)
KIO	Kachin Independence Organization
KKY	Ka Kwe Ye
KNDO	Karen National Defence Organization
KNLA	Karen National Liberation Army
KNU	Karen National Union
LAD	*The Legislative Assembly Debates*
LDP	League for Democracy and Peace
LORC	Law and Order Restoration Council(s)
MIS	Military Intelligence Service
MNDO	Mon National Defence Organization
MP	Member of Parliament
MPT	Myanmar Post and Telecommunications
MTA	Mong Tai Army
NAB	*News Agency Burma*
NBW	*New Burma Weekly*
NDF	National Democratic Front
NGO	Non-Governmental Organization
NLD	National League for Democracy
NSA	National Solidarity Association(s)
NUF	National United Front
NUP	National Unity Party
NYT	*New York Times*
PBLC	*Proceedings*, Burma Legislative Council
PDC	Parliament, House of Commons, *Debates*
PDP	Parliamentary Democracy Party
PRC	People's Republic of China
PVO	People's Volunteer Organization

PWG	*People's Workers' Gazette*
RASU	Rangoon Arts and Sciences University
RDT	Rangoon Development Trust
RHS	Rangoon Home Service
RIT	Rangoon Institute of Technology
RU	Rangoon University
RUSU	Rangoon University Students Union
SAC	Security and Administrative Committee
SLORC	State Law and Order Restoration Council
SPDC	State Peace and Development Council
SUA	Shan United Army
UN	United Nations
UNICEF	United Nations Children's Fund
UNLF	United National Liberation Front
US	United States
USAID	United States Agency for International Development
USDA	Union Solidarity and Development Association
VOA	Voice of America
VOM	Voice of Myanmar
VOPB	Voice of the People of Burma
YMBA	Young Men's Buddhist Association

Introduction

This book examines approximately 122 years of Burmese history, from the annexation of Upper Burma by the British at the beginning of January 1886 until the devastation of Cyclone Nargis in 2008. The main reason for writing this book has been to provide the story of modern Burma as the country moved from the era of high colonialism, through the Japanese occupation and the Cold War, to the present. Although it is sometimes claimed that there is a paucity of research on the country, a view no doubt strengthened by very real limitations placed by the current government on access to government archives and even to everyday Burmese people, in reality both Burmese and foreign scholars have persevered. The body of specialized work on the country is huge, diverse, and valuable. Perhaps because of the enormity of the task of bringing this research together, few general histories of modern Burma have emerged since the works of John F. Cady and D. G. E. Hall half a century ago. Thus there is a need for a general history encompassing the colonial and postcolonial periods. Despite government censorship and political suppression, international interest in the country, awakened mainly by the events of 1988, 1990, and 2007 and fed by the work of indefatigable political activists, NGOs, foreign governments, and Burmese political organizations inside and outside the country, has not diminished. This book has been written to provide a general view of the country's experiences, often relating events as they unfolded, for both the nonspecialist audience and for undergraduates who might find the specialized literature too inaccessible to develop what in popular parlance is referred to as "the big picture."

The present history is divided into chapters according to the major phases of the modern Burmese experience. While colonial rule in Burma did not begin in 1886, this year marked the beginning of what is generally understood as "colonial Burma," when the major institutions of colonial rule were in place. Stepping back any further would necessitate a lengthy diversion into the politics, economy, and society of the Konbaung Dynasty, Burma's last, and its competition with the areas of Burma under British rule that would eventually be welded together into British Burma. This would have expanded the volume to an unwieldy size, and in any case this period has already been more than satisfactorily covered by other histories, some of them very recent. Instead, the first two chapters of the present history focus on the 1886–1937 period, when Burma was a part of British India, a colonial possession within a colonial possession and when Burmese were not only under the British, but also at the bottom of a social hierarchy headed by Europeans and a range of Asian immigrant minorities. During this period, liberation meant not only separation from London but also separation from India. The division of this period into two chapters is intended to address the unique position of Rangoon (present-day Yangon) in the colony both as a foreign city on Burmese soil and in terms of its central position in the narrative of Burmese anti-colonialism and early nationalism. By contrast with the wealth, large colonial buildings, and feisty "big city" politicians of Rangoon, rural Burma was another world, closer to fields, the monastic order, and to Burmese Buddhist traditions. The third chapter, covering the period from 1937 to 1947, was perhaps the most volatile and certainly one with the most serious ramifications for the future political history of the country. Although not completely independent, Burmese were subject to two different kinds of limited self-rule, one British and one Japanese, that attempted to mask very real foreign control. This period might also justifiably be called the "era of Aung San," for it saw this student leader rise to head an army and then a nation, before he fell to an assassin's bullet shortly before Burma achieved true independence. His death, as much as his life, would remain the focal point of Burmese understandings of the birth of their nation.

The four decades between 1948 and 1988 have been divided into four chapters according to the different regimes that held sway over the country. The main reason for doing so is not to provide an essentially political history, but in recognition of the fact that a succession of different social, economic, and cultural policies accompanied political change, often influenced to a degree by the changing international context or the direction in the tide of a civil war that figured prominently in the concerns of most Burmese. Chapter 4 examines the first democratic period, from 1948 until 1958, which saw a regime fight desperately to preserve itself from powerful political and ethnic insurgencies, in the face of the threat of a spillover of the Cold War across its borders, plagued as well by political infighting and the challenges of erecting a socialist system in the country.

The consequences, explored in Chapter 5, were the establishment of a military caretaker regime (1958–1960), its more Western-oriented economic policies, and its succession by a new democratic government that compromised on such issues as the separation of church and state and rejected the economic reforms only recently introduced. From 1962 until 1988 Ne Win dominated Burma, in two essentially separate but not easily delineated periods. Chapter 6 examines the first, the military government of the Revolutionary Council, which sought to build a new Burma from scratch eschewing democratic principles and civil liberties in favor of fostering tight national unity. One of Ne Win's underlings, Tin Pe, helped pave the way to economic disaster as he sponsored a Marxist reworking of the economy. A new ideology, intended to give the Revolutionary Council "revolutionary" credentials, provided justification for political, intellectual, and social suppression. This period established the foundations for the Burma Socialist Program Party (BSPP) government years, discussed in Chapter 7, when new constitutional arrangements gave an apparently civilian face to what remained essentially a one-man dictatorship. Nonetheless, Burma's economic problems increased and by the end of the BSPP years, Burma had become one of the least developed of third world nations.

The period from 1988 to the present is divided into two chapters. Revolutionary Council and BSPP rule led to a popular revolution in 1988 and national elections in 1990, this volatile two-year period being the subject of Chapter 8. Dire economic performance, political and intellectual suppression, and outright atrocities against Burmese students and others led to mass protests and violent confrontations with Burmese soldiers and police. Under the weight of domestic opposition and a crumbling economy, Ne Win had run out of ideas and his regime folded. The popular revolution brought to the fore of Burmese politics new leaders, especially Aung San Suu Kyi, and even returned some from a previous era, like U Nu. This revolution was not just about "bread and butter" issues, but also about the desire for genuine recognition of the principles of Burmese nationalism voiced since the days of anti-colonialism, especially for a return of representative, elected government and the return of civil liberties. In a bid to prevent the erosion of their power, the military, influenced or controlled by Ne Win behind the scenes, seized power to buy time to erode popular opposition. Although Aung San Suu Kyi's political party, the National League for Democracy (NLD), won an overwhelming electoral victory in 1990, the regime stepped back from its promises and refused to transfer power. Chapter 9 examines the two decades that followed. In what might best be referred to as the "politics of delay," the military regime, referring to itself at first as the State Law and Order Restoration Council (SLORC) and then the State Peace and Development Council (SPDC) spent these years attempting to intimidate, remove, and otherwise erode popular support for the NLD. It has simultaneously engaged in a circular series of face changes and constitutional steps apparently designed to prolong its hold on power rather than to make meaningful progress. When and how this period will end remains unpredictable, although the "Saffron Revolution," in which monks led mass protests against the regime in September 2007, has made it clear that popular hopes for freedom and democracy have not diminished since the Burmese took to the streets in 1988.

While this book is structured according to periods of Burmese history, certain themes transcending these phases dominate its coverage. These include the struggle between civilian politicians bent on representative, democratic rule and those favoring authoritarian rule over the country, whether in the form of British colonialists or indigenous military officers; the political division of the country between essentially lowland Burma and highland Burma, both during the colonial period and the civil war; monastic opposition to state supervision and control; the attempts by Burma's political leaders, both civilian and military, to separate domestic politics from foreign influence, and the chronic failure to foster economic prosperity. These themes will be brought together in the Conclusion, which will focus on the "rhythm" of modern Burmese history.

CHAPTER I

Burma under colonial rule

A century and a quarter ago, the British annexed the last vestiges of the kingdom of Burma, what had once been mainland Southeast Asia's greatest empire. Burma was carved up by the British in three Anglo-Burmese wars (1824–1826, 1852–1853, and 1885) and for much of the nineteenth century there were two competing Burmas, a shrinking independent state in the north and an expanding colonial entity in the south. While a desperate Burmese court raced to introduce administrative reforms and to modernize with the latest Western technologies, court politics and a poorly developed economy ensured its ultimate defeat.

Colonial rule created much of the "Burma" seen by the outside world today. The extension of the Great Trigonometrical Survey of India into Burma in the late nineteenth century defined Burma's political geography and recorded its topography. Western writers associated in one way or another with the colonial state produced representations of Burmese culture, how Burmese thought, and how they behaved, that have shaped contemporary understandings. It could be suggested that perhaps more foreigners over the years have read George Orwell's *Burmese Days* than any other single publication about the country. D. A. Ahuja who ran a photographic studio in Rangoon in the first quarter of the twentieth century produced by far the most popular series of postcards of Burma, amounting to over 800 "scenes" of Burmese pagodas, architecture, and people. Mailed out to locations throughout the British Empire, the English-speaking world was provided with snapshots of what "typical" Shan, Burman, Kachin, Mon, Karen, and other peoples looked like and how they dressed.

The foreign imagining of Burma had little to do with how Burmese viewed their own country – that is, how Burma was viewed from the inside. For the most part, indigenous chronicles and literature, the local monastery or spirit shrine, the general continuity of precolonial material culture, and a range of other survivors of the British annexation continued to shape daily life and perspectives on the vast rural landscape well into the twentieth century. The most serious challenges to the continuity of precolonial social and cultural life would occur in the colonial capital at Rangoon, as we shall see in the following chapter. Nonetheless, important changes did occur for rural Burmese with the arrival of colonial rule and these involved mainly administrative and economic transformations.

RURAL ECONOMIC CHANGE

Colonial rule disrupted traditional reciprocal relationships between the landed gentry and the peasants. The basic unit of administration and realm of social life throughout rural Burma was the village. While the precolonial state had exercised tighter administrative control over the country than any of its predecessors, it had touched upon village life only lightly and indirectly. The village headman acted not only as an agent of the state or of the revenue-grantee, but also as a representative or protector of the village community. When harvests were bad, he could work through a chain of patron–client ties to soften the revenue demands for that year. The village headman was responsible for supplying the necessities for village festivals and a range of other communal needs. In return, villagers provided a pool of labor for working his land or for supporting him at times of conflict, whether in cases of contributing men to local contingents required by the throne for war or for more personal conflicts with other powerful men in the local landscape.[1]

Economic change connected to the political reconfiguration of Burma from the mid nineteenth century encouraged the initial breakdown of the rural society. The piecemeal annexation of Burma by the British and the economic reforms in Upper Burma together changed the face of rural society in Burma. The eventual emergence of a large rice-exporting economy in Lower Burma after the mid-1850s led to a 600 percent increase in acreage under cultivation in Lower Burma between 1860 and the end of the 1920s, with most of this growth occurring between 1870 and 1910. Moreover, cultivation was intense, leading to a twenty-three-fold increase in the volume of rice cultivated over the course of the same period. The growth of the rice export economy in the south encouraged a massive migration of cultivators from the north into the delta, attracted by growing prosperity. Because of Lower Burma's sparse settlement, there was a yet unexploited rice frontier in the south that could be opened up for rice cultivation by northern settlers. Over the course of the next few decades tens of thousands of villagers packed up their possessions and with their draft animals in tow resettled in the delta.[2]

SUBMISSION TO THE COLONIAL STATE

For those Burmese who moved south between the 1850s and 1880s and for Burmese who came under British rule after 1885, life under colonial rule meant the loss of the headman as an important mediating buffer between themselves and the state. An even more unfortunate development was the colonial Village Act. Under its terms, all Burmese, except for Buddhist monks, had to *shikho* (a salutation reserved for important elders, monks, and the Buddha) British officers, as a demonstration of their recognition of submission to British mastery. Villagers were required to erect thorn walls around their villages and serve rounds as nightwatchmen. Villagers were also required to provide inter-village transport, as well as food and firewood, on the appearance of colonial military or civil officers. More importantly, the village headman was now an appointee of the government and was transformed into an agent who relied solely on the state for his status, income, and property rights and now owed his responsibilities to the colonial state alone. Villagers were required to attend upon the village headman upon the beat of his gong and to perform whatever service he demanded or be punished with twenty-four hours in stocks. With the end of the protective buffer of the village headman, the rural population also became more vulnerable in times of poor harvests and revenue demands were now marked by their regularity and uniformity rather than their flexibility in response to local and temporary conditions. Moreover, villagers suspected of theft could be imprisoned for a year without trial.[3]

The colonial authorities expected that they would receive the same obedience from the Burmese as the indigenous court had enjoyed and urged them to retain their "natural traits" of obedience to authority. When Lord Curzon, Viceroy of India, visited Mandalay in 1901, he held an audience for chiefs from the southern Shan states, the chief notables of Upper Burma, and other "native gentlemen of Burma." He did so in the West Throne-room of the former royal palace, seemingly presenting himself in the same position of authority as the old indigenous rulers of the kingdom. After speaking to the Shan chiefs, the first time a Viceroy of India had done so, he turned to the Burman attendees and explained to them (in English, which was then translated into Burmese) that

the British . . . do not . . . wish that the people should lose the characteristics and traditions . . . of their own race . . . The Burmans were celebrated in former times for their sense of respect – respect for parents, respect for elders, respect for teachers, respect for those in authority. No society can exist in a healthy state without reverence. It is the becoming tribute paid by an inferior to a superior . . . The most loyal subject of the King-Emperor in Burma, the Burman whom I would most like to honour, is not the cleverest mimic of a European, but the man who is truest to all that is most simple, most dutiful, and of best repute in the instincts and the customs of an ancient and attractive people.[4]

Colonial authority was backed by the broad intrusion of foreign institutions and practices that regulated or interfered with rural life to a degree greater than any indigenous, central institution had attempted in the precolonial past. The degree to which paper now governed life was astounding. Relationships with local administrators, the resolution of gripes with one's neighbors, the establishment of land titles, the payment of taxes, and a range of other activities now required the completion of a myriad of forms, visits to township or district law courts, and submission to information-gathering by government clerks and investigators on a regular basis and everywhere, customary arrangements gave way to legal ones. Births and deaths now had to be officially registered locally.

The colonial state, through a series of censuses taken in 1872, 1881, and every tenth year thereafter until 1931 demanded information on every aspect of people's lives, from their occupation to their religion, and about every member of the household. The collection of census data was problematic. In many spheres of Burmese life, identities and identifications that were fluid, syncretic, multiple, or even undefined were common. Whether in terms of religion, ethnicity, or culture, it was not unusual for an individual or a group to change their self-identifications in different contexts. "Karens," or rather, "Kayins," for example, might be freely used by writers and others; these terms were vague and masked significant diversity. Colonial administrators and writers differed in their approach as they brought an understanding developed in the West that national, racial, and other identifications had to be essentialized so that they could be incorporated into classificatory schemes for people, following the same approach adopted for the classification of animals and plants. Thus, as one scholar notes, and despite the substantial cultural, linguistic, and religious differences among Karen groups, a Karen identification based on the practices of only one group, that of the Christianized Sgaw Karen, was applied to the Karen in general, in large part because this community had more records than others and because they had been the main subject of missionary reports.[5] These generalizations would remain current in scholarship well into the twentieth century, with Karens often being referred to as Christians, and many would be surprised when, in the 1990s, Buddhist Karen rebelled against their Baptist leadership.

In keeping with European practices, the colonial census required Burmese to give single, unqualified answers as to their affiliation with a pre-scribed set of exclusive ethnic categories. Although the Burmese language had generally become the main medium of daily intercourse throughout the Irrawaddy Valley, many who, to foreigners, appeared to be Burmese, dressed like Burmese, and spoke Burmese, would not, in fact, have consid-ered themselves to be Burmese. Likewise, precolonial Burman migration into the Lower Delta was especially intense in the last half of the eigh-teenth century and there was significant intermarriage between different ethnic groups, so that individuals who could claim ancestry from among the Mon, the Burmans, the Karens, and numerous other ethnic groups were very common in the delta. Given these two situations, one in which non-Burmese might be confused as being Burmese and another in which an individual could claim multiple ethnic origins, problems necessarily ensued when census-takers sometimes asked headmen or others to inform them about the ethnic identity of people in the area or required that inter-viewees tell them exactly which particular ethnic group they belonged to. Census data collected on religion, ethnicity, language, and a range of other identifications thus presented an artificially rigid, and largely incorrect, picture of rural society and its components.[6]

Especially resented by rural Burmese was the required submission to the colonial medical establishment, particularly when it came to epidemic diseases such as smallpox. The practice of inoculation was common in rural Burma from the late eighteenth century and by the colonial period had emerged as the method of choice in preventing smallpox. Colonial medical authorities, largely dismissing indigenous medicine as quackery, preferred to impose on Burmese society a visually very similar but fundamentally dif-ferent procedure: vaccination. The actual differences between inoculation and vaccination are largely irrelevant to the present discussion, as regardless of vaccination's eventually demonstrated advantages, the indigenous popu-lation preferred to be treated by indigenous inoculators by accepted means rather than submit to foreigners applying an equally foreign method. In the 1920s, the colonial medical establishment, stymied by the continued popularity of inoculators, turned to legislation as a means of enforcing vaccination. In the absence of significant efforts to persuade them on an intellectual basis of the advantages of vaccination, the Burmese were faced with fines and imprisonment by colonial authorities that preferred to force submission. Not surprisingly, when rural Burmese set up organizations to fight colonial courts and agents, as well as moneylenders, in the 1920s, these organizations also interfered with the work of colonial vaccinators.[7]

PEASANT CULTIVATORS

Although colonial rule alienated some segments of the population and introduced – by some accounts – over-intrusive regulation, it also presented economic opportunity. The main concern of colonial authorities was how to produce enough revenue to pay for the costs of administration. Ultimately this meant developing a large rural class of cultivator-owners. This was achieved with some degree of success in the early twentieth century. Participation in the rice-exporting economy provided cash incomes that could be used to pay land taxes and purchase the necessities of life, and even then many of the otherwise most costly requirements, such as building materials for homes, and fish and vegetables to supplement a diet of rice, were readily acquired from the local environment at little or no cost. Cash also provided opportunities to purchase a few luxuries, either products of indigenous cottage industries or even Western goods. On the other hand, the rigidity of the colonial taxation system, which rarely afforded relief during bad harvests, and dependence upon a single crop in the context of fluctuating world markets meant that a cultivator's economic situation could change dramatically from one year to the next. Moreover, the costs of opening up land and maintaining cultivation of a surplus for export, beyond personal subsistence, were high. To meet these demands, Burmese cultivators (see Fig. 1.1) increasingly found themselves turning to moneylenders.

LAND ALIENATION

From the 1890s on, rural agricultural land was gradually alienated to moneylenders. This problem is sometimes attributed to the nefarious practices of the Indian Chettyars. The Chettyars were a moneylending caste indigenous to Chettinad in the Madras Presidency. Although their business dealings in the colonial period extended throughout much of Southeast Asia as well as in Sri Lanka, their main area of interest was Burma. Their presence was uneven, however; in some districts they maintained a small presence, while in a few others, such as Hanthawaddy and Tharrawaddy, they were the overwhelming source of loans for Burmese agriculturalists. The Chettyars operated through widely cast family networks that could channel capital easily between India and Burma. These networks were geared toward taking reasonable risks in moneylending and hence loaned out money at low rates of interest to cultivators who appeared capable of paying the money back. The goal was to use the profits from moneylending

Figure 1.1 Burmese village scene today

in Burma to build up further capital for financial reinvestment or to purchase land in India, and if land was acquired in Burma it was mainly to
avoid or prevent the complete loss of return on a bad loan. The Chettyars
were not the only foreign moneylenders, for other Indians and Chinese
were also involved, though not to anything like the same extent as the
Chettyars. In terms of land alienation, however, the most significant cul-
prits prior to the Great Depression were Burmese moneylenders. They
more commonly made risky loans and charged higher rates of interest.
Although their main purpose was also not to foreclose, they frequently
acquired land in default of repayment of a loan because the loans made
had been so risky in the first place.[8]

The colonial authorities were slow to respond, but from 1900 to 1930
two solutions were put forward to resolve the problem of land alienation.
The first sought to curb the practice through legislation on the grounds
that the Burmese were incapable of exercising self-control in the economic
arena. The second – which advocated cooperation rather than compulsion –
recommended educating the Burmese in the ways and means of combating
land alienation. In the end, regardless of these efforts, and largely as a
consequence of the Great Depression, more and more land was handed

over to the moneylenders, even though the the latter would have preferred the repayment of their loans.[9]

In the early 1920s, village associations emerged in response to a diverse range of interests. The conventional view is that these organizations were prompted by encouragement from the General Council of Burmese Associations (GCBA) to promote rural-based nationalist agitation. Many organized or joined other rural associations, however, to resolve serious rural economic or legal problems, especially colonial tax demands and exploitation by moneylenders. In an effort to empower the rural population, the village associations also sought to appropriate for themselves the authority claimed by colonial law courts and local government officers. In some villages, associations formed their own "courts" and encouraged the population to resort to them rather than to colonial judicial authorities. Such village courts, headed by indigenous "judges," handled the full range of peasant disputes, assigned penalties, and ordered the payment of damages.

The village associations also opposed the local agents of the colonial regime, the village headman and his close relations, as well as moneylenders. Although monks also cooperated with these associations in social sanctions and were frequently portrayed as the instigators of this activity, it was sometimes the case that local associations merely made use of the moral authority of the monk to legitimize their actions. In one case, an eighty-year-old monk was made the chair of a village association meeting at which a social boycott of an offending villager was decided. Although the monk "seemed to be deaf, inactive and not much interested in what the meeting resolved," he was put on trial for the offense.[10]

From the beginning, village associations encouraged the general population to boycott foreign goods and to revert to traditional, indigenous ways. They urged Burmese not to buy imported British textiles but to rely instead on homespun, and home-products exhibitions were set up at conferences to encourage home industry. Burmese cheroots were to be smoked instead of Virginia cigarettes, the population was discouraged from using Burma Oil Company candles to light Buddhist shrines, no one was to wear coats, boots, or shoes exceeding the value of twenty rupees, and the hair was to be worn long as in precolonial times. In keeping with Buddhist scriptures, the eating of meat, the drinking of alcohol, and the taking of opium were all proscribed. The village associations were able to enforce the boycott of colonial taxation and the purchase of foreign goods by applying social pressure. Villagers who collaborated with the government or the moneylenders, for example, faced social ostracism, the stoning of their homes, denial of help in planting, being banned from employment, the maiming of their cattle, destruction of their crops, and even death. Further, although both Burmese and Chettyar moneylenders were targeted, Chettyars were especially despised for being foreign.[11]

Rather than deal with the economic roots of the problem, the colonial regime focussed its criticism on the village associations. In a speech in October 1924, Governor Sir Spencer Harcourt Butler accused an unnamed central organization of encouraging village associations to resist colonial decrees, thereby undermining governmental authority. The village associations, he argued, prevented free speech and actions and thus he promised the government would use all available powers to suppress them. Citing examples of intimidation, including two murders, the government accused the organizers of attempting to establish "a kind of reign of terror." It then strengthened the police force and declared a number of important Burmese associations to be unlawful. Another tool utilized by the colonial state was the Anti-Boycott Act under the terms of which the village headman only needed to persuade one of the villagers to make a complaint in order to bring charges against the president or committee members of a particular village association. Additional instructions in reference to the Act provided for the public acknowledgement by offenders of the wrongs they had committed against the colonial regime and the propagation of the confessions of their guilt in order to avoid prosecution.[12]

THE *HSAYA* SAN REBELLION

Although the *hsaya* San rebellion that broke out in late 1930 is often seen as the first armed rebellion in rural Burma in the twentieth century, it had numerous predecessors, including a 1910 rebellion of petty cultivators at Sagaing, Shwebo, and Lower Chindwin Districts, the Mayoka uprising of 1913, and a miscarried rebellion in Tharrawaddy in early 1928.[13]

Hsaya (teacher) San, a one-time traditional medical practitioner, had been born into a rural family in independent Burma in 1879 and had published books urging the Burmese not to accept expensive Western medicine and to rely instead on Burmese traditional medicine, which was cheaper and more reliable. He traveled around rural Burma where he observed the poverty of Burmese cultivators in the colonial economy and joined the GCBA sometime after its foundation in 1920. At its annual conference in 1925 at Paungde, the congress of the GCBA turned to San as a literate peasant with a clear dislike of British rule to investigate the problems of Burma's rural population. San thus became the head of the enquiry commission whose purpose was to examine peasant complaints about the collection of taxes. From 1927 to 1928, San and the commission toured districts where clashes had reportedly occurred between peasants and government forces. The completed report related ill treatment of Burmese cultivators and disrespect for Buddhism. The report recommended that the capitation tax and the Thathameda tax be resisted and that forest laws which prevented peasants from collecting bamboo and timber should be opposed by nonviolent means. When the annual conference of the Soe Thein branch of the GCBA (which had by then divided into different organizations, many retaining the GCBA label) met in 1929, however, San was dismayed that no proposal was made to take action on his report. He made a motion in favor of organizing "People's Volunteers" to defy the colonial government, but was opposed by monks who argued that this amounted to sedition. This prompted yet another division in the organization and, on the grounds that the association was too weakened to be effective, San resigned, and planned an armed uprising.[14]

There is considerable controversy regarding the nature of the *hsaya* San rebellion and the timing of its outbreak. The controversy can be divided into two different, but intimately connected, issues. The first issue is the timing of the rebellion and the debate focusses on whether or not it was sparked by the Depression and the parlous economic circumstances of peasants unable to pay colonial taxes or, alternatively, whether the rebellion was a millenarian revolt and thus a response to the displacement by colonial rule of the traditional, precolonial moral order; or that it represented a transition into a new stage of rural anti-colonial politics, supported by new political networking.[15] These propositions are not mutually exclusive, for the underlying motives of or methods deployed by the rebellion's leader, San, and the reasons for his success in mobilizing large numbers of rural cultivators to rebel may have been very different. Moreover, a new discussion is emerging over the sources for understanding this rebellion. Conventional dependence upon colonial records frequently means that the participants in the rebellion, mostly illiterate peasants, have no voice. Some of the key documents regarding the rebellion, for example, have been shown to be dubious.[16]

Although some scholars have argued that the rebellion represented a millenarian revolt or the fruition of one man's political maneuvering through the village associations that dominated rural politics in the 1920s, it is difficult to deny that the outbreak was intimately connected with the effects of the World Depression that gradually hit Burma over the course of 1930. During that year, the price of rice paddy per 100 baskets dropped from

145 rupees in April to 94 rupees in December. Paddy sellers, frightened of fluctuating prices, disposed of their rice paddy stocks at lowered rates. Cultivators in Tharrawaddy District petitioned the government not to reduce taxes but rather to postpone their collection until May. On 22 December, the acting governor, Sir J. A. Maung Gyi, told Tharrawaddy residents that no delay could be granted because of the government's difficult financial position. The rebellion broke out later the same day.[17]

San's personal motivations or beliefs also seem irrelevant in explaining why so many Burmese responded to the call to revolt. Regardless of whether San was a manipulative politician or a sincere believer in Burmese traditional politics, for example, he mobilized peasants using a vocabulary and symbols that would be meaningful to rural Burmese. Reportedly, in early January 1930 San began organizing "galon" *athins*, secret societies, in rural villages in Upper Burma and on 18 January he went to Tharrawaddy to recruit a *galon* army. The *galon* was a mythical bird that kills *nagas* (snakes) and San characterized foreigners, especially the British, as *nagas*. The *galon* emblem would be tattooed on members of his army and they would be required to take an oath to the *galon athin*. At the end of November, San is reported to have claimed *minlaung* (a king to be) status with the title of Thapannakate Galuna Raja, while his wife became the chief queen and the *galon* army became the royal army. On 5 December, the foundation stone was laid at Alan Taung for the construction of his royal capital, naming it Buddha Raja. San now prepared for the forthcoming war with the British. Village blacksmiths made small arms and cannon, as well as swords and spears, which were stored in the royal armory; uniforms and war flags with the emblem of the *galon* defeating a *naga* were made for the army, and amulets and charms that would provide invulnerability (including immunity from bullets) were distributed.[18]

The rebellion began with an attack on government officials in Tharrawaddy district but soon spread to the other districts. William Louis Barretto, the Deputy Commissioner for Pyapon, was responsible for suppressing the rebellion once it reached Pyapon. A well-known Burmaphile who had written a play, in Burmese, on the Cooperative Movement, he was not inclined to inflict unnecessary casualties. When confronted with a rebel group, he ordered his men to first fire above their heads rather than to shoot to kill. Seeing that the guns had been discharged and yet no one was hurt, the rebels believed that they were immune to bullets; they then charged and many were killed. As a result of this incident, the Riots Manual was thoroughly revised. Despite their assumed immunity, the fighting went poorly for San's army after the British called in reinforcements from India and San's forces began to suffer from dysentery and fever during the 1931 rainy season. At the same time, bandits took advantage of the situation, also calling themselves *galon*, and under the pretence of being rebels, stole from the Burmese.[19]

San, disguised as a monk named U Nyana, had meanwhile abandoned his capital and had arrived in the Northern Shan State in early March 1931 to mobilize Shan peasants into another army. After organizing this army, he chose the site for his new royal capital and appointed new generals. By this time, however, the rebellion was dying out. San's soldiers were poorly armed to face British machine guns and government officials dispatched Buddhist monks to rural areas to urge peace and persuade peasants that the struggle was futile. In early August, San was captured and, over the course of the following year, colonial soldiers and police gradually suppressed the rebellion. However, their methods created long-term resentment among the Burmese, especially those in rural areas. In order to make an example of the rebels and warn others, photographs of their decapitated heads were posted at the main police stations throughout the country. As the police had mistreated villagers during the rebellion, local dislike of the British government and especially of the police lingered at least into the late 1930s.[20]

San's trial before a special tribunal arranged at Tharrawaddy provided a martyr for Burmese nationalism. Despite the efforts of his defense counsel, Dr. Ba Maw, to portray the rebellion as a riot, which was a lesser offense, San was sentenced to death and hanged in the Tharrawaddy jail on 28 November 1931. The main political impact of the *hsaya* San rebellion was that it helped to further encourage the nationalist movement and this process was aided substantially by the Burmese press, for various newspapers, including *The Sun* and *The New Light of Burma*, had published the news about the fighting between the *galons* and the British, sometimes exaggerated and biassed in favor of the rebels. The colonial government reacted with censorship and the imposition of substantial fines. San's trial also reaffirmed the nationalist credentials of Ba Maw who would eventually become the Prime Minister of Burma.[21]

CONCLUSION

The political and economic transformation of rural Burmese society began in the mid-nineteenth century well before the British arrived. Some might say that the problems associated with that transformation would also have occurred under indigenous rule, given late precolonial reforms, the emerging world market, and political centralization. Nevertheless, the economic opportunities that accompanied colonization had their downside.

First, of course, was the blight of foreign rule as well as the decision to rely on Indians and ethnic minorities in the administration and defense of the colony more than on the Burmans. The feelings of alienation and disenfranchisement in their own country that led to the rise of village associations in the 1920s and the mishandling of a rural situation that spawned the *hsaya* San rebellion were likewise poor choices for which the colonial administration was at fault. On the other hand, British rule also brought to rural Burma new economic opportunities, better transportation infrastructure, and some of the benefits of Western medicine, whether or not the Burmese appreciated the way in which the latter was introduced. The rural Burmese experience, both positive and negative, would connect with the urban experience, especially in the colonial center at Rangoon, to provide the context for the push for separation from India and limited self-rule from 1937, as well as the cooperation of some Burmese nationalists with the Japanese Imperial Army in 1942, as will be discussed in the next two chapters.

CHAPTER 2

The colonial center

Rangoon was not colonial Burma's only urban center, nor the only center for British settlement, administration, or commercial operations. Different centers had been important at earlier stages of colonial rule, such as Akyab and Moulmein, while Mandalay played a role in the north – though to a lesser degree – akin to that of Rangoon in the south. However, Rangoon was the most significant center for the colony as a whole as well as the colonial capital.

More importantly, Rangoon was a foreign city erected on Burmese soil. It was here, to the exclusion of anywhere else save for a few hill stations, that Burmese life was thoroughly pushed to one side. In its imposing architecture, its physical arrangement, its landscaped gardens, its focus on the harbor and maritime trade, the ethnic division of its population, and in many other ways, Rangoon was a mimeograph of dozens of port cities scattered throughout colonial South and Southeast Asia. A person only had to squint to be confused as to whether he or she was standing in Singapore, Penang, Calcutta, or elsewhere.

Colonial Rangoon became not so much a melting pot as a pressure cooker, where Burmese witnessed both the positive and, mostly, the negative consequences, direct and indirect, of the growing colonial economy and foreign rule. Rangoon clarified the social distinctions between the ruler and the ruled: the perception of all foreigners, European and Asian alike, as being economic exploiters; the sense of political disenfranchisement, and moral indignation regarding prostitution and other vices. In this context, Rangoon saw the emergence of new generations of Burmese leaders who pushed the colonial regime for political concessions and greater respect for Burmese traditional institutions and culture.

THE BIG CITY

Prior to the British acquisition of Rangoon in 1852 (they had briefly occupied the town from 1824 to 1826), Rangoon had experienced nearly a hundred years of indigenous rule since its establishment by King Alaungh-paya (r. 1752–1760) in 1755. European travel accounts during this long period typically begin with the arrival of a European mission at Rangoon, at the time known as Yangon, and the governor of Hanthawaddy, who ruled the town, was the first major Burmese official encountered by European visitors. Despite its importance to European visitors and its economic importance as Burma's preeminent maritime port, however, its scale and grandeur were far from those of the royal capital. The town had always been, by Burmese and European standards alike, a run-down port area, dominated by palm-leaf huts and timber shacks. Roads within the town were mere muddy tracks that were so formidable to pedestrian travel that planks had to be thrown over and around them to allow residents to walk without drowning in a mixture of mud, filth, and animal excrement. For many years after its colonial makeover in the 1850s, Rangoon remained a small town, quickly overtaking Akyab as the key exit point for rice exports, and, from 1862, became the administrative center for all of British Burma. The new Rangoon was completely different from its predecessor, for the British laid out their capital on a square grid pattern that replaced the haphazard layout of the old city.

Rangoon's modest proportions were rapidly transformed by new waves of merchants and laborers. Immigration took place on such a scale that it made Rangoon the world's leading port of entry for immigrants, topping even New York City.[1] One consequence of rapid population growth and a strong colonial economy was the rise of new buildings. During the building boom of the late 1880s and 1890s, wooden houses quickly gave way to masonry buildings in the downtown area (reinforced concrete structures were not introduced in Rangoon until 1911). The annexation of Upper Burma gradually brought more wealth into the colonial capital, but it also brought an expansion in the administration and thus new commercial and government buildings were constructed. Rangoon opened its new, grand town hall in November 1886, the Dufferin Hospital was opened in 1887, a new Secretariat building was constructed between 1890 and 1905, a new Government House was built between 1892 and 1895, and the Diamond Jubilee Hall was completed in December 1898. Rangoon as it would appear for the remainder of the colonial period was beginning to take its final form. While the colonial government and merchant areas of the capital were turning to masonry, colonial land policy was a deterrent to such a transformation in outlying areas of the town. The short-term leases granted to urban residents prevented any substantial investment in housing and thus residential areas remained flimsy, wooden structures. The town's

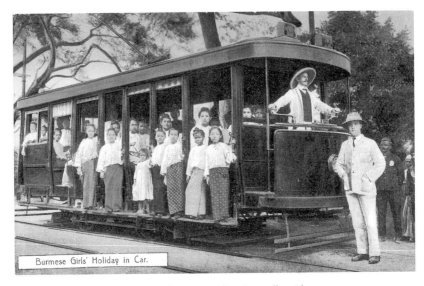

Figure 2.1 Burmese girls enjoy trolley ride

water supply was not extended to many of these areas, making sanitation a serious challenge.[2]

As Rangoon underwent its steady transformation from colonial outpost to modern metropolis, it adopted what at the time was state-of-the-art transportation technology. Until the 1880s, land transportation in Rangoon was limited to horse-drawn vehicles. In 1884 J. W. Darwood laid the lines for steam tramways in the city and built a depot where Bogyoke Aung San Market now stands, fifteen locomotives being put into service to carry passengers along the central business district. At the end of the nineteenth century, however, the streets were still lit by oil lamps and the tramlines had fallen into serious disrepair. From 1900 onward the Rangoon Municipality sought to reverse this situation by electrifying everything from transportation (see Fig. 2.1) to lighting. A power station was built at Ahlone on the Rangoon River in 1906, the steam trams were replaced with electric trams between 1906 and 1908, and electric street-lighting was extended around the city between 1907 and 1911.[3] It was very much a "city of light" that contrasted sharply with rural Burma, where such conveniences would remain unavailable, in many areas even to this day. Such disparities helped lend weight to emerging impressions that whatever prosperity the colonial order offered was not for the benefit of the Burmese.

Developments in urban transportation were mainly limited to the center of Rangoon, preventing the population from moving outwards and encouraging overcrowding. The introduction of the private automobile, which first appeared in Burma in 1905, followed by the motor bus in 1913, made an expansion of urban settlement possible. Alongside automobiles, horse-drawn vehicles continued in operation but became more of a nuisance because of the excessive use of powerful double-toned gongs, which became common by 1907. By 1915, Rangoon had 8 buses, 139 motorcycles, 28 taxicabs, and 426 private cars and lorries, operating on 183 miles of road. By 1936, trolley buses (electric buses running on tires rather than rails) began to replace Rangoon's electric trams, marking the last major transportation initiative in the municipality before the Japanese occupation.[4]

The expanding limits of settlement in Rangoon and the need to develop better roads for the growing number of motor vehicles went beyond the capabilities of the Reclamation Advisory Committee. Further, overpopulation in central Rangoon naturally raised the costs of housing. Two other factors propelled these costs to the extreme. First, in order to clear land for development, many poorer residents of Rangoon were evicted from their homes over the course of the first two decades of the twentieth century if they refused to accept the terms of the new ninety-nine-year leases.[5] Lacking resources to purchase new property many became renters. But land speculation accompanied development, driving up property prices and thus rents, and bringing misery to Rangoon renters. This was especially a problem during the land boom of 1903–1904, when many of Rangoon's largest government and commercial buildings were erected, such as the Chief Court buildings (see Fig. 2.2) and Messrs. Rowe & Company. Second, most could not afford motor transport, especially when buses were withdrawn from service in 1915.[6]

In 1920 the Municipal Government placed the Government Estate, the powers to develop this estate, and the authority to acquire land for development into the hands of the newly created Rangoon Development Trust (RDT). Over the course of the next two decades, the RDT would reclaim land to the east and west of the city center and build roads that encouraged the development of suburbs. The RDT's stated purpose was to eradicate swampy and unsanitary settlements and provide housing to Rangoon's poorer occupants. Its activities also included opening up new markets, such as Scott Market (today, the Bogyoke Aung San Market) in 1926. Nevertheless, the RDT's activities also remapped European settlement in the municipality, relocating the Agri-Horticultural Gardens and the Rangoon Turf Club. Several RDT projects substantially benefited Rangoon's wealthier

Chief Court · Burma.

Figure 2.2 The Chief Court Buildings under construction

inhabitants, as in the cases of the suburbs of Windermere Park and Golden Valley, two enclaves of Europeans and rich Chinese and Indian merchants. Burmese resentment at the loss of Burmese land to wealthy "foreigners" was spelled out in words and illustrated in cartoons in the vernacular press.[7]

IMMIGRANTS

According to the Census of August 1872, over two-thirds of Rangoon's population was Burmese. The Burmese proportion of Rangoon's population steadily shrank, however, and by 1937, of Rangoon's 400,000 residents, only 127,000 were Burmese. Thousands among the Burmese residents were more or less permanent immigrants from Upper Burma, while several thousand others were itinerant boatmen or seasonal laborers such as millhands. The "floating" population as a whole probably numbered as many as 20,000, as the reports of headmen, who did not include this population on their rolls, produced a total population for Rangoon of 77,777 in 1872, compared to a return of 98,745 by the official census for that year, which included everyone.[8]

The diverse origins of the immigration that consumed Rangoon produced a social and cultural milieu comparable to other British colonial port towns such as Singapore and Penang. Most of Rangoon's immigrants came from Southeastern India and Southeastern China, particularly the Hokkien and Guangdong. Straits Chinese and Europeans provided smaller, though important, increments to population growth. Chinese settlers entered Burma both from Yunnan in the northeast and through Rangoon and other ports in the south. The former often moved back and forth across the border in conjunction with the caravan trade, while the latter became more or less permanent residents, whether they intended to remain or not. The most significant Chinese population in Burma was to be found in Rangoon, numbering about 24,000 people in 1921. Indian immigrants included Chittagonians from Bengal, Ooriyas from Ganjam, Bihar, and Orissa, Tamils from the southern Madras Presidency, Telugus from the Coromandel Coast, and other groups, whether Hindu or Muslim, considered together by colonial authorities under the general heading of "Hindustani," mainly from the United Provinces of northern India. Although the Indian population was widely distributed geographically, mainly in Lower Burma, its concentration was in Rangoon, where it made up the majority of Rangoon's population (55 percent in 1921). Indeed, before World War II, the majority of Rangoon's population came from South Asia (the modern independent countries of Bangladesh, India, and Pakistan, with smaller contributions from Nepal and Sri Lanka).[9]

Being considered by the colonial administration as too backward for equal treatment with the Indians, as well as too lazy to compete with them for manual labor, and too inept to compete commercially with the Chinese, Burmese easily associated their complaints against colonial rule with the Asian immigrant communities. J. S. Furnivall, who would later develop the idea of plural society, found when he arrived in Rangoon in 1908 a city focussed on profit only and uninterested in the welfare of Burma generally. As he observed in one letter:

the only link between all these individuals of different nationalities has been the lust of acquisition, immediate and personal profit has been the aim of almost every one of them, a crowd of greedy folk recognizing no duty to the country where they have been striving to make their fortunes, no common principle to which they owe allegiance but the single principle of making money. There has not even been the check of complying with the traditions of the country; those of the Burmans are of no account, and the impersonal rule of an official hierarchy has no effectual tradition save that of leaving things alone . . . and the Burman who would talk with the European in the Rangoon streets must speak in Hindustani.[10]

Burmese feelings of exclusion were bolstered by immigrant dominance in commerce, industry, and administration. Hindustani, for example, emerged as the lingua franca of the colonial capital and Europeans in government (and often even commercial) service were required to pass exams in this language and not Burmese. As colonial Burma was administered as part of British India until 1937 and many of those British companies that dominated commercial life in Rangoon had already emerged within the Indian context, Indians found it easier than Burmese to dominate middle and lower echelon commercial and government positions. Brahmin Hindus, for example, monopolized the cash departments of British companies in the city. Other immigrant groups were able to bring skills learned at home to monopolize particular occupational niches. Thus, Ooriyas living in Rangoon worked mainly on the docks or on the railways; Tamils who did not venture into the countryside to become field laborers worked the Rangoon rice mills or became government or commercial clerks; Chittagonians worked on the river boats, including the big river steamers of the Irrawaddy Flotilla Company, and Telugus provided muscle for factories, mills, and transport.[11] Among Chinese immigrants, people from Guangdong Province dominated the construction industry and the Hokkien dialect group from Fujian Province dominated gold selling and other trades. Above everyone sat the European population of the city.

The Burmese who attempted to make a life for themselves in Rangoon were the outsiders in a very real sense. As former British residents remembered, Rangoon was unique in the social segregation of different ethnic communities. The critical mass of foreign settlement meant that it was possible in Rangoon, to a degree not found elsewhere in the colony, to recreate "home" in miniature, where one did not have to – or perhaps should not – interact intimately with members of other communities. The two most prominent Chinese dialect groups were the Guangdong and the Hokkien, for example, and they lived in two symmetrical blocks of the town opposite each other along Dalhousie Street (today Mahabandula Street).

There were many immigrant success stories that helped to make Burmese economic disenfranchisement clear by comparison. One of the most famous Chinese success stories was the family of Chan Mah Phee. In 1861 Chan Mah Phee, a Hokkien, left Xiamen (Amoy) in Southeastern China to take up small trading in the Straits Settlements. After two years he resettled in Burma where he spent a decade trading in piece goods in independent Burma. In 1883, he established the firm Taik Leong in Rangoon, trading in oil, rice, and tobacco. As his business expanded, he bought city land, built houses and shops on it, and then rented them out, becoming the largest landowner among the Chinese community in Burma. In the late 1890s he also became the most important Chinese rice dealer in Burma. Part of

Chan Mah Phee's success can be attributed to the fact that although he did not speak English, he had married a Burmese farmer's daughter and undertook patronage of the Shwedagon Pagoda, aiding him in building up local connections that transcended the Chinese community. His son, Chan Chor Khine (born in 1886), maintained and expanded his empire while maintaining a balance between colonial Rangoon high society and his Chinese roots. The younger Chan initially received an English education at St. Paul's Institution in Rangoon, where his interest in sports was fostered and would provide the background for his position on the Rangoon Turf Club Committee and his personal collection of prize-winning racehorses. Upon the completion of his education in Rangoon, Chan's father sent him for a second education in China. After his return, Chan joined his father's company and became sole manager upon the latter's retirement. At the same time, he served as Honorary Magistrate, Councilor on the board of the Corporation of Rangoon, and member of the Burma Legislative Council. Chan's well-endowed estate, "the Brightlands," located opposite Dalhousie Park and the Royal Lakes, as well as his membership of the Orient Club, reflected his wealth and place among the general colonial elite. Nevertheless, he made certain to keep a conspicuous place at the top of Chinese society in Rangoon, serving as a trustee or president of many of the city's Chinese associations and providing patronage, such as his gift of ten acres for the construction of the Chinese High School.[12]

The promise of new opportunities and higher incomes, and the potential for a new beginning, certainly played a role in attracting immigrants to the colony. These expectations were buoyed by the well-known immigrant success stories mentioned above. However, once in Burma, particularly in Rangoon, poorer immigrants found a rougher side to life in the Big City. Many immigrant Asians in Rangoon lived and worked in such miserable conditions that they soon found the notion that life was any better in Rangoon surprising. The accommodation available was poor, a discomfort made obligatory by the low wages and debt burden of contract laborers. Often they amounted to barracks with no ventilation, poor drainage, and insufficient provision of latrines.[13]

Ethnic tensions in Rangoon would make themselves strongly felt with the impact of the Great Depression in 1930, when Rangoon experienced several major communal riots. On 5 May 1930, a severe earthquake rocked Rangoon, causing severe damage made worse by the slow colonial response, and news was received of Gandhi's arrest in India. The combination of these two events created excitement that resulted in a stoppage of dock work on 6 May, strikers demanding a pay increase. Between 14 and 22 May, two thousand Burmans were brought in to replace Indian dockworkers. The two groups came to blows on 26 May and the fighting spread into the town, leading to four days of communal rioting, bringing Rangoon to a stop. The complaint was rooted in economics, as in Rangoon Burmese were being denied dock labor in favor of imported South Indian coolies, who were preferred by the British because they were cheaper. In January 1931, Rangoon experienced another riot, this time between Burmans and Chinese, resulting in twelve deaths.[14]

RANGOON VICE

Until the last few decades of the nineteenth century, Rangoon could still be viewed as a kind of frontier town, boomtown, or at least a colonial outpost. Crime, opium, gambling, and a range of other vices were part of everyday life. As Rangoon's European population and that of Westernized Burmese, Chinese, and Indians grew, late Victorian values gradually began to influence colonial legislation. Opium had been targeted in the 1890s, after controversy over its medicinal value in the middle of the decade. Opium dens, filled with "torn mats . . . [and] grimy pillows soaked in perspiration" thrived in Rangoon into the 1930s.[15] The early twentieth century also saw a rapid increase in the use of another drug, cocaine, which colonial lawmakers argued was much worse than opium. Arguing that cocaine caused permanent problems such as loss of memory and mental control and often resulted in insanity, the Lieutenant-Governor's Council decided to bring cocaine under control in the same way as other intoxicating agents, according to the Excise Act of 1896.[16]

Another important feature of daily life in central Rangoon also became a major concern of the government. Much of the life in Rangoon after work and evening meals revolved around sex, particularly paid sex, and Rangoon saw the growth of a lively commercial sex industry; its red-light district was reportedly the largest in British India. Numerous brothels emerged around the town, becoming sites of remunerative liaisons typically between European, Indian, Chinese, and Burmese men, on the one hand, and Burmese women, on the other. Chinese, British, German, Russian, and Japanese sex workers also arrived in Rangoon to service male clientele with particular ethnic tastes and the means to indulge them.[17]

The overwhelming majority of Asian immigrants were male. In 1911, for example, among Chinese residents in Rangoon, the ratio was about one female to every five males, although by 1931 the gap had shrunk to about one in two. The disparity among Indian immigrants remained higher in

Rangoon, mainly because of the kinds of labor in which they were engaged and the fact that most of them were temporary immigrants, who sought to return to India when it became economically feasible.[18]

While many more prosperous immigrant males married Burmese women, most immigrants remained too poor to afford a family or had a family at home to support. In such circumstances, many immigrant males often turned to prostitutes. While this pattern was shared by all immigrant communities in Rangoon, a more conspicuous clientele were the British and Indian soldiers garrisoned in the town. In 1901, the Rangoon Municipal Council considered ways to resolve the problem of people loitering around the military cantonment to solicit for prostitution. This was not a problem found in Rangoon alone, for it was seen wherever military stations were found in the colony, such as at Mandalay and Thayetmyo. Nevertheless, visiting prostitutes was or became a regular activity for many Burmese males traveling to the "big city" in search of work or schooling.[19]

Prostitution in colonial Burma was legal, but frowned upon by colonial authorities and it became a recurring issue. Under the Rangoon Police Act of 1899, law enforcement was only permitted to keep prostitutes off the main streets and to act elsewhere if they had become a public annoyance. From 1901, the government adopted a segregation policy, giving powers to local government to identify prostitution-free areas where no brothels would be allowed, and thus force prostitutes to remote areas of the town. Brothels were restricted to a particular area of town and subject to closure elsewhere upon complaint. From 1914, the whole of Rangoon fell under notification, so the Commissioner of Police was authorized to close brothels at his own discretion, a power rarely exercised. An amendment in 1902 limited prostitution within central Rangoon to two areas, 33rd and 34th Streets between Fraser and Montgomery Streets and 27th, 28th, and 29th Streets between Dalhousie and Montgomery Streets.[20]

There was considerable hypocrisy in the colonial concern for isolating brothels, a reflection of earlier imported Victorian-era puritanical values. It was not uncommon for colonial officers and businessmen to keep Burmese concubines, much like Flory in George Orwell's *Burmese Days*. One man who did so was John Cowen, who had been brought to Rangoon by the local Bishop to stamp out prostitution as a sinful practice. Nonetheless, Cowen launched a vigorous propaganda campaign that targeted the civilian side of the trade, the government's complicity in making prostitution available to the troops by sanctioning prostitution areas near the barracks, and even concubinage, of which he himself was a practitioner! There were also very real health concerns regarding the spread of venereal disease, endemic but not limited to the sex trade. In one school, all Burmese boys over the age of fifteen were believed to have contracted one or another venereal disease.[21]

Rarely was the negative impact on the lives of the women drawn into the trade reflected upon until the 1920s. In 1921, with the argument that brothels were a source of venereal disease, that women kept in the brothels lived in virtual slavery, and that the operation of brothels encouraged the continual trafficking of poor Burmese girls from rural areas into the city for the purpose of prostitution, members of the Legislative Council introduced the Burma Suppression of Brothels Bill. The resulting Act made the closure of brothels not discretionary but mandatory, making it a crime for a man to live off of the earnings of a prostitute, to manage a brothel, or to traffic women and girls for immoral purposes. The Act, however, specifically limited itself to brothels and refused to penalize prostitutes themselves, for at the very least they were independent women. In 1925, the provincial government also targeted the sources of prostitutes. Attempts were made to end the trafficking of girls under fourteen years of age from impoverished families in Tavoy into Rangoon to work as servants, sometimes under work agreements, but in several cases sold outright. Such girls frequently ran away from abuse and were believed to have entered illicit Rangoon brothels. Gambling, alcohol, and drinking establishments also emerged as targets for social reform. In the first decade of the twentieth century, billiard-saloons and ring-throwing establishments provided public entertainment but also opportunities, it was claimed, for drinking and gambling, and in addition to being on the increase, a number had opened near schools and colleges in the city. Rangoon lawmakers also banned the employment of women as barmaids in liquor bars, because of the "evils which have been found to attend the employment of barmaids in Rangoon," although this was lifted sometime afterwards under pressure from angry liquor bar proprietors.[22]

THE BURMESE

Although a minority in Rangoon, the Burmese population still dominated the outer wards and had a noticeable presence in the city center. It was largely Burmese who carted in agricultural produce and other resources that were not ferried in on barges or by rail, helping to sustain the urban population and supplying the factories and commercial firms. Rangoon represented a new order of things in which the Burmese occupied the lowest rung of a colonial hierarchy that sought not to give, but to take. The best railway carriages were designated "Europeans only." Regulations stipulated that headmasters and superintendents of Anglo-Vernacular Government High Schools had to be British. Burmese names on tax revenue receipts and summonses bore inferior prefixes such as "Nga" and "Mi."[23]

Especially conspicuous in Rangoon was a small but growing group of Western-educated Burmese who were joining the lower and middle echelons of the colonial administration and Rangoon-based commercial enterprises. Rangoon's concentration of so much wealth and people in a single city encouraged a new consumerism and exposure to new, Western-oriented intellectual currents. Books and newspapers drawn from every corner of the British Empire flooded news stands and bookshops, while Western cigarettes and Virginia pipe tobaccos, the latest Western clothing fashions, and a rich medley of international foods all added to the flavor of life in central Rangoon, merely noticed by Burmese laborers, but embraced by their upwardly mobile, elite compatriots.[24]

A good example of the emerging Westernized Burmese middle class was U Kyaw Min, a prominent member of the Orient Club, the Pegu Club, and the Rangoon Golf Club. Born at Akyab in 1899 into a family of Cambridge-educated lawyers, Kyaw Min was educated in St. Anne's convent at Akyab and St. Xavier's College, Calcutta before joining Trinity Hall in Cambridge in 1918. There he became President of the Cambridge University Billiards Club and co-founded the "Crocodiles Club" which he served as treasurer and then as president; received College honours for hockey, was a first-string track runner for the college, and undertook radio communications as a hobby, before receiving his B.A. in 1921 and his law degree in 1922. He took the ICS competitive examinations in August 1922 and passed on his first attempt, becoming Headquarters Assistant, the only Burman in the ICS at the time to have qualified by competitive examination. His rise up the administrative ladder was rapid, from a subdivisional officer in 1924 to Deputy Commissioner in 1931, and to Deputy Secretary of the Education Department in 1936. After limited self-rule was inaugurated in 1937 he became Secretary of the Forest Department. Tellingly, when the Japanese invaded Burma in 1942, he chose not to remain in Burma but to retreat with the Government of Burma to Simla in India, where he spent the entire war. He served the returned Government of Burma as a commissioner from 1945 to 1947.[25] Cooperative, capable, sporting, and Western-educated, he represented the kind of Burmese that colonial authorities sought to foster.

Among those members of the Burmese middle class who participated in government service, either in Rangoon or on tour in one of the rural districts, feelings of social isolation were probably common. Until the mid-1930s, Burmese officers had mimicked the dress of their European counterparts, complete with trousers and coat. This was partly to prevent the Burmese official from being confused with other Burmese and thus of inferior social status. Learning English was perceived as the key to professional and social advancement, so much so that some "attached so much importance to acquiring the correct English accent that they had succeeded in learning very little else." Even so, throughout Burma there had always been a bar to Burmese participation in the social life of colonial officialdom. European and Burmese officers had separate clubs. While Europeans belonged to Gymkhana Clubs in different government stations, Burmese joined Burmese officer clubs, and if there were none of the latter, they joined the Rotary Club, the oldest club in Burma. Although Europeans might sponsor a Burmese, if he had effectively adopted European manners, for membership in the Gymkhana Club, social interaction with other club members was often minimal. Club activities were beyond the normal experiences of Burmese and some had not yet become skilled in playing bridge, tennis, golf, or polo. As one Burmese officer remembered, "It was an artificial life as there was very little in common between me and the non-Burmese members of the Club." Constitutional change would encourage changes in the ways in which Burmese officers perceived their place in colonial society. In the mid-1930s, as Burma headed toward home rule, younger Burmese officers had begun to abandon European dress and instead wear *longyis* and *gaungbaungs* (a turban-like headdress). While some did so for nationalist reasons, others did so for comfort after deciding that it was no longer necessary to prove social equality with British officers.[26]

While the colonial government grappled with prostitution, city planning, and increasing state revenues, this emerging class of educated Burmese was more concerned about the degradation of their culture and the decline of Buddhism under British rule. As an ethnic minority in the country's largest and most important city, there was an increasing awareness among them of their own vulnerability to becoming lost in the multicultural urban milieu, especially under foreign rulers uninterested in involvement in such matters. As the Burmese language was no longer the medium of commerce and administration, it became more closely linked to ethnic identity, just as Buddhism, no longer the state religion, had also become a mark of being Burmese. Growing self-awareness contributed to and was strengthened by the emergence of a vernacular press.[27]

The sense of alienation and second-rate status in Rangoon and other important towns intersected with this clarification or production of ethnic identity to contribute to Burmese Buddhist communalism and the realization that if they were to be preserved under colonial rule, the Burmese had to act to save themselves. From the late nineteenth and early twentieth centuries onward, Buddhist lay organizations began to emerge everywhere, often founded and led by Burmese who had been educated in Western or Anglo-Vernacular Schools and who were able to mobilize Western organizational techniques and media (such as the new vernacular newspapers) to promote traditional culture and Buddhism. Many such organizations soon reorganized into a larger body, the Young Men's Buddhist Association (YMBA), which was founded in 1906.[28] The YMBA's chief concern was the decline of Burmese civilization. As one of its founders complained in 1908:

On all sides we see the ceaseless, ebbless tide of foreign civilization and learning steadily creeping over the land, and it seems to me that unless we prepare ourselves to meet it, to overcome it, and to apply it to our own needs, our national character, our institutions, our very existence as a distinct nationality will be swept away, submerged, irretrievably lost.[29]

Direct confrontation with the government took place as a result of the "shoe question." In 1916, a young lawyer, U Thein Maung, found a sign at the Shwe Sandaw Pagoda in Prome that read "No one permitted to wear shoes in this Pagoda but Englishmen and Asiatic Europeans." He replaced the sign with another that banned footwear for everyone and refused to take it down a few months later. The local deputy commissioner demanded that Thein Maung provide scriptural evidence regarding footwear removal. The *Thathanabaing*, a government appointee, refused to intercede and Thein Maung brought the matter before the YMBA. The YMBA passed two resolutions. First, it would protest the use by foreign companies of the Buddha and pagodas in their trade or brand marks. Second, it would protest the wearing of footwear in religious precincts and order members to put up signs to this effect at all religious places. As the pagodas throughout Burma began to put up signs, tensions grew. One angry monk even took a knife and cut the face of an offending European who had walked upon the sacred ground of the Mahamuni Shrine in Mandalay with his shoes on. In May 1918, the YMBA also demanded the removal of the British war cemetery and cantonment on Shwedagon Hill in Rangoon. After the government raised questions about whether the YMBA had the right to engage in political activity, for the shoe question had now become a political issue, older members of the YMBA including many government servants were pressured to leave the association. Younger, more radical members would soon form a new political organization to continue the struggle over the shoe question and to push for Burmese home rule.[30]

Some scholars have argued that pacification was never complete and that Burmese resistance to British rule continued until the latter left. Nevertheless, modern nationalism was indeed new and unfamiliar to the bulk of Burma's general population. So too were the organizational techniques of Western politics. It would take several decades for a handful of Burmese thinkers and political activists to develop popular acceptance of and participation in both. Modern Burmese nationalism slowly emerged over the first few decades of the twentieth century. The defeat of a European power by an Asian one in the Russo-Japanese War of 1904–05 was one source of encouragement. In 1908, a Japanese movie exhibition brought gas-lit projectors and a film of the actual fighting in that war to Rangoon. The film, shown in darkened areas on the streets, was the first movie ever shown in Burma.[31]

An especially important figure in the early stages of Burmese nationalism was the Buddhist monk, U Ottama (1879–1939). Ottama was an Arakanese monk who had gone to India to teach Pali and Buddhism at the National College and was eventually drawn into the Indian National Congress, which spearheaded Indian anti-colonial efforts. Ottama thus gained familiarity with modern political campaigning. He soon left India and traveled to various countries, including China, Korea, Vietnam, the United States, Britain, and Japan, observing their contemporary condition relative to Burma, before returning to Burma in 1918. Ottama had been particularly struck by the example of modernization in Japan, another Asian country. Both in his writings and in speeches (re-circulated in the vernacular press) during his tours of the colony, Ottama informed Burmese of Japan's ongoing industrialization and urged them to follow Japan's example of self-development.[32]

Ottama was imprisoned in 1921 for denouncing imperialism in a speech, but immediately resumed his anti-government activities within weeks of his release from prison in August 1924. In Mandalay, police stopped a procession organized by Ottama leading to violence that left several dead and many wounded. Ottama ran into trouble again in early October when he was charged with sedition for two speeches he made in Rangoon and imprisoned for three years with hard labor. His sentence was viewed as too harsh for a monk and led to a demonstration in Fytche Square in downtown

Rangoon by a crowd led by outraged monks. After three warnings to disperse were ignored, aside from booing, Rangoon City Mounted Police were then ordered to charge the crowd. In the ensuing violence, in which the monks resisted the police, a number of monks were injured. When popular demands were made for an inquiry into police behavior, the colonial government refused, arguing that no inquiry was needed because no one had been hurt in the incident. In reality, the wounded had not gone to hospital for fear of arrest. The Rangoon authorities then banned all public meetings in Rangoon for a month. After the Fytche Square Incident, Governor Sir Spencer Harcourt Butler received a telegraph from an assembly of monks at Moulmein calling Ottama's arrest unlawful, for it interfered with the Buddhist religion. The monks offered to take Ottama's place in prison and demanded the repeal of the section of the Penal Code by which Ottama was convicted. The Governor responded that it did not amount to interference with religion, as none of Burma's residents were above the law, and he argued that it was against Buddhist tenets to spread hatred for the established government. Monks in Rangoon took more direct action. After confronting non-European police officers on patrol and threatening to kill them if they did not resign, gangs of monks knifed four Europeans in a series of attacks. As for Ottama, he was imprisoned again and would remain there until his death behind bars in 1939.[33]

The delay by colonial authorities in responding to indigenous desires for participation in the administration of the colony helped to sustain Ottama's early activism and popularity. The Secretary of State for India, Lord Montagu, was partly to blame for Burmese disappointment. He had made a declaration on 21 August 1917 in the House of Commons that included the possibility of Indian self-government. As Burma was a province of India, some Burmese believed that self-rule was on its way for their country as well. Subsequent Burmese demands for reform may have come as a surprise to British authorities, for colonial authorities such as the former Lieutenant-Governor of Burma (1910–1915), Harvey Adamson, believed that the Burmese were unprepared educationally or politically for self-rule; Adamson argued at the time that the Burmese intelligentsia were fifty years behind that of India. The joint report drawn up by Lords Montagu and Chelmsford (thus known as the Montagu–Chelmsford reforms), which led to the Government of India Act, 1919, excluded Burma, declaring that its political development would be left aside as a separate issue to be dealt with at some point in the future.[34]

Burmese advocates of Home Rule continued to press for the same concessions for Burma as were granted to India in the Montagu–Chelmsford scheme. Lieutenant-Governor Sir Reginald Craddock disliked the proposed reforms and suggested a modified scheme in May 1919 that called for indirect election to the Legislative Council for rural areas and direct election for special constituencies and towns. The Executive would consist of four boards and heading each board would be a non-official member of the Legislative Council who would not be responsible to the legislature. As Craddock further elaborated in April 1920, he was also against Burma's separation from India. It was probable that Burma would ultimately separate from India, after further political development. In the meantime, if that view was taken and reasonable recognition was given of Burma's differences with the Indian Provinces, Burma would benefit from its continued membership in the Government of India's "family of provinces." Indians who lived in Burma, he argued, had no reason to fear ultimate separation, for there were no measures in preparation to restrict any of their privileges as British subjects in Burma. Nevertheless, Indians, he continued, should remember their obligations regarding living in Burma and not disturb the "calm atmosphere" of Burma with essentially Indian problems.[35]

In early 1920, Burma was shaken by a large number of unrelated labor strikes. In this volatile context, the University Act Bill was submitted for discussion in the Legislative Council. Many Burmese viewed the proposed Act, and the requirement that classes be taught in English, as a means of preventing them from overcoming the claims of the Montagu–Chelmsford reform scheme. Although rural Burmese had contributed to the University Endowment Fund by collections at festivals held all over Burma, they had little hope of sending their children to the university. Burmese political associations asked that passage of the bill be suspended until the Reformed Legislative Council was put in place, but the Lieutenant-Governor refused. Instead, he opted to enlarge the Legislative Council with the inclusion of prominent Burmans who were associated with opposition to the bill. Although the latter fought in the Legislative Council for additional concessions, the bill was made law anyway.[36]

Rangoon College students went on strike on 5 December 1920. The students were going to "smash" the University Act because, they argued, it was nothing more than a government instrument to "keep the nation in chains." Burma, they claimed, needed a "national college" where the kind of education that was suited to the "sons of the soil" could be given. In part their complaints were over issues of powers and representation. Students had not been asked for their views on the Act and now they demanded that the university council and senate should represent all classes of people and views and that students should have representation as well. Moreover, the

Chancellor's power should be less arbitrary and he should not be able to appoint professors directly. The demands also related to university requirements and costs. The university, for example, was to be residential, making the cost prohibitive to poor Burmese. More importantly, the fact that instruction would be in English not only disadvantaged Burmese and Indian students but also lengthened the term and thus the cost of study because it meant a preliminary year course in English had to be undertaken.[37]

As the student boycott movement spread throughout the colony and soon involved virtually all government schools, it became the vanguard of political unrest directed at colonial rule. Strikers organized ninety national schools all over Burma and a national college in Rangoon.[38] Ultimately, the strike helped to foster greater political awareness and solidarity among Burmese across the colony, a development that pushed the British to grant the colony greater political concessions than it had formerly been willing to make.

The political awakening that was occurring among Burmese was soon channeled into electoral politics. In 1921, the Secretary of State for India finally recommended to Parliament the extension of the Act of 1919 to Burma. Under diarchy, certain non-critical areas of government would be "transferred" to two Burmese ministers chosen by the Legislative Council, while all other areas of importance to the Indian Government would be "reserved" and remain under the control of the Governor (who would replace the lieutenant-governorship on the establishment of diarchy in 1923). A committee under Sir A. F. Whyte visited Burma in 1922 to examine the degree of self-rule that would be appropriate to Burma and how to determine "reserved" and "transferred" subjects. The Committee's proposed Draft Rules were accepted with minor modification by Parliament and were put into force with the arrival of Harcourt Butler as Governor on 2 January 1923. The irony, as pointed out by one scholar, was that although the British had originally intended to give Burma less than was given to India, the terms of the extension of this Act to Burma in 1923 proved to be more liberal than those that had been granted to India. First, women were given complete equality with men because of their allegedly high social status in Burma. Second, the franchise was much wider than in India because of the greater diffusion in Burma of elementary education. Under the "diarchy" system, the executive authority was vested in the Executive Council, called the Governor-in-Council. This consisted of two members in control of transferred subjects, including Agriculture, Education, Excise and Forests, Local Self-Government, and Public Health, and two members in control of reserved subjects, including Finance, General and Judicial Administration,

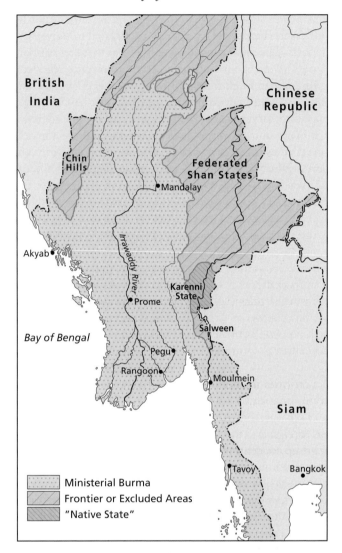

Map 1 Colonial Burma

Police, and Revenue. The former were designated Ministers and were chosen from and responsible to the Legislative Council, while the latter were responsible to the Governor and not to the Legislative Council.[39]

Diarchy was not for everyone. The colonial authorities had other plans for the ethnic minorities in the hill areas. There, according to colonial authorities, "racial" and local administrative peculiarity meant that integrating them with the rest of Burma would be a bad idea. There was probably also some truth to claims that the authorities were responding to local desires, for these areas had always enjoyed substantial autonomy from precolonial central control and this autonomy, including the local authority of the Shan *sawbwas*, had been preserved thus far under colonial rule. Under diarchy, local autonomy might easily be eroded by a Burman majority that would presumably dominate the forthcoming Legislative Assembly, despite significant and automatic representation of several ethnic groups in that body (the so-called "reserved seats"). In 1922, the Kachin Hills, the Chin Hills, and the Shan states were thus placed under a new civil service called the Burma Frontier Service. The Shan states were divided into two newly created administrative units, the Northern Shan State and the Southern Shan State, and these two halves were joined together in another new administrative unit called the Federated Shan States, headed by an advisory council, and administered through a commissioner appointed by the Governor of Burma. This arrangement would isolate the Shans and others from further constitutional reforms granted to what became ministerial Burma until the end of the colonial period. Even during the Japanese occupation period, the Shan states and the other frontier areas would remain separate from the lowland Burmese administration.[40] In the longer term, it set the stage for the continuity of divisions that have fueled an ongoing civil war.

Ethnic minorities in the hill areas were not the only ones who feared Burmese domination. There were of course the substantial Chinese and Indian communities, both of which Burmese nationalists increasingly characterized as foreign and unwanted in the country. A smaller, though very important group concentrated in Rangoon were the Anglo-Burmans, often the children of unions between European men and Burmese women, but sometimes vice versa. They sat uneasily between two worlds, one Burmese-speaking and indigenous and the other English-speaking and foreign. Many Burmese nationalists viewed them as part of the colonial elite, benefiting from advantages in commerce and administration that stemmed from their connexion with the British colonial establishment, their Western education, or both. After independence, many would lose their businesses with the introduction of Burmanization programs. Many Anglo-Burmans had indeed become successful in the colonial period, but, like many of their Westernized Burmese compatriots, they also served as an intellectual bridge between the West and Burma. Still, fear of being overwhelmed or cast out by majority Burmese rule would lead them to seek special recognition and legal protection when Burma headed for self-rule in the years ahead.[41]

Aside from the university strike and the introduction of diarchy, the most important political development in colonial Burma in the 1920s was the emergence and then fissure of the General Council of Burmese Associations (GCBA). In September 1920, the aforementioned YMBA split into two groups. The younger, more radical, and larger group established a new organization, the GCBA, which supported the university boycott. Two men soon came to dominate the GCBA, the great orator, Tharrawaddy U Pu, who served as president and the forty-three-year-old U Chit Hlaing (1879–1952), the son of a teak merchant educated in London with a degree in law, who served as secretary. The GCBA experienced its own division in 1922 over the issue of how to react to the diarchy reforms. While the main GCBA leadership opposed cooperation with the government and sought immediate dominion status for Burma, twenty-one prominent members who disagreed with this policy and sought to fight for concessions within the forthcoming Burma Legislative Council left the GCBA and formed the Nationalist Party. The GCBA, however, clung to non-cooperation. This proved a disaster for the GCBA in the long run. First, staying out of the Council meant that the GCBA was steadily deprived of supporters from among the more anxious urban politicians who sought to legitimate their nationalist credentials, in the eyes of the government, through open election. Second, by virtually abandoning the Council and the urban electorate to opposing parties, the GCBA found that it increasingly depended upon rural and small town branches of the party. When GCBA politicians preached Home Rule to villagers, they quickly learned that the latter misunderstood the call to mean the abolition of taxes and the restoration of the monarchy. Party leaders thus often found themselves outside their element.[42]

In 1925, the GCBA finally resolved to fight for Home Rule both within and without the Council. It would also encourage Burmese to resist and thus make rule through the Legislative Council impossible. The party now sought to purge the GCBA of title and place-hunters, promote the election of Home Rule candidates who would obstruct the work of the Council if their demands were not met, to organize Burmese labor, to improve industry and agriculture, and, hopefully, to affiliate with the British Labor Party, who had the means to guarantee that Parliament would hear about Burmese grievances.[43]

BURMESE WOMEN

Although, as mentioned, Burmese women were accorded higher status under diarchy than their counterparts in India, the position of women in colonial Burmese society was by no means equal to that of men. While they could vote under the new system, they could not yet hold office and hot debates broke out in the Legislative Council as to whether they should be accorded this right as well. On this issue, the extension of further constitutional rights was favored more by Rangoon-based representatives, both Burmese and non-Burmese alike, than by representatives elected by constituencies outside Rangoon. The main reason for this divide was that the image of women and their proper place in Burmese society differed between the cosmopolitan, foreign-oriented world of Rangoon and the tradition-entrenched world of the village whose grip even included important towns like Mandalay.

Western observers had early on remarked on what they saw as the independence of Burmese women.[44] Positioned as the mirror image of Burmese men, whom the colonial discourse tended to portray as lazy and backward, women were portrayed as hardworking and industrious. Indeed, as the country's small traders they were highly visible to Europeans in the urban centers, who rarely stepped outside the confines of town even to notice Burmese men at work in the fields, though of course women were hard at work here too. Colonial photography and literature eventually emphasized the "exotic" Burmese beauty and replaced images of women pounding unhusked rice with studio shots of brightly clad women posing with parasols and long cheroots. Orwell in *Burmese Days* and other writings contributed as well to a notion of the sexual accessibility of Burmese women, which was strengthened by Rangoon's growing reputation as the main center for prostitution in British India. Even so, Europeans and Western-educated Asians in Rangoon never questioned the intellectual independence of the Burmese woman.

In the later 1920s, Western-educated Burmese politicians argued forcefully that Burmese women should have full political equality with men.[45] Burmese politicians from rural constituencies, however, fought to counter such views. In traditional Burmese Buddhist society, they argued, Burmese women were not equal to men. As U Kyaw Dun (representative of Mandalay Rural) argued before the Burma Legislative Council in 1927,

The faults of women mentioned by the Buddha are too numerous . . . Women have seven [sic] inherent faults, namely, untruthfulness, artfulness, indiscretion, vanity, uncleanliness and cruelty. The wise and the virtuous have never placed women on the same footing as men. Placing women in the same position as men amounts to damnation of women to hell. According to the time honoured Buddhist custom, a woman has to walk behind a man in travelling. She has to sleep and eat after her husband. All these prove woman's inferiority . . . Western customs have been

introduced into our country. I beg you not to adopt them wholesale. Our customs
are quite different from those of the Western countries . . . [46]

Kyaw Dun's argument was not unrepresentative of the prevailing views
of Burmese men who eschewed "Western" influences. Their continuity
with the precolonial past is indicated in part by the late-1870s writings
of U Po Hlaing, in then independent Upper Burma, who made the same
general observations about the proper role of Burmese women in Burmese
Buddhist society.[47] These views, including the importance of preventing
Western notions from influencing Burmese society, would persist beyond
independence and six decades later would echo among the many argu-
ments set forth by a military government attempting to prevent a Western-
educated Burmese woman, Aung San Suu Kyi, from gaining leadership
over the country.

SEPARATION FROM INDIA

The Government of India Act of 1919 had stipulated that after ten years a
Statutory Commission would be appointed for examining progress made
in education and representative institutions and on the working of the
government system. Sir John Simon was appointed as the Chairman in
1928. The Simon Commission, which visited Burma in 1928–1929 as part
of its mandate to examine representative institutions in India, including Burma, recommended abolishing the diarchy system and increasing
provincial autonomy as much as possible. The first Indian Round Table
Conference held in London in 1930–1931 supported Burma's separation
from India. A special Burma Round Table Conference was held in London
in 1931–1932 where nearly all of the Burmese participants confirmed that
they favored separation in principle, but disagreed on certain details.[48]

The 1932 Burma Legislative Council elections largely focussed on the
question of separation. Some Burmese politicians favored separation, while
others formed a noisy anti-separationist alliance. The latter argued that
Burma's connection with India should continue until India had achieved
full dominion status; otherwise Burma would be relegated, as a crown
colony, to a status inferior to that of India, should the latter become a
dominion. The anti-separationists won a majority of the seats and the new
Legislative Council adopted a resolution opposing either separation from
or federation with India. Parliament decided that since the Burmese could
not settle the separation issue, the British government would decide for
them, resulting in the India Act, 1935 (reenacted separately for Burma as

the Government of Burma Act, 1935), which included a new constitution for Burma. Burma was now to be a unitary state separate from India.[49]

The Government of Burma Act of 1935, not put into force until 1937, established a new structure of government, in which the Governor remained the head of the executive with the assistance of a ten-member Council of Ministers. The Governor also chose these ministers, including the Chief Minister, who was called the Prime Minister. The Legislature was expanded to two houses. The Senate consisted of thirty-six members, half elected by members of the House of Representatives and the other half nominated by the Governor. The House consisted of 132 members elected by different geographical, ethnic, organizational, and commercial constituencies. The qualifications for franchise were reduced. Now, the payment of any municipal tax qualified a member of a municipality to vote, while the rural vote was limited to the payment of tax or the possession of land revenue of not less than five rupees. Any laws passed by the legislature were subject to veto, first by the Governor, and, second, by the Secretary of State.[50]

A NEW GENERATION

A new, more cosmopolitan generation of Burmese leaders was emerging from Rangoon University (RU) in the early Depression years. Some were conservative and Western looking. They bought English pipes, then in fashion among their peers, at department stores such as Rowe & Co. in downtown Rangoon, and pinned their hopes for future success on winning positions in the Indian Civil Service. Other students and graduates looked at the colonial government and the West in a different, more critical way. In 1930, students and recent graduates of RU formed the Dobama Asiayone (We Burmans Association). They protested against British rule and called for the creation of a national organization to put forth demands for Burmese rights. They made their rejection of subservient status to the colonizers known by abandoning the use of Maung or Ko before their names and replacing it with Thakin, or "Master," indicating that they were the masters in their own country. This was highly symbolic; as in the case of "sahib" in India, "thakin" was the term that Burmese were expected to use in addressing the British. They also wrote and sang the Dobama song as their anthem (which would later become the national anthem of independent Burma) and replaced the peacock of the Burmese royal household with a tricolor flag representing the Burmese nation as their banner. Some British observers and conservative Burmese condemned the Thakins as hotheaded young men, but they emerged as popular leaders among the Burmese in general. The Thakins organized cultivators, laborers, education circles, and itinerant libraries, as well as a parliamentary political group, the Ko Min Ko Chin Party. However, the Thakins lacked any coherent ideology, loosely borrowing ideas from the Irish Sinn Fein, Hitler, Mussolini, Lenin, and Kemal Ataturk.[51]

As many of Burma's future leaders spent the early and mid-1930s together in RU, their experiences there in student organizations and their development of strategies to deal with the Principal, the hard-working but stubborn D. J. Sloss, were an important influence in shaping how Burmese leaders would deal with British diplomats after the war and with parliamentary democracy and state building from 1948. As U Nu, Burma's future prime minister and an RU alumnus, later admitted, at this time everything British school authorities did was perceived as imperialist in intent, and RUSU leaders took it upon themselves to protest Sloss's efforts to develop the university into a world-class institution. When Sloss rejected their attempts to reverse a decision he had made for preliminary examinations, on the grounds that he refused to be intimidated by RUSU, Nu and his friends used their connexions to editors at Burmese newspapers to plant stories that Sloss had actually rejected Burmese political parties and Burmese political leadership in general. Although Sloss demanded a retraction, the newspapers refused. The RUSU leaders then began to make speeches to mass meetings in and outside of Rangoon (see Fig. 2.3), calling for Sloss's resignation. The Governing Board of the University soon caved in and canceled the preliminary examinations.[52]

The students rose to national prominence as nationalist leaders as a result of the university strike at RU in 1936. Among the organizers and leaders of the strike were many of the main national leaders of post-war Burma. The main force behind the strike was the RUSU. Nu was elected to the post of President of RUSU in August 1935. He stood out partly because he was a few years older than the other students, for he was a graduate of the university, who had returned for a law degree. One of the powers behind the scene in the election was U Kyaw Nyein, Nu's future political rival, who chose not to stand for election and among the other candidates elected for the nine posts on the RUSU executive committee was Ko Aung San, the future father of Burmese independence. Aung San was selected by the committee to serve as editor for RUSU's magazine, the *Oway*. Among others involved in the magazine was the future Communist leader, Thakin Than Tun, who provided material for publication.[53]

Figure 2.3 Colonial architecture in Rangoon today

RUSU became involved in several disputes between students and the university in late 1935. The most important occurred as a result of the publication in *Oway* in late February of an article written under a pseudonym by one of Aung San's friends. The article, entitled "Hell Hound at Large," was a satirical treatment of the sexual advances of an unnamed Burmese member of the university administrative staff to female students. As the article described the administrator: "A pimping knave with avuncular pretensions to some cheap wiggling wenches from a well-known hostel . . . His only distinguishing marks were buboes and ulcers due to errant whoring." Although Sloss was said to be aware of the author's identity, Aung San refused to confirm it.[54]

With Nu already expelled and an order to expel Aung San from the university imminent, the other seven members of the RUSU Executive Committee made two resolutions. First, they would refuse to sit for the University examinations. Second, they would hold a general meeting of the student body in Union Hall on 26 February 1936 to inform them of the first resolution. At the meeting, the students determined to undertake strike action at the Shwedagon Pagoda in downtown Rangoon. There, the strikers would remain for the next two months. To provide for supreme authority over the student strikers, a Boycotter's Council was created, consisting of the nine members of the RUSU Executive Council and two representatives each from the twelve university hostels. Due to its large size, a smaller inner council was created, with Nu as President, U Raschid as Vice-President, and Aung San as Secretary. Rangoon's general population supported the strikers materially and in spirit. They were also supported by the Burmese press – and were criticized by the two English newspapers in town.[55]

On the day of the examinations, Raschid was sent with 600 strikers to picket the university entrances. Although some students did sit for the exams, these were very few in number, leading to a postponement of the examinations. The inner council now determined on making formal demands and publicizing them to the Burmese public. The demands included the reinstatement of expelled students, changes in the University Act to allow the RUSU to seat two representatives on the University Council, the holding of examinations a month after the end of the strike, and a greater role for students in the management of campus hostels. The University finally conceded on most of these demands and the strike was officially called off on 10 May 1936. Ultimately, Professor Pe Maung Tin replaced Sloss as the principal of the university, becoming the first Burmese to head the institution.[56]

The RUSU strike brought to the fore of Burmese politics a new generation of Burmese leaders. Aung San, Nu, Than Tun, and others were able to use Western institutions and political tactics against the British, as were more established politicians such as Ba Maw. What set the RUSU protestors apart was their solidarity, their ability to mobilize themselves and others without the complications of overdeveloped egos. While the Burmese politicians of the 1920s often sought to promote themselves at the expense of national solidarity, the student leaders acted more as comrades than as political competitors. This new attitude and willingness to suppress individual rivalries for the national cause would contribute heavily to the forging of alliances that carried Burma to independence a decade later.

CONCLUSION

Colonial Rangoon's place as the center of colonial life and politics naturally made it the site for some of the most important confrontations between the Burmese and the British. The position of the Burmese as a minority in the city contributed to the mounting tension. It was thus in Rangoon that the impact of British rule and the economic domination of Western commerce and Asian immigrant minorities was clearest, or at least in the case of the latter this image was most easily manufactured, and most despised. These perceptions would be carried into the countryside, often by the vernacular press, but more frequently by Rangoon-based Burmese politicians.

At the same time, colonial Rangoon was included in a circuit of colonial ports that connected Burma with intellectual and material flows emanating from Europe, and particularly from Britain. New consumer items, the latest fashions, new political ideas, and news from around the globe contributed to the emergence of a new Burmese self-awareness that no longer merely drew upon Burma's precolonial past, but also on the international present. Westernization became equated with modernization and advancement. Burmese attraction to industrializing Japan, for example, was not due to the continuity of Japanese traditional culture, but the fact that an Asian people could develop a state and economy that was equal to those of the Europeans. This did not mean that the "colonial" Burmese were not informed to a strong degree by the precolonial past. Instead, recognition of the importance of the latter was cultivated in new lay associations built upon Western organizational models.

Rangoon thus made an important transition in the colonial period, from a foreign control center, to the center of Burmese nationalist activity. In the years that lay ahead, Rangoon would maintain its place as the center of the Burmese state for well over half a century. Nevertheless, its "foreignness" would remain an important issue throughout the post-independence period.

CHAPTER 3

Self-government without independence, 1937–1947

Historians usually view the late 1930s and the Japanese occupation period (1942–1945) separately. Certainly, in the context of the greater Asia-Pacific region, Burma can be viewed as an example of a colony that was shaken and redirected by Japanese wartime occupation. From the perspective of Burmese efforts to achieve independence from Britain, however, late 1930s parliamentarianism and "independence" under the Japanese between 1942 and 1945 were part of a single period in which unique circumstances allowed the Burmese to gain fluctuating degrees of independence and experiment with different models of government and political control. Thus examining the 1937–1947 years as a single period makes good sense, at least in terms of Burma's political history.

During this period, the Burmese experienced different political arrangements under the British and the Japanese that allowed for limited self-rule, but never complete independence. The main reason was that the controlling power, whether Britain or Japan, was reluctant either to lose control of the Burmese economy and Burma's resources or to compromise broader regional security (in Britain's case, the security of India; in Japan's, its strategic position in wartime Southeast Asia). At no point prior to 1947 was Burma a unified whole, the Scheduled Areas (later renamed the Frontier Areas) remaining separate from parliamentary (lowland) Burma under both the British and the Japanese.

Given the entrenched British interests in Burma, it would be difficult to imagine the constitutional situation being any better during these years had World War II not broken out. At the same time, while the Japanese occupation did not create the nationalist forces that would drive Burma to independence in 1948, it did help to clear the political field of conservative and moderate politicians who might have provided more competition to Aung San and other leftwing politicians. The Japanese occupation and its collapse also ruined the reputation of Ba Maw, arguably pre-war Burma's foremost political leader. Ultimately, the assassination of Aung San thrust into the forefront of national politics the unlikely figure of Nu, both charismatic and erratic. Another impact of the war was that Burma was laid waste by both sides as the colony became a battleground. The ruination of the colonial economy would hamper Burma's post-war economic recovery in the decades ahead. This was indeed a decade of important and unpredictable change.

THE BA MAW, PU, AND SAW GOVERNMENTS

Separation from India occurred with a perhaps unexpected ease. Upon the commencement of separation, Burmese members simply vacated their seats in the Indian Legislative Assembly. It also had little impact on the colonial administrators in Burma itself. Since Burma was no longer part of India, ICS officers posted to Burma had the choice to retire, to transfer to India, or to join the new Burma Civil Service, and the vast majority chose the third option, mainly because they were familiar with Burma and did not want to be burdened with adjusting to a new linguistic and cultural environment. Indians and other minorities living in Burma were concerned about their status and security in a Burmese-ruled state. These concerns grew when Burmese politicians turned their attention to taking control over the Rangoon Corporation. In 1937, the thirty-three councilors managing the Corporation consisted of two Chinese, three Anglo-Indians, nine Indians, eight Europeans, and eleven Burmese. Now, Burmese politicians pushed through a bill in the House of Representatives to increase Burmese representation on the Council to 50 percent.[1] As separation turned to nationalization, Asian immigrant communities in Rangoon grew concerned about how far the new Burmese government would go.

In reality, the new Burmese government was saddled with too many other problems, including its own instability, to present an important threat to anyone. U Ba Pe's United Party had won the most seats in the 1936 election and Ba Pe was thus asked to form a government. Over the course of the next two months, however, Ba Pe proved either unable or unwilling to negotiate with other parties and proposed only members of the United Party for cabinet positions. Ba Maw, who had campaigned to wreck the Constitution, dropped this course of action and joined a coalition of seven parties, leading by March to his selection as Prime Minister of the prospective government, although at Ba Maw's request this title was changed to that of Premier. Ba Maw's government, however, never proved to be very stable and in 1938 found itself increasingly mired in strike actions by labour, especially by oilfield workers. Rioting broke out in July between Burmese and Indians as the result of the publication of a pamphlet, deriding Gotama Buddha, authored by a Burmese Muslim. In December, the arrest of two university students led the RUSU to launch a protest demonstration at the Government Secretariat. After police brutally broke up the student demonstration, the death of one student was taken up as a cause by the Burmese press and student strikes now broke out throughout the country. In February 1939, police fired on demonstrators in Mandalay, killing seventeen, including many Buddhist monks. The Ba Maw coalition government could no longer maintain its position and by the end of the month, U Pu became the new premier.[2]

In September 1939, World War II broke out in Europe when Germany invaded Poland. This event changed London's attitude to the Burmese government as Britain now sought solidarity in the empire for the fight against fascism. Governor Sir Archibald Cochrane requested that Pu solicit a formal declaration of war from the Burmese legislature, but Pu refused, on the grounds that it would split his party. On 18 November 1939, the Thakins, the All-Burma Students' Organization, and the Sinyetha Party of Dr. Ba Maw created the Burma Freedom Bloc Organization under the secretaryship of Aung San, to push the British to set a definite date for Burmese independence in exchange for Burmese participation on the Allied side in the war. Winston Churchill, who had replaced Neville Chamberlain as British Prime Minister shortly after the outbreak of war, however, rejected the demand. Churchill, an unashamed imperialist, would resist any move toward independence in the colonies, as he would again in Burma after the war. The Freedom Bloc organization thus launched an anti-war campaign on the grounds that the war was an imperialist war and was unrelated to the issue of Burmese independence. In its first few months, the activities of the Freedom Bloc consisted of mass meetings and anti-war demonstrations in Rangoon. The government responded by suspending civil liberties in the colony, and arrested and imprisoned leaders and members of the Freedom Bloc, forcing the Thakins and others underground.[3]

In these conditions and as a result of its own problems with the British Government, the Pu Government fell in September 1940. U Saw, the head of the Myochit Party, now became Premier. Political rivals viewed Saw as a man with fascist tendencies, especially since he had a small private army, known as the Galon Tat, which sometimes came to blows in the districts with the Thakins' own volunteer organization. Saw, like other Burmese nationalists, hoped that cooperation with the British during the war would bring complete independence and flew to London in October 1941 to gain political concessions. In a meeting with Churchill, Saw promised

Burma's loyalty in the war, but demanded the application of the third clause of the Atlantic Charter, the right of self-determination of nations, to Burma. On this basis, Saw demanded a British promise of the grant of dominion status to Burma at the end of the war. However, Burma was not promised dominion status, Churchill merely repeating the vague promise of discussions on self-government at some point after the conclusion of hostilities. Saw then turned his hopes to convincing US President Franklin D. Roosevelt to put pressure on Churchill to give in, but without success. Disappointed, Saw flew from Washington DC to Hawaii, where he would continue on to Burma. By coincidence, his plane landed in Honolulu on the night of 7 December 1941. He thus witnessed the confusion and devastation just wreaked on the US naval base there, including the crippled Pacific Fleet, many of whose surviving or destroyed vessels were still burning, and the significant casualties. The effect must have been alarming. Blocked from returning to Burma by the western route, Saw now flew east. Landing in Lisbon, he went to the Japanese embassy and reportedly offered Japan Burma's cooperation in the war. In early January 1942, as he flew on to Palestine, the British, who had become aware of the meeting, intercepted his plane in mid-air and forced it down. Saw was then sent to Uganda where he was interned in a detention camp for the duration of the war. His Myochit Party could not survive without him and disappeared from Burma's mainstream nationalist struggle. His place as Premier was given to Sir Paw Tun, who held it briefly until the government was forced to flee to India a few months later.[4]

THE THIRTY COMRADES

Although Burma had separated from India and now had limited self-government, these gains remained unsatisfactory for many Burmese nationalists. The British Governor still controlled major areas of the government and a colonial elite dominated by Europeans, Eurasians, and Asian minorities controlled the economic wealth of the country and dominated the capital, in which the Burmese population remained a minority in 1937. Burma was not yet fully extricated from a colonial empire in which "things British" remained the measure of civilization and modernization. Another model of modernization, one that was Asian and hostile to European colonialism, was Japan. British accounts of the Second World War frequently suggest surprise at the rapid pace of the Japanese conquest of Burma in 1942 and a disbelief that the Burmese would cooperate with the Japanese invader. Since the Japanese victory against the Russians in 1905, however,

Japan had been admired by nationalists throughout Southeast Asia as an Asian country that could not only adopt the best that Europe had to offer, but also use Western weaponry with success against the Europeans. Burmese intellectuals attempted to draw the attention of literate Burmese to Japan's success in everything from business to medicine. One such effort came in 1937, when Maung Khin Maung published his Burmese-language account and photographs of the machinery and factories of Nagoya, Japan, in *The Sun*.[5]

Finding little hope for his vision of complete Burmese independence in continued association with the British and, indeed, pursued by the police at home, Aung San sought support, not from the anti-Communist Japanese government, but from the Chinese Communists. On 8 August 1940, Aung San and a comrade thus slipped out of Burma on a steamer to Amoy, China. There is disagreement over whether Ba Maw and other nationalists at home had meanwhile made arrangements with the Japanese to "find" Aung San at Amoy or whether Aung San changed tactics once he was arrested by the Japanese there. In either case, Aung San now fully accepted Japanese patronage.[6]

One can easily imagine the excitement with which Aung San prepared for the liberation of Burma, a dream repeatedly stymied by the colonial authorities. In November 1940, he flew to Tokyo where he spent the next few months at the War Office with Colonel Keiji Suzuki (Bo Mogyo) outlining plans for the campaign. He would return to Burma four times between February and June 1941 to see whether the Freedom Bloc would ally with Japan and, if so, to recruit Burmese for military training by the Japanese. Aung San found among the Thakins twenty-nine recruits, soon to be known, along with Aung San as the Thirty Comrades. He secreted them out of Burma in groups during each of the four trips for Japanese training in warfare and administration. The twenty-nine members of the Thirty Comrades (one, Thakin Than Tin, had died during training on Formosa [Taiwan]) were organized into the Burma Independence Army (BIA) in Bangkok in December, in preparation for the Japanese invasion of Burma (Japan declared war on Britain on 8 December). The BIA followed the Japanese invasion route, first into Tenasserim, and then from Tavoy and Moulmein to Rangoon in March 1942 and its numbers eventually grew to 50,000 – almost as many as the Japanese invasion force of 60,000 men.[7]

Britain's neglect of Burma in the interests of India proved a decisive factor. One of the main reasons for the quick British defeat was the failure to develop a Burmese army that had an incentive to defend their own land. Separation from India had required breaking down the Indian Army of which some Burmese units were a part. Upon separation, for example, the Indian Army lost four battalions of the Burma Rifles, three units of the Indian Territorial Force, and five units of the Auxiliary Force. The British government promised, however, that Indian troops would "not normally be employed in Burma," aside from a few minor units that would remain until Burma could raise comparable units of its own. This had left the issue open as to whether the Indian Army would in future be available for the defense of Burma, which remained under consideration. To augment local forces for Burma's defense, the governor, who was still responsible for matters of defense, began to recruit soldiers for a "frontier force" from non-Burman ethnic minorities, such as the Chins, Kachins, and Karens, although this was opposed by some missionary elements in the colony.[8] Such efforts did not come to fruition by the time of the invasion and the Indian Army viewed Burma as expendable.

When a BIA unit under the command of Ne Win entered Rangoon, they found it largely deserted. The Japanese had made a devastating air attack on Rangoon on 23 December 1941, prompting a mass exodus of 75 percent of the municipality's population. While Burmese were left to fend for themselves and fled to the villages, British authorities appointed "Evacuation Officers of the Indian Evacuees" to aid the Indian population that began to "walk" to India along the Rangoon–Prome Road (some 180 miles long) and then across the Arakan Mountains. The hardships of the evacuation led to the deaths of thousands from exposure and exhaustion. British Advanced Army Headquarters, as well as administrative units and all troops not assigned to demolition, withdrew from Rangoon on 7 March 1942. As Burma was to be sacrificed to the Japanese for the better defense of India, British demolition teams were put to the task of destroying much of Rangoon's economic and transportation infrastructure. The BIA and the Japanese took Rangoon the following day. One Burmese town after another was similarly sacrificed as the British continued to retreat toward the Indian frontier. The Japanese took Prome after the British withdrawal on 2 April, and then repulsed the Chinese Fifth Army that had only recently taken up the defense of Toungoo. Mandalay, Maymyo, and many other towns fell soon after, followed by the Arakan region, until the Japanese reached the difficult, mountainous terrain to the northwest. Topography more than British military prowess halted the Japanese advance. Burma was now a land laid waste by both sides in the war. More destruction would follow.[9]

Those Allied troops captured in Burma and elsewhere were soon put to work on building a railway to supply the Japanese Army in Burma overland from Thailand. As was typical of most European colonies, the transportation infrastructure was oriented toward taking raw materials and agricultural produce to the main port to be shipped back home (and conversely to bring imports in from the colonial metropole), rather than to encouraging overland trade with neighboring colonies, one of the colonial legacies that would hamper development in the post-war years. The Japanese trans-Burma railway was thus a major feat, built across rugged terrain, in a very short period. It would run from October 1943 until very nearly the end of the war, carrying a maximum of 500 tons per day.[10] Nevertheless, this line, popularly remembered as the "death railway," caused the deaths of thousands of prisoners of war, who were worked, starved, and beaten to death in their struggle to build it, and whose graves can still be found on both sides of the Burmese-Thai border.

"SELF-RULE" UNDER THE JAPANESE

The Japanese were never really interested in Burma for itself. The real prizes of Southeast Asia were Indonesia for its oil and the Malay Peninsula for its tin and rubber. In fact the Japanese would create a lot of misery in the country when they tried to get Burma to produce something useful for the war effort, such as cotton, because rice could be had nearly everywhere else. Burma's main place in Japanese wartime planning was first as a springboard into India and second, as the western wall of a "fortress Asia" when Japanese fortunes declined (incidentally, very early in the war). Hence the Japanese Army was given considerable latitude in handling Burma and the Japanese Military Administration (JMA) could afford to make political concessions there, as well as in the Philippines, that it was unwilling to give in other areas of Southeast Asia until 1945 when the end of the war approached.

The Japanese had given permission for the BIA to organize the administration of liberated villages, towns, and districts and when Thakins under Thakin Tun Oke reached Rangoon, they organized the Bama Baho government. This made economic concessions to the Japanese and promised to pay 3,000 rupees for every Japanese killed in Burma during the war. The Thakins, however, began pushing for more independence than the Japanese were willing to concede. Moreover, the Thakins' small experience in administration made them poor rulers and they proved unable to keep law and order. The Japanese Commander-in-Chief in Burma, General Shojiro Iida, thus abolished the Bama Baho government on 5 June 1942 (he would disband the BIA the following month), turning to Burma's older, more experienced leaders instead. One day earlier, Iida had called a meeting at Maymyo of important Burmese leaders who remained in the country. He promised that in return for Burmese cooperation in the war and participation in the Greater East Asia Co-Prosperity Sphere, they could set up a Central Government under Japanese military control and later would be given independence. Ba Maw agreed and set up an interim government. A preparatory committee was then established, chaired by Ba Maw, to prepare for the creation of a Central Government. The interim government would last from 5 June to 1 August. This was replaced, from August 1942 until August 1943, by the Burmese Executive Administration, again under Ba Maw, who served as Chief Administrator as well as Executive for Internal Affairs. Soon after, the name of the committee was changed to the Provisional Government of Burma and Ba Maw was named as Prime Minister. Under the Burma Executive Administration, the whole administration, including the Chief Administrator, were under the authority of the Japanese Commander-in-Chief. Beneath him was a shadow hierarchy of Japanese officers attached to the central office of each department as well as to Burmese district officers. Burmese administrative autonomy was a myth.[11]

The Burmese Executive Administration launched countrywide campaigns in support of Japan. These claimed that the "Japanese and the Burmans were brothers, being Asiatics, that they were also of the same race and same religion, and that, therefore, they must move together with Nippon as the mighty leader." A totalitarian order would have to be established in order to win the war. Political parties were then abolished and a new unitary party was established, the Dobama Sinyetha Party, later renamed the Maha Bama Sinyetha Party. Three thousand men of the BIA, which had been disbanded in July, were remobilized under the title of the Burma Defence Army (BDA) under the command of Aung San. This army underwent instruction from Japanese officers, whom many found to be too overbearing. There were also complaints that they were underpaid.[12]

The Burmese who had welcomed the Japanese into the colony waited anxiously for independence. Movement in this direction began in early 1943. In January, the Japanese Prime Minister, General Tojo, announced before the Imperial Diet that he intended to grant Burma independence within one year. In March, Ba Maw headed a delegation, including Aung San, which flew to Tokyo to discuss the issue. The Japanese Army agreed to speed up the transition to independence in order to use Burma as an example to stimulate rebellion in India. Later in March, General Iida appointed a Supreme Court in Burma and in April he set up the twenty-two-member

Burma Independence Preparatory Committee under Ba Maw, to draft a new constitution. This body soon operated as Burma's Constituent Assembly.[13]

On 1 August, the new Constitution was finally promulgated, creating the office of *Adipati* ("dictator"), a cabinet of ministers, and a thirty-member privy council to serve as a consultative body. After Ba Maw was chosen as *Adipati*, he declared Burmese independence, formally ending the JMA. As the capital of the now independent "Bama" state, the Rangoon Municipality was eloquently renamed "Rangoon Naypyidaw." Colonel Ne Win was appointed as the commander of the new Burma National Army (BNA) that replaced the BDA, while Aung San, the Minister of Defense, devoted himself to developing the BNA into a genuine fighting force. A significant number of Burmese were then sent to the Imperial Military College in Japan.[14] Despite the formal declaration of independence, the Burmese government remained under close Japanese "guidance."

THE "OTHER" BURMA

The development of independence out of liberation required a definition of what Burma was and what it was not. The Japanese had to act both pragmatically and politically. Thailand was a wartime Japanese ally and was rewarded with various territorial concessions, including Western Laos and Western Cambodia, which were transferred from French Indochina to Thai control. Thai nationalists, borrowing from the examples of Fascist ethno-centered views of history being played out in Europe, also sought to reconnect the Thai with other branches of the "Tai race" who made up the main population of the Shan states. Ultimately, the Japanese transferred ownership of Kengtung and Mongpan States to the Thai Government.[15]

The Japanese-sponsored redefinition of Burma reinforced the rough division between ministerial Burma and the "Scheduled Areas" inherited from the pre-1942 period. The Japanese recognized the political autonomy of the Shan *sawbwas* in the states and these states were thus left out of the newly "independent" Burma under Ba Maw. Likewise, Ba Maw's Burma did not include the Karenni States, which had always enjoyed the status of a "native state" under the British. Although the Japanese could afford no major ethnic rebellions within a major war front area, which Burma constituted, ethnic tensions were perhaps unavoidable. In 1940, two years before the invasion, Burmans made up only about 12 percent of the Burma Army, while the Kachins and Chins each made up about 23 percent of the troops, and the Karens nearly 30 percent.[16]

By contrast, the BIA was largely recruited from urban areas in Lower Burma and it generally did not recruit from either the Asian immigrant minorities, such as the Chinese and Indians, or the hill tribes. Almost by default, the BIA became an armed Burman ethno-nationalist force and, as a result of colonial favor to the Karens and the legacy of colonial generalizations of the Karen on the basis of the Christian Sgaw Karen, the BIA closely associated the Karens in general with the British, whom they had just removed from Burma with Japanese help. When the BIA began to disarm Karens in Myaungmya, fighting broke out, Burmans and Karens burning scores of villages on each side. In order to restore stability behind their lines, the Japanese Army moved in to stop the violence that now swept through the delta. The Myaungmya violence was not the only reason many Karen favored the Allies in the war; many Karen from the colonial army who had remained behind in Burma, particularly in the hill areas, after the British withdrew, were already hostile to both the BIA and the Japanese and would become key to the organization of Karen attacks on the Japanese later in the war. The Kachins also lent their support to the anti-Japanese cause by joining the US Office of Strategic Services' Detachment 101 in the north. Operating from mountain outposts, they were mainly involved in destroying the transportation infrastructure and gathering intelligence, but in the process reportedly killed over 5,000 Japanese soldiers.[17]

The emergence of the BIA and its successors, the BDA and the BNA, under the Burmese together with support for the Allies among the ethnic minorities, on the one hand, and the constitutional division of Burma, under the Japanese, into a Burman state and ethnic hill areas, on the other hand, fostered an ethnic dimension to the war that would contribute both to the prolonged duration of negotiations for independence once the British returned in 1945, and the civil war early after independence. As one scholar observes, among some of Burma's hill minorities, the heritage of World War II was the rise of their own ethno-nationalism and expectations that they would be rewarded, after the Allied victory, for their wartime service. Among some Karen leaders, these expectations included the establishment of an independent Karen state.[18]

THE SOCIAL AND ECONOMIC IMPACT OF OCCUPATION

Under Japanese rule, civil liberties were severely curtailed and promised freedoms for which the Thakins had agreed to aid the Japanese were denied. The Burmese were particularly upset over the way in which Japanese soldiers would publicly slap them across the face for petty offenses. The

Japanese secret police (*Kenpeitai*) scoured the country for opponents to the Ba Maw Government and, as the war dragged on and the Allies began their advance into Burma, the Japanese adopted stricter security measures. Among these were restrictions on the movements of Burmese who were now required to carry passes issued by local headmen when traveling outside their own towns and villages. The Ba Maw Government re-imposed the system of communal responsibility under which families and sometimes the whole village were held responsible for the misbehavior of a single individual. From April 1943, the Japanese also required local Burmese officials to recruit *heiho* (auxiliary troops) to help provide local security, but most were sent to Rangoon to serve as laborers for the Japanese Army. Although formally a volunteer force, difficulties in recruitment led to coercion. Many Burmese naturally deserted whenever the opportunity presented itself.[19]

The Japanese were also concerned that the disappearance of the export market would create political problems when Burmese farmers were left with too much excess paddy on their hands or problems for the Japanese if Burmese farmers reduced their production to meet self-sufficiency alone. Without the export market, much of the 1941–1942 crop went unutilized and the same was true for the 1942–1943 crop. In June 1943, Agriculture Minister Than Tun announced the Purchase of Paddy Scheme under which the state would purchase the whole of the surplus of the paddy crop from the 1942–1943 season from thirteen districts, thus reducing agriculturalists' hardships, restoring the desire to cultivate crops for the 1943–1944 season, and encouraging the circulation of funds to support the economy. Little preparation was made for the scheme and only 160 officials, given only one day's training, were mobilized to carry out the program. By the end of 1943, the Ba Maw Government had given out in loans only a quarter of the funds needed to finance the paddy crop and cultivation declined. In early 1944, Rangoon Radio broadcast a one-act play in Burmese in which a mother taught her daughters to cook grass as well as explaining the nutritional value of grass and that it could be eaten in difficult times such as the present. As agriculture continued to collapse, Nu, the Foreign Minister, complained that it was difficult to find food even to give to the monks.[20]

THE ANTI-FASCIST PEOPLE'S FREEDOM LEAGUE

Although Tojo decorated both Ba Maw and Aung San in Tokyo in mid-1944, Aung San had already gone far in preparations for turning against the Japanese. The war minister had begun to send representatives in secret across the front to make contact with the Allies in India from December 1943. The Allies eventually promised to train Burmese troops to work as a fifth column and promised to include arms for the Burmese in future air drops. Force 136 entered Burma to establish resistance bases in Karen areas. By August 1944, the Anti-Fascist People's Freedom League (AFPFL, also known as the Anti-Fascist Organization to the Allies, as well as the Burma Patriotic Front in India) was formed to prepare for the Allied invasion. In preparation for the uprising to meet it, Aung San ordered the officers and men of the BNA to cease shaving their heads, as the Japanese had required, and wear their hair long like other Burmese men so they could merge easily with the general population when the time for revolt came.[21]

The war on the northwestern front quickly turned against the Japanese in late 1944 and early 1945 and Aung San prepared to make his move. On 24 March 1945, Aung San made a pledge at the Shwedagon Pagoda to begin the BNA's campaign against the Allies, while a Japanese military band provided the rhythm for the BNA units that marched out in the direction of the front. Once out of Rangoon, these units dispersed to pre-designated base areas in six zones throughout Central and Lower Burma and on the prearranged day, 27 March, they began their attack on Japanese forces. Before the end of May, Aung San's forces had fought 1,000 engagements and claimed, with considerable exaggeration, to have killed as many as 20,000 Japanese soldiers. Lt.-General William Slim's Fourteenth Army finally captured Rangoon on 3 May and talks began with Aung San two weeks later. Slim was impressed with Aung San and took him to be a genuine nationalist and an honest man. Aung San liked Slim as well and promised him that he would continue to support the Allies militarily and delay talk of independence until the Japanese defeat.[22]

As they had been cut off from communications with Japan during the Allied advance, Japanese soldiers in Burma, as in many other areas of Asia, fought on for weeks after the surrender of Japan. On 16 August, the Allies began airdropping leaflets across Burma informing Japanese soldiers that the war was indeed over. Still, Japanese soldiers fought on (and Allied planes were greeted with anti-aircraft fire from the ground), in the belief that this was simply enemy propaganda. Finally, on 24 October, the Japanese commander of the Burma area, General Kimura, formally surrendered his sword to Lt.-General Sir Montagu Stopford (Twelfth Army) at Rangoon University.[23]

THE BRITISH MILITARY ADMINISTRATION

The war had devastated Burma. As one observer commented after it had ended, "I believe there was a higher degree of destruction in [Burma] than in any other area in the East."[24] Two major campaigns had been fought across the entirety of the country, first by the Japanese to push the British out and then by the Allies, joined later by the AFPFL, to drive the Japanese out. In early March 1942, the British set fire to oil refineries in the vicinity of Rangoon and later burned Prome, they scuttled 95 percent of the five hundred steamer fleet of the Irrawaddy Flotilla Company, destroyed bridges, and engaged in a range of other efforts to "deny all to the enemy." While Japanese and later Allied planes would pound remaining installations and towns into rubble, after occupying the country, the Japanese engaged in no major wartime reconstruction, beyond the needs of the Japanese Army. Alongside the Japanese Army, Japanese companies were brought in to help in the procurement of supplies. Some of these, especially those in front-line areas, relied on harsh measures to achieve this. As a result of commandeering, the number of cattle in Burma dropped by two-thirds, severely hurting agricultural output. Japanese currency used to buy commodities quickly became inflated. Clothing became scarce and expensive. Things worsened as Japanese forces, cut off from supplies from abroad due to Allied submarines and aircraft, took all available resources.[25]

In the last months of the war, underground movements also began destroying bridges, communications, and harbors in order to pin the Japanese Army down. In Rangoon, the port and the railway station had been put out of commission. Half of the public and commercial buildings and one-third of homes had been ruined. Of those buildings that remained, they were empty shells after all their windows, doors, furniture, and electrical and sanitary fittings had been removed. It was estimated that 80 percent of the city had to be rebuilt. Myingyan, Meiktila, Prome, and Myitkyina had been completely flattened. Of Burma's 1,200 passenger railcars only 12 remained, 200 of its 250 locomotives had been destroyed, only two-thirds of its freight wagons survived, and as late as December 1945, only 800 out of 2,000 miles of railway track had been reopened. Bridges throughout the country had been destroyed and roads were in serious disrepair. Oil production and mining operations had completely stopped. Burma's rice acreage had also been cut in half, from thirteen million acres to a little over six million acres. Disease and starvation plagued the country.[26]

The immediate task of reconstruction fell to the British Military Administration (BMA), whose tenure ran from 6 May until 16 October 1945.

Although the British occupation had brought with them Indian notes stamped with a Burmese inscription as well as pre-war Burmese notes, they were not yet in general circulation and Burmese had continued to use the Japanese notes because they were the only widely distributed form of currency. In late May, as Burma quickly fell under re-occupation, the British Army issued Proclamation No. 6, which declared Japanese currency invalid without any offer of compensation or exchange. This declaration wiped out overnight whatever Burmese had saved over the past three and a half years, impoverishing all indigenous classes except for those who had fled to India (who had lost much themselves in the 1942 exodus). Riots broke out, shops closed, and crafty town-dwellers drove trucks full of Japanese notes into the countryside to buy goods from peasants who had not yet learned about the proclamation. For Burmese families, the cost of living index had risen to 679 by November (based on the figure of 100 for 1941).[27]

Impoverished civilians poured into Rangoon, which had become nearly deserted over the course of the war, for shelter. They found little left. Timber housing in the city had all gone up in flames. Besides their destroyed homes, the military had occupied all of the best surviving buildings, including the schools and the RU Campus. British troops are remembered to have been "greater vandals than the Japanese." They scoured buildings for flooring and stairs that could be used for firewood and broke up surviving bungalows for this purpose as well. Even the famous Minto Mansions Hotel, which had remained in fair condition, was demolished for masonry to exchange a dirt floor for a solid foundation in a depot one unit occupied. The BMA appears to have given low priority to finding shelter for the Burmese. Thus, thousands were forced to erect mat huts in every available space, especially pavements, which made better flooring than muddy soil. The Royal Lakes now became hidden by shanty towns and the main streets of Rangoon were lined with huts: "Rangoon was a veritable metropolis of matting and thatch."[28]

The BMA established the Civil Affairs Service (Burma) or CASB which set up a system of government projects. A consortium of pre-war British and Indian commercial firms, working as agents of the government and employing their skilled workers to rebuild industries in the areas of civil supplies, transport, timber, and rice, ran each project. The projects were designed so that the industries so revived could eventually be transferred to the ownership of the commercial firms involved. The Civil Supplies Board (CSB), for example, was established on 27 August 1945 and was given "dictatorial powers," being responsible only to the CSB and then to the governor on his return. The CSB had powers to search for goods, make compulsory purchases, and control the transport of commodities. Further, it nominated certain commercial firms as its agents and "liquidated" any competition. As boats and steamers came back into service, they were run for the government by the Irrawaddy Flotilla Company, at government expense, with the agreement that when water transport had returned to normal the company had the right to take over ownership of the craft "at a value." The projects continued to be run by the CASB until 1 April 1946, when responsibility was transferred to the governor.[29]

Although other projects were agreed in principle with companies, they were not wholly put into operation immediately because commercial firms refused to rebuild their installations until Britain agreed to compensation for wartime damage. They also refused to invest new capital in Burma until the government had established a clear policy on these lines. The projects would also be severely criticized by Burmese leaders. Burmese were not informed of the "policy, organization, and the actual working of these government projects." The CASB operated with a kind of secrecy, according to Burmese critics, and they were not told how the commercial firms were benefiting from their participation in the projects, whether or not (and if so, how much) the CASB was profiting from the sale of Burmese rice in India, or what the ultimate policy of the government would be regarding the projects and the commercial firms. The information gap left much room for the Burmese to suspect the intentions of the British government and many Burmese understandably interpreted these projects to be British support for a return of British and Indian commercial domination.[30]

THE EXECUTIVE COUNCIL

In October 1945, the BMA was ended and the government in exile (in Simla) was reinstated under Governor Sir Reginald Dorman-Smith. While Dorman-Smith would be personally blamed for the faults of the returned colonial administration, the evidence indicates that he often disagreed with the policies he was ordered to pursue and his suggestions to government on making concessions were just as frequently rejected.

The British plan was for the governor to rule with emergency powers until the pre-war Burmese government could be reestablished and this government, elected under the 1937 Constitution, would determine Burma's future. Dorman-Smith announced on 17 October 1945, the day after he arrived in Burma, that he would create a fifteen-member Executive Council as an advisory body and a fifty-member Legislative Council. He invited the AFPFL to join. A week later, the League's Supreme Council adopted a resolution that it would cooperate if the governor filled eleven of the fifteen seats with League nominees, leaving four seats for him to select. The eleven League-nominated members would have to be allowed to work as a team, decide the allocation of portfolios among themselves, and to resign as a group if the League decided by a 75 percent vote that they should do so, or if at any point they felt they were not accomplishing their objectives within the Executive Council. The League also resolved that the Executive Council would have to prepare for a general election based on universal suffrage for a constituent assembly rather than for a legislature, and also act as a "popular Government and undertake other tasks" that were not specified. Aung San later repeated these demands to the governor, further requiring that a League member should control the Home Affairs portfolio. By 28 October, talks with Dorman-Smith broke down and he approached other politicians in order to appoint an Executive Council, now reduced to eleven members, without the League for the time being. He then filled the Executive Council with pro-British Burmese with no popular appeal, as well as a British general and a British civilian official by mid-November.[31]

Dorman-Smith proposed to London in March 1946 to increase the powers of the Executive Council and the Legislature prior to the planned elections, but these measures were refused. Dorman-Smith also proposed including Aung San in the Executive Council, but London denied permission for this move as well, citing outstanding murder charges against the AFPFL leader. In response, Dorman-Smith sent a strong protest to London, arguing that "rigid adherence" to these rulings might provoke an "open rebellion."[32]

Since the British continued to prove reluctant to grant independence, Aung San now began a constitutional struggle, demanding the creation of an interim representative government with full powers over the affairs of the colony. Aung San also called for Burmese non-cooperation in matters of the payment of rent and taxes, and the sale of rice to official government purchasing agents. In June, Dorman-Smith was recalled to London to report to the government on the situation in Burma. He did so in early August, and resigned afterwards. The AFPFL interpreted the recall as an indication of British weakness. Emboldened, the League now promised to support all public service personnel in their demands against the government; it would force the latter to restore press freedom and civil liberties, and ordered all League branches to fly only the party flag and celebrate "national" days it identified.[33]

The new governor, Major General Sir Hubert Rance, the former head of the CASB, faced a seemingly hopeless situation when he arrived in Rangoon at the end of August 1946. He was tasked with ending the strikes, bringing the AFPFL to heel, and establishing the conditions necessary to continue with reconstruction. Yet more obstacles were already in the works. Burmese nationalists were already remobilizing their paramilitary forces, including Aung San's People's Volunteer Organization (PVO) and Saw's Myochit Party's paramilitary wing. More strikes were also being organized. On 1 September, at a time when "dacoity" was everywhere, police officers went on strike in Rangoon and in several rural districts. Despite the tensions now boiling over, Rance held firm and announced what the British government was prepared to allow. There would be no "epoch making changes." The powers of the Executive Council would not be increased, the country would be prepared for dominion status rather than outright independence, and the government would seek the participation of both the Myochit Party and the League. His government's three main objectives included reconstruction and rehabilitation, the creation of the conditions necessary to hold elections in the spring of 1947, and the restoration of law and order.[34]

Despite the unyielding rhetoric, perhaps intended to please politicians at home, Rance in actuality abandoned non-cooperation and adopted a more conciliatory approach than had Dorman-Smith. On 21 September 1946, Rance met with Burmese leaders to discuss the membership of the reformed Executive Council. To ensure that there would be no colonial backpedaling, Aung San increased the pressure. During the negotiations, the strikes continued and were joined by employees of the Postal Department and the Central Government Press, while Aung San simultaneously called for a general strike to take place on 23 September. The governor caved in completely and announced that a new Executive Council had been formed, giving the AFPFL a majority of six members in the nine-member Executive Council, under his own chairmanship. League members only accepted the concessions on the understanding that the Council would operate as a normal Council of Ministers and that the governor's veto would be used as sparingly as possible. Most of the strikes ended within a week.[35]

THE LONDON AGREEMENT

Burmese politicians remained frustrated by the White Paper issued by the Conservative government on 17 May 1945, which offered a three-stage independence plan. First, for a three-year interim period, until or before 9 December 1948, Burma would be governed under the rules of the emergency administration set up in 1942. However, there would also be an executive council including Burmese and perhaps a colonial legislature. By the close of this period, an election would be held for a government like that granted under the Government of Burma Act, 1935. The Burmese would then write a new constitution and negotiate with Britain regarding what the latter would continue to control, such as the Scheduled Areas (the Frontier Areas), after final independence. At a yet undetermined time (suggested by some as being about mid-1953), Burma would gain independence within the British Commonwealth with limitations that had been determined in the second stage.[36]

The Executive Council complained of the "leisurely and protracted" pace of preparations for independence outlined in the White Paper and the more "energetic" program regarding the creation of an interim government and a constituent assembly to replace it in India. There was also some unhappiness that the White Paper did not limit the term for the governor's discretionary powers. Nor was there any provision for a Burmese-led interim government to rule the country until the promulgation of a constitution. Instead of the White Paper's program, the Executive Council, following the resolutions made by the AFPFL Working Committee in early November 1946, demanded

(1) the immediate establishment of an interim national government with the governor serving as constitutional head;
(2) a British promise by 31 January 1947 to grant independence in one year;
(3) a firm statement by the British that the Burmese had the right to decide whether or not Burma would join the Commonwealth;
(4) use of the scheduled forthcoming elections for a colonial legislature for the election of a constituent assembly instead;
(5) an inquiry into how to fit the Frontier Areas into independent Burma;
(6) that all British financial projects be restructured or ended prior to 31 January 1947,

and promised that if the British did not concede on all of these points, all of the League members of the Executive Council would resign.[37]

Changing political fortunes in Britain favored the successful outcome of AFPFL demands. By December 1946, a Labour government had replaced the Conservatives in Britain and Clement Attlee was now Prime Minister. On 20 December, Attlee announced that Britain would review its policy regarding Burma. Britain did not want people in the Commonwealth against their will, he explained, and Burmese nationals should frame their own constitution after the election of a constituent assembly, "on the analogy of what has already been done in India." Furthermore, in the meantime, the British Government would not interfere in the way in which the Burmese members of the Executive Council handled everyday administration. In January 1947, a Burmese delegation led by Aung San went to Britain for negotiations with the government and determined on reaching a settlement. Stopping in New Delhi in the first week of January on his way to London, Aung San took time to study how the interim government was working in India, in order to prepare for one in Burma. Aung San warned from the outset of the negotiations that he had to reach a settlement by the end of January or he would go back to Burma and there would be a political deadlock. He also added to previous AFPFL demands that the Executive Council have free access to the Frontier Areas to persuade the people there to join Burma. The British and the Burmese delegations eventually arrived at an agreement, the London or Anglo-Burmese Agreement, on 27 January. The Agreement promised independence to Burma and that she could decide whether or not to join the Commonwealth but did not mention when independence would be granted.[38]

While the Burmese delegation had achieved most of its objectives, not all Burmese were satisfied. At home, some Burmese claimed the delegation had achieved nothing, while others said, figuratively, that it had achieved 75 percent of its goals. There was dissent among the delegation. At 11:15 P.M. on 26 January 1947, after the parties had agreed on all the major points, Saw and U Ba Sein, having given no indication of opposition previously, suddenly announced that they did not wish to sign the agreement. When Attlee and Aung San both pressed the pair for an explanation, they simply said that the agreement "did not go far enough." Saw eventually relented and gave a quick, ill-thought-out response that he wanted elections for the legislature, even though the agreement had gone far beyond this. When Aung San suggested their immediate resignations, the British side said the matter could be resolved when the Burmese delegation returned to Burma. A British critic of Saw and Ba Sein conjectured that their move had something to do with their frequent meetings with former governor Reginald Dorman-Smith and an effort by right-wing British politicians to sabotage Burmese reconstruction. In early February, both Saw and Ba Sein resigned from the Executive Council.[39]

Elections for the Constituent Assembly were held on 9 April 1947. The AFPFL won a landslide victory, taking 248 of 255 seats, while the Burma Communist Party took the remaining seven. U Saw's Myochit Party, Ba Maw's Maha Bama (Sinyetha) Party, and Thakin Ba Sein's Dobama Asi-ayone had boycotted the election, as they could expect only a small share of the vote. The Assembly finally met on 9 June. Soon after, Nu was elected President of the body, Aung San's resolution outlining the seven main points on which to draw up the Constitution was passed, and the Assembly created a fifteen-member select committee to draft the Constitution.[40]

THE FRONTIER AREAS

According to the British White Paper of May 1945, the Scheduled Areas of which the Shan states were a part were renamed the Frontier Areas and remained, as before, outside of "ministerial" Burma and thus outside the authority of the Executive Council and directly under that of the governor. A separate Frontier Areas administration was then set up in 1946 under the Director of Frontier Areas. The first Frontier Areas' Conference, also being the first such meeting between Burmese and "Frontier Areas" leaders, was held at Panglong from 27 March to 2 April 1946. Shan leaders of the thirty-four federated Shan states, presided over by the *Sawbwa* of Tong Peng, met to discuss their goals regarding trade, culture, and welfare. The conference had also invited Karen, Kachin, and Chin representatives, several Burmese leaders, including Saw and Thakin Nu, and the governor (who did not attend due to illness) to discuss future relations between the Frontier Areas in general and the Shan states in particular with ministerial Burma. The Director of Frontier Areas announced the creation of Regional Councils to advise British residents and State Councils to advise the *sawbwas*. Saw also gave a speech urging the representatives of the Frontier Areas' peoples to agree as soon as possible to unity with ministerial Burma regarding economy and defense, promising autonomy in all other matters. The second Frontier Areas' Conference (usually remembered as *the* Panglong Conference), mentioned in the London Agreement, was held at Panglong from 9 to 12 February 1947. The conference was to determine Frontier Area representation in the Executive Council and the forthcoming Constituent Assembly. The Chins and Kachins wanted separate, autonomous states, under a central government that handled defence and foreign policy. The Shans, already having the Shan States Federation, wanted to negotiate their relationship with the future central government.[41]

Under the agreement reached and put into operation at the end of March 1947, during the interim period, the Frontier Areas would be brought within the authority of the Executive Council on matters of "common interest," in such cases as defence and external affairs, "but without prejudice to full internal autonomy." The Agreement also preserved the existing

Frontier Areas' internal administrative autonomy. The Agreement did not change the status of financial assistance to the Chin and Kachin Hills and the financial autonomy of the Shan States Federation. The Executive Council would now include a member representing the "frontier peoples" and this member would be appointed by the governor on the recommendation of the Supreme Council of the United Hills Peoples. Since there were three ethnic groups or "races" to be represented, after the councilor was selected, the two "races" which he did not belong to would be represented by two councilors who would assist him and act on the principle of joint responsibility and would be able to attend the Executive Council meetings when their areas were under discussion. The first appointees included a Shan *sawbwa* as councilor, along with a Chin and a Kachin deputy councilor. The Agreement guaranteed the citizens of the Frontier Areas "the rights and privileges which are regarded as fundamental in democratic countries." The Panglong Agreement also created the Frontier Areas Enquiry Commission, planned for in the London Agreement. The commission visited the Frontier Areas and conducted numerous interviews and on this basis submitted a unanimous report that asserted that representatives "of all states, districts and local areas" wished to be associated with the forthcoming Constituent Assembly. It also recommended increasing the size of the Assembly by the creation of an additional forty-five seats, all reserved for the Frontier Areas.[42]

While the Shans, Chins, and Kachins occupied ethnically identifiable and distinct zones in the Frontier Areas, the situation of the Karens was more problematic. Relatively small pockets did exist that could be identified as Karen, the largest being the Salween District, but these were scattered in the hill districts of the Frontier Areas. A failed plan to establish a semi-autonomous Karen state in August 1947, for example, suggested that it should include the Salween District, the Karenni States, and the Toungoo Karen Hills. Such a state would lack geographic connectivity and be unworkable as an administrative unit, in addition to lacking, it was argued at the time, an economically stable basis for survival. Further, most Karens lived in the Burmese lowlands, intermixed with other ethnic groups, especially the Burmans. Erecting an integrated Karen homeland was thus more problematic than for the Shans, the Kachins, or the Chins. The biggest challenge, however, was the bifurcation of Karen leadership between those who favored integration with Burma and those who preferred to establish an independent state. This made a united Karen front impossible. Although Karen leaders were not included in the delegation that negotiated the London Agreement, pro-union Karens supported it, since that Agreement proposed to double the number of seats reserved for the plains Karens from twelve in the old colonial legislature to twenty-four in the forthcoming Constituent Assembly. A boycott of the Panglong negotiations by some Karen leaders meant that only a small body of Hill Karens attended the conference and even they did not participate in the proceedings. Consultations were then begun between the various Karen groups to determine what their position was relative to the Panglong Agreement.[43]

The Karen National Union (KNU) was formed in 1947 out of the remnants of the Karen Central Organization, founded in 1945, which in turn had succeeded the Karen National Association founded in 1881. The KNU's purpose was to represent those Karens who saw no future for themselves in a united and independent Burma. They were not alone, for the Mons also sought independence from the forthcoming Union of Burma and began writing to different governments for help at about the same time. The KNU announced that it would not take part in the April elections because the Karens had been allotted insufficient seats in the forthcoming Constituent Assembly. Instead, they pressured Saw Ba U Gyi, a member of the Executive Council, to resign and sent a deputation to the Frontier Areas Commission of Inquiry to lodge a complaint. After the KNU pulled its candidates from the election, the AFPFL nominated twenty-four members of the Karen Youth League to run for election. Thus, pro-union Karens swept the polls for the reserved Karen seats. Further, the two Karen seats in the Executive Council both went to pro-union Karen leaders.[44]

The anxieties of anti-union Karens would become feverish by October. Karen separatists sent to Governor Rance a letter they wanted him to forward to Prime Minister Attlee that claimed that they had arms and would not surrender. Rance refused to send this officially to the government, but did forward it on an informal basis. Although the AFPFL was aware of the situation, it downplayed its significance, choosing instead a policy of placating the Karens by putting them into important positions of authority. In Karen areas, administrative offices were given to Karens. The League had also determined to replace the commander of the Burma Army, General Thomas Latter, with Smith Dun, a Karen and a graduate of Sandhurst Military Academy, when the British Military Mission withdrew in the forthcoming months. The Karens remained concerned, however, since future Burmese leaders might entertain a different policy. Despite the League's awareness of the crisis emerging regarding the Karens, it delayed on recovering weapons from the Karens.[45]

As a result of both the London Agreement and the prospective Anglo-Burmese Treaty, some parties formed an opposition bloc. This included Saw and his Myochit Party, Ba Sein and his Dobama Party, and Ba Maw's Sinyetha Party. Their opposition was not mainly ideological, but grew out of personal jealousy of Aung San. Of these leaders, Saw would emerge as the most notorious. Saw had become a sad figure since his pre-occupation days when he had been Prime Minister. He had spent the war in a detention camp and after his return to Burma a jeep pulled up alongside his car and a revolver was fired at him at close range. A window had deflected the bullet, but shattered glass hit Saw in the face and lodged in one eye, for which reason he wore dark glasses in public. Saw struggled to find his place in the new Burma and was frustrated by the popularity of the AFPFL that made a serious political comeback difficult. He deeply distrusted Aung San, whom he saw as nothing more than a Japanese collaborator, and strongly felt that Rance made a serious mistake in giving Aung San leadership rather than himself.[46]

Claims later emerged that Saw had attempted to assassinate Aung San in February 1947 and had given six months of weapons training to members of his Myochit Party for a second attempt in the future. Conservative elements in Britain also disliked Aung San. Winston Churchill continued to deride Aung San, even after his death, as a "traitor rebel leader," the organizer of a "Quisling army," and a man guilty of "great cruelties" against loyal Burmese during the war. Only when the British Army advanced into Burma did Aung San, "whose hands were dyed with British blood and loyal Burmese blood," conveniently switch to the Allied side.[47]

At 10:00 A.M. on the morning of Saturday, 19 July 1947, the Governor's Executive Council held a meeting to discuss national security regarding the theft of 200 Bren guns from the Ordnance Depot a week earlier. The session, presided over by the Council Deputy Chairman, the thirty-three-year-old Aung San, was held in the Council Chamber of the Secretariat Building. As usual, Aung San, who had exchanged his military uniform for a silk jacket and a Bangkok *longyi*, seated himself at the center of the large u-shaped table, whose mouth faced the entrance. On the north side of the table sat Thakin Mya, Mahn Ba Khaing, Deedok U Ba Choe, A. Razak, and U Ba Win (Aung San's elder brother). On the south side sat Sao Sam Htun (the *Sawbwa* of Mong Pawn), U Ba Gyan (Member for Rehabilitation and Public Works), U Aung Zan Wei, and Pyawbwe U Mya. Shortly before 10:30 A.M., five men dressed in the jungle-green uniforms of the

Twelfth Army pulled up to the Secretariat Building in a jeep bearing a false license plate. Police waved them in without much thought. In Rangoon and elsewhere in Burma, old military uniforms were worn regularly by many, even within the Secretariat, and PVO members and the militia of other organizations could be seen everywhere, many armed. The men got out at the entrance to the Shan State Ministry and went up to the first floor, while their jeep waited with the engine running. As they did so, the Deputy Secretary of the Ministry of Transport and Communications, U Ohn Maung, entered the chamber to submit a report to the Council. At about 10:37 A.M., the men, led by one Hmon Gyi, approached the Council Chamber. With their three Bren guns and one Sten gun in hand, they knocked down a guard at the door, pushed it open, and entered the room, shouting "Don't run away!" As Aung San rose to face the men, they opened fire, dropping him to the floor. They sprayed gunfire first across the middle of the table, killing Ohn Maung, and then across the table's north-ern half, killing three of the ministers, and mortally wounding a fourth (Ba Choe died later the same day), seated on this end. As the gunmen then swung their guns toward the southern side of the table, the ministers on this end fell to the floor in a split second, saving their lives, with the exception of the *Sawbwa* of Mong Pawn who was wounded in the face (and died on the operating table the following day). After three more rounds of firing, the assassins fled the area, mortally wounding Razak's personal bodyguard on the stairs as he rushed up to see what had happened. Seven of the ten men in the room were dead or dying. As the survivors ran out, they left behind a miserable scene that would alter the course of Burma's history forever: the smell of carbide, blood-stained floors, spent cartridge cases, and the bodies of the father of Burmese independence and some of his closest associates. Although another pair of assassins had also been sent out to kill Nu, they were unable to find him that morning.[48]

Colonial officials at first believed that the assassinations had been the work of the Communists. On 19 July, however, government forces raided Saw's house and arrested both him and four men who were ultimately accused of having carried out the attack. U Ba Nyun, a witness for the prosecution in the trial that followed, explained that the jeep had returned immediately to Saw's house, where the license plate was replaced and the jeep's genuine number was now painted once again on its side. The men then changed their clothes and began drinking alcohol in celebration. Saw was even reported to have drunk alcohol from the barrel of the gun that had killed Aung San. The guns and license plate were then dumped into Inya Lake near where Saw lived, and the discarded uniforms burned.

Police action against Saw had been quick, because he had been under secret surveillance by the police on another matter for some time and the departure and return of the jeep had been noted. Eight hundred others would eventually be arrested in the investigation as well. A British police officer (Burma was still a colony) was put in charge of the investigation. The police found that the jeep was still covered in wet paint, divers recovered the guns and ammunition from the lake, and remnants of burned uniforms were found in the kitchen fireplace. A bevy of witnesses came forward to provide evidence of Saw's complicity in the conspiracy.[49]

Ironically, the existence of an orgy of evidence that too clearly identified Saw as the killer has led to speculation that the assassination was carried out by the British government, another political rival to Aung San, or both. Some, such as the BCP leader (and Aung San's brother-in-law) Than Tun, accused the British of ordering the assassination through counter-revolutionary allies. A British Labour MP even told Parliament that members of the British Conservative opposition bore more "moral guilt of the assassination" than the gunmen for having encouraged Saw to carry out "treachery and sabotage." As rumours of British involvement grew, the Government of Burma made a public declaration that neither the British Government nor Rance were in any way connected with the killings. Saw's defense attorney argued that he was being framed, for how could someone of his intelligence entertain the murderers at his home shortly after the crime took place? Saw himself testified that the man who had turned King's evidence, Ba Nyun, and other followers had suggested at one point that AFPFL members should be "wiped out," but that he himself, despite having had numerous political rivals over the course of his career, had never considered killing any of them. After hearing the case, a tribunal convicted Saw of the murder. After appeals failed, Saw was hanged.[50]

Steps toward independence moved very quickly after Aung San's assassination. The draft constitution was put before the Constituent Assembly on 31 July and was unanimously approved on 24 September. The following day, this body also unanimously elected Sao Shwe Taik, the *Sawbwa* of Yawnghwe, and Nu as Provisional President and Prime Minister, respectively. Meanwhile, the formalities of severance from Britain continued to proceed. The Constituent Assembly also voted unanimously not to participate in the British Commonwealth, despite Rance's encouragement to join it. The Anglo-Burmese Treaty setting out the terms of Burma's relationship with Britain was finally signed on 18 October 1947. The Burma Independence Act was then put before the Parliament and was approved against strong Conservative opposition. Independence was finally declared on 4 January 1948.[51]

CONCLUSION

The Burmese had several tastes of independence during the 1937–1947 period. From 1937 to 1942, the Burmese had limited self-rule without formal independence; under the Japanese, from 1942 to 1945, they had formal independence and less self-rule, while during the 1945–1947 period, although formal independence was taken away, they nearly had de facto control of the colony, made clear by the general strike. These years included many potential watersheds, or lost opportunities. One wonders if, had the British granted dominion status to Burma, as Saw demanded in 1941, or if the war had not broken out at all, a conservative nationalist leadership would have led independent Burma. On the other hand, the Japanese invasion ensured that whatever concessions were made, it was Aung San and his comrades who were assured supreme nationalist credentials. When the British returned, whatever they were willing to offer was irrelevant as Burma's course to independence had already been established by the actions of the AFPFL in early 1945.

More importantly, the 1937–1947 period served as a long trial run for independence. All of Burma's major political leaders for the next four decades emerged on the national scene during these years, held commanding positions in the state or army, and gained the kind of administrative experience necessary for the challenges ahead. The period also saw the end of the careers of the leading members of Burma's pre-independence national leadership: Aung San, who was assassinated; Saw, who was hanged; and Ba Maw, who was politically dead due to his close collaboration with the Japanese. With the charismatic center of Burma's leadership gone, their lieutenants would lead Burma headlong into one of the world's longest civil wars.

CHAPTER 4

The democratic experiment, 1948–1958

Aung San's assassination in 1947 cast a long shadow over independent Burma. Nu was handed the task of leading Burma in an experiment with democracy that ended badly. This was partly due to the fact that Nu lacked much of the single-minded focus, political skills, and organizational ability of his predecessor. Perhaps more blame could be directed at the myriad political, ethnic, and institutional forces set loose. It could be said that by comparison to the 1945–1947 period, when the Burmese had unity, but not independence, that under Nu, Burma had independence, but not unity. The Burmese had achieved independence without a revolution, which prevented the emergence of internal solidarity or the squeezing out of rival groups and ideologies that occurred, for example, with the Vietminh in the face of French military efforts to reestablish their control in the First Indochina War. Whereas the Vietminh were provided with the opportunity to cultivate the political solidarity originally developed to oppose the Japanese and Vichy French, after World War II, in Burma the old political rivalries reemerged very quickly, especially as the British left.

To make matters worse, guns and other weaponry were everywhere, whether abandoned by the British in 1942 or by the Japanese in 1945, or supplied to the men of the BIA. Around the country were PVO soldiers, consisting mainly of men demobilized from the BIA and then remobilized but kept in a virtual limbo to give Aung San potential muscle in his negotiations with the British. With Aung San gone, the PVOs were directionless, although mostly left-leaning, and looking for a cause. Communists, rightists, Karens, Mons, and a number of other groups, several of whom had begun revolt under the British and now determined to continue against the Nu regime, thus had the means available to make war on the young government.[1]

It is impossible to understand the Nu years, or indeed any period of post-independence Burma without considering the ongoing civil war. Among the Nu government's most serious challengers were the Communists. Aung San had helped organize the Burmese Communist Party prior to the outbreak of World War II. The Communists overtly split into two factions in 1945, but the leadership had already begun to divide with the beginning of the Japanese occupation. While Aung San and Than Tun collaborated with the Japanese and accepted positions in the various Ba Maw regimes, the more radical and doctrinaire Thakin Soe spent the war years moving around rural Burma, building up an organization and spreading propaganda geared toward revolution against either the Japanese or the British when the war was over. In mid-1945, Than Tun was able to oust Soe from the party leadership, creating a split between the more moderate and larger Burma Communist Party (BCP) "White Flags" under Than Tun and the smaller and more radical Communist Party of Burma (CPB), also known as the "Red Flags," led by Soe. Both groups were popular among the peasantry, for they had both advocated alleviating rural problems, but differed over cooperation with the AFPFL in negotiating independence from Britain. The gap widened when the British declared the CPB illegal, marking the beginning of its insurgency.[2]

Prior to independence, Nu's impression of BCP leaders was that they were nationalists and not directed by the Soviet Union. Nevertheless, Nu was confident that they would never get strong support from the general population because of the latter's religiosity. In November 1947, AFPFL willingness to negotiate with the BCP for reconciliation died and Nu canceled planned talks between the two. Nu had considered inviting the BCP back into the League after they disarmed, although he was wary that they might attempt to seize power from within the AFPFL. The BCP, it was asserted, talked about unity with the League, on the one hand, but had actively tried to undermine the credibility of the AFPFL by supporting student strikes and looting of rice, on the other. When the AFPFL announced on 17 November that it could no longer consider the re-inclusion of the BCP, its leader Than Tun accused the League's leadership of being rightwing and of seeking every opportunity to prevent reconciliation. In May 1948, the Nu government botched an attempt to arrest its leadership, marking the beginning of the BCP insurgency.[3]

After the failure of negotiations with the BCP, Nu announced his plan to create the Marxist League, fusing together the Socialist Party and the

PVO, the two strongest constituent parts of the AFPFL, with moderate Communists in order to stabilize the government and draw support away from the BCP. In order to accomplish the political fusion, the PVO would cease as an independent organization and its members would have to disarm and become civilians. Negotiations with the PVO faltered, however, and although the Marxist League plan was floated as one part of the Leftist Unity Programme in 1948, it was dropped from the program in order to win over moderate Communists. Political infighting followed and even this plan failed by July 1949, when the majority of the PVOs rebelled. As with the Communists, their loyalties were represented by the government in colors, with those who rebelled becoming known as the "White Band" PVOs and the more moderate and loyal faction, the "Yellow Band" PVOs. The sheer numbers and dispersement of the White Band PVOs (they could be found in most local areas) and their military experience, for they were all ex-soldiers, made them a potentially greater threat to the government than the Communists, with whom many now joined or cooperated.[4]

Thus far, rebellions against the Nu government were mainly limited to local ones, such as in Arakan, inherited from the pre-independence period, or ideological ones, such as the Communist and PVO rebellions. Within six months, major ethnic rebellions broke out as well. The armed wing of the KNU, known as the Karen National Defence Organization (KNDO), became one of the most important and most durable armed ethnic forces facing the Burmese state. Initially, the Karen, Kachin, and Chin units had remained loyal when desertions to the BCP began in mid-1948. In November, however, the KNU, along with two Mon separatist groups demanded the grant of independence to a Karen–Mon State, consisting of much of Lower and Southeastern Burma. From December, when the government refused the request, numerous Karen soldiers and police officers joined an unofficial KNU rebellion, followed by the Third Battalion Karen Rifles and then the First Kachin Rifles.[5] The rebellion became official in January.

Karen Christians dominated the KNU leadership, but much of the rank and file consisted of Karen Buddhists. Ethnic affinities, shared traditions of relative autonomy from central control, and the memory of harsh treatment at the hands of the BIA in the early months of the Japanese occupation were thus far more important than religion in mobilizing Karens against the Nu government. Moreover, not all Karens supported the Karen rebellion, for there were many others fighting on the side of the Rangoon regime. The Karens, sometimes in cooperation with BCP (with whom they took Mandalay) and White Band PVO units, launched a lightning sweep

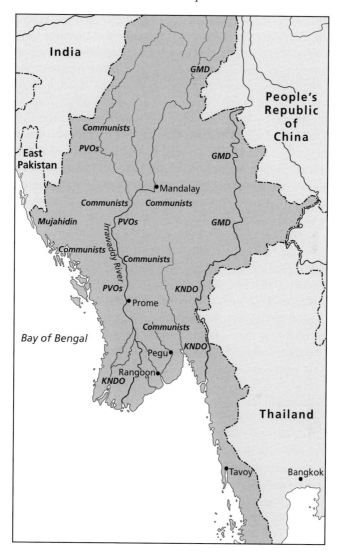

Map 2 Civil war in the early 1950s

through the Lower Burma delta region and very nearly took Rangoon.[6] Although the KNU was soon forced back away from the capital, their near success in toppling the Nu regime made certain that suppressing domestic rebels would remain a chief priority, whether in words or in fact, of every government after independence.

After the early years of the civil war, however, the insurgents faced a number of disadvantages in their fight against the Burmese government. In many ways, these weaknesses paralleled those facing the opponents of the Communist regime in the Russian Civil War between 1918 and 1921. In that war, the "White forces" had two fundamental flaws. First, they consisted of a myriad of tsarists, ethnic groups, and foreign interventionists who were only very weakly united in their opposition to the Communist regime. Unlike the Communists, they lacked a common ideology that would help to bind their forces together and mobilize the general population on their behalf. Second, they were unable to wrest control of the transportation infrastructure, which allowed Leon Trotsky, as overall Commander of the Red Army, to move his forces from one front to another with great speed. Trotsky was thus able to hit them quickly at their weakest points, exploit their geographical dispersement, and eliminate them one at a time. These flaws were essentially true of Burma's ethnic insurgents as well, although the BCP did have the potential (never realized) to compete for national leadership. This is not to say that the insurgents did not attempt to organize. In 1956, they created the Democratic National United Front followed by the National Democratic United Front in May 1959. The latter included the Karenni Progressive Party, the All-Burma Chin National League, and the Mon State Party, as well as the BCP.[7] Yet another united front emerged in 1960, when the National Liberation Alliance was formed.

In each case, the insurgent alliances proved temporary, due to differences in goals and the same kinds of personal conflicts that plagued the Nu regime. Unable to effect external unity, the insurgent groups were frequently unable, as the Communists had demonstrated even before independence, to maintain internal unity. In mid-1958, for example, several of the insurgent groups agreed to return to the legal fold. In late July, members of the People's Comrade Party (the former PVO) began to surrender, as did the Mon National Defence Organization (MNDO). Nevertheless much of this represented merely a fragmentation within these organizations, as one faction would make the arrangement and follow through with it, but others continued to resist in the name of the organization or joined other, ongoing insurgencies. The MNDO, for example, split between those who wanted autonomy within a federal system and those who would be happy with nothing less than a completely independent Mon state centered on Moulmein. Thus, while Nu's promise of autonomy was an incentive for many in the MNDO to surrender, it had little appeal for others, some of whom formed the insurgent New Mon State Party.[8]

In response to early rebel gains, Ne Win, who replaced Smith Dun as commander of the Armed Forces in 1949, began a dramatic expansion and improvement of the army. Burma was under martial law during 1948–1950, viewed as the worst years of the civil war for the government. By 1951, the Burmese Armed Forces were still insufficient in number to end armed opposition to the government. According to a CIA report, the Burmese Armed Forces were "small, inadequately trained, and poorly equipped." It was mainly an infantry force, consisting of about 43,000 regular and auxiliary troops. Although the Navy had been able to effect control over the delta and main waterways, it was small and composed only of coastal and river craft. The Air Force was also small and only capable of limited tactical reconnaissance and ground support. The armed forces controlled the central valley, where they were concentrated, while insurgents were scattered on the edge of the central valley, which meant that any attempt to concentrate Burmese forces against one or another rebel group would mean dangerous vulnerability somewhere else.[9]

In response to the challenge, Ne Win oversaw an expansion of the Army, focussed on improving its weaponry and the efficiency of its command and administration, and mobilized new resources for the war effort. Colonel (later Brigadier) Aung Gyi and Lt.-Colonel Ba Shin, for example, launched the Women's Auxiliary Corps as a means of mobilizing women for the war effort. They were to serve first in the Armed Forces secretarial branches and would later be "fully militarized." The nucleus of the corps was formed in April 1953 with forty-five women (soon expanded to over eighty). In the next five years, the experiment was considered a success and each of the branches of the Armed Forces began recruiting and training its own female wing.[10]

Slowly, the Army was able to return much of lowland Burma to central control and increasingly to isolate the insurgents to pockets around the northern and eastern rim of the country. The impact of the intersection of the insurgencies, the Cold War, and the growth of the Army on regional autonomy was significant. As in the colonial period, the Shan states had remained under the authority of local Shan *sawbwas* who exercised considerable political authority and maintained their own police forces. The fact that, in 1949 and 1950, parts of the Shan states had been overrun both by the Guomindang as it moved back and forth across the border with Yunnan and by the KNDO in its struggle with government troops forced the Army to assert its control over the area to avoid compromising its own strategic situation. In 1952, martial law was again declared, the *sawbwas'* governments were brought under Army administration, their police forces were integrated into those of the state, and the *sawbwas* agreed that after the termination of the military government (which occurred in 1954), their authority would be replaced by democratic government. Despite these developments, and the effecting of some centralizing reforms, the *sawbwas* remained in place, albeit with more circumspect authority. Their vulnerability at the hands of the Army, however, encouraged their establishment of the Social Democratic Party in 1955, to protect their position from further erosion. Nonetheless, in 1958–1959, they and the Karenni (Kayah) *sawbwas* handed their formal power over to the government, although they would continue to exert substantial, informal influence in their former domains.[11]

As the 1950s progressed and Nu became more confident that the rebellions were on the wane, he took a harder line on negotiations with the rebels. In a March 1957 speech on government policy before the Chamber of Deputies, Nu separated himself from the opposition, which favored a negotiated peace with the rebels. Nu believed that the rebels and their offers of peace could not be trusted; peace could not be had by negotiation, as the rebels, currently relying on outdated arms, would only remain above ground until a new opportunity for rebellion arose. If the government did make peace with them, the government would be betraying those, such as the armed forces, who were laying down their lives to save the union. Nu predicted that after such a peace, when the rebels went underground again, as he expected, those now supporting the government would refuse to help again, turning down the request with an "I told you so," and the country would be doomed. Instead, Nu proclaimed, if the rebels were sincere about peace, they would have to lay down their arms and subject themselves to legal prosecution. Their act of surrender would be considered as a mitigating circumstance, for those sentenced to death, the state would not actually execute them, and others would not have to serve full prison terms. Only after this and their abandonment of the "cult of the gun" would their political organizations be legalized.[12]

THE COLD WAR

The Nu government also had to respond to the pressures from both the Communist and non-Communist blocs to draw Burma into the Cold War, an agenda that was not shared by most of the insurgent groups, with the exception of the Communists. Nu's solution was neutrality in international affairs. Very early on, Nu had joined Jawaharlal Nehru and Sukarno in their opposition to alignment in the Cold War on the grounds that participation by young states in Africa and Asia would distract them from the more important challenges of developing their economies and ensuring political stability and the promotion of social welfare. Moreover, the Cold War powers were seen as possibly replacing old-style European colonialism with neocolonialism.

Nu also had concerns specifically related to Burma's ongoing domestic insurgencies, in that Cold War alignment would invite external intervention and possible connection with domestic insurgents. Burma had already faced the likelihood of the intersection of the Cold War and its own civil war in 1949, after Guomindang (GMD) remnants from China's own civil war fled into the Shan State, which they used as a base for several attempts to reinvade Yunnan. Repulsed by the People's Liberation Army, the GMD settled in for a longer stay in Burma, supplied by Taiwan and the CIA. Nu's concerns that a prolonged GMD presence in northeastern Burma would invite PRC intervention, a fear shared by the Burmese Army, were realized when the PRC began making threats about resolving the problem if Burma could not (and briefly invaded under the pretext of a boundary dispute). Nu successfully waged a diplomatic offensive in the UN that led to a nominal withdrawal of GMD forces, although many of its officers and soldiers would remain for decades, playing a significant role in the opium trade. Through shrewd political maneuvering, Nu was able to maintain an effectively neutral position between the PRC and the US into the mid-1950s, frequently supporting the PRC internationally, although criticizing in the UN Communist aggression, such as the North Korean invasion of South Korea that sparked the Korean War. The last incident reminded Nu of how precarious was his bifurcation of Burma's problems into internal and external spheres. When the government supported UN action in Korea in 1951, for example, the pro-Communist Socialists in the AFPFL who opposed the move were removed from the AFPFL and they organized the opposition Burma Workers' and Peasants' Party (BWPP).[13]

Despite US and Taiwanese promises to the contrary, GMD forces were never fully withdrawn and the responsibility for suppressing them fell back on the Army. The Army was generally successful in defeating the GMD in the field, but the difficult terrain of the Shan State that made insurgencies generally difficult to put down also worked in the GMD's favor. With each GMD defeat, the Nu government had been able to convince the UN to put pressure on Taiwan and more troops would be withdrawn, such withdrawals occurring in 1953, 1954, and 1961 but the GMD core continued to revitalize itself with local Shan and Wa recruits. Even as late as 1961 it still numbered up to three thousand men. The GMD was also slowly undergoing two transitions. First, it was changing shape from a foreign army to a local insurgent force, on the one hand, and a drug operation, on the other. The GMD had initially become involved in opium smuggling, soon bringing 90 percent of Burma's opium exports under their control, in order to finance themselves as US and Taiwanese support became irregular. After the 1961 defeat, the GMD withdrew first to Laos and then into Northwestern Thailand, along the Burmese border, where they recommenced their involvement in opium trafficking.[14]

Nu's policy of neutrality had successfully warded off serious attempts by the US to mobilize Burma against the Communists. It had also reduced the potential for PRC intervention to suppress the GMD. Nevertheless, the US continued to prepare for the time when, it hoped, Nu would change his mind. The revised US Cold War strategy in Burma was laid out in the National Security Council's statement of policy on US "Objectives and Courses of Action with Respect to Southeast Asia," adopted in January 1954. The US would make clear to the Nu government that it was interested in resolving the GMD issue and would be prepared to provide logistical support to accomplish this task. The US would act quickly on a recent agreement to supply arms and supplies to the Burmese Army, would be ready to recommence economic and technical assistance if asked to do so, and would urge Nu's cooperation with anti-Communist countries. As long as the Burmese government remained non-communist, the US should step lightly to prevent alienation of that government. In the meantime, the US would raise Burmese awareness of the PRC threat and the need for military defense, including "coordinated military action with other Southeast Asian countries." The US should also take steps to prepare alternative anti-Communist forces in case the Nu government was unable to stem the Communist advance. The US should develop cooperation among indigenous anti-Communist groups in the country, prepare for the organization among "suitable" ethnic groups of guerrilla forces, and activate the latter if local Communists made a large-scale attempt to seize power. If the PRC made an overt assault on Burma, the US would support a Burmese appeal to the UN, take military action against the PRC "as part of a UN collective action or in conjunction with France and the United Kingdom and any other friendly governments," and employ GMD forces in China proper, Korea, or Southeast Asia. If all or a substantial part of Burma were to fall to Communism, the US would support reliable anti-Communist resistance. When the Eisenhower Administration attempted to attract Burma into its new collective security arrangement in the region, the South East Asia Treaty Organization (SEATO), in 1954, Nu resisted.[15]

Burma had a number of reasons not to join SEATO. It had only recently gained the upper hand against domestic Communist rebels; it was still weak militarily and economically and first had to "set its own house in order." Even if Burma joined such a grouping, it would be unable to make a military contribution. It was not in the position to provoke the PRC, with which it had a 1,000-mile common border. It also remained unclear if there was strictly PRC aggression yet and it was still too difficult to differentiate between covert subversion and manifest invasion when assessing the nature of the PRC threat.[16] Nu extended an uncompromising view of extreme neutralism to the Non-Aligned Movement as well, for although he was willing to promote the principles of the Bandung Conference (1955), he was unwilling to join another bloc of states, even one built on the principle of non-alignment. To Nu, this would still represent a form of alignment.

BURMESE SOCIALISM

As one scholar points out, there is a myth that pervades historiography on the Nu period. In attempting to emphasize the catastrophic economic consequences of prolonged military rule, the Nu period is characterized as a time of prosperity. In reality, Nu's Burma was from the start an economic nightmare, though how much of this was due to the legacy of World War II destruction, the devastation of the early years of the civil war, or a combination of both is unclear.[17] Regardless of the government's unfortunate economic starting position, Nu and many of his associates viewed unbridled capitalism as a serious obstacle to reinvigorating the economy. Before independence, the Burmese experience with capitalism was inseparably intertwined with that of colonial rule, which had introduced it. For the average Burmese, at the root of colonial exploitation was the ruthlessness of foreign capital, the cruelties of the world capitalist order, and the greedy intentions of agents of foreign companies. Moreover, those non-European elites in the cities, whether Chinese, Indian, or Eurasian, owed their greater prosperity vis-à-vis the Burmese to capitalism. Burmese nationalism since the 1920s had been directed toward gaining self-rule and then independence, not so much to gain democratic freedoms, of which the average villager understood very little, but to alleviate the burdens of colonial economic exploitation.

Aung San had laid out the principles for the economy of independent Burma in May 1947 at the Sorrento Villa Conference, promising that capitalism would never again dominate Burma. Aung San understood, however, that there could be no sweeping, overnight economic revolution and that, in reality, private property could never be abolished. He instead called for the careful construction of a socialist state. At first, the state would merely control the country's sources of natural power, its communications and transportation infrastructure, its teak forests, and its mineral wealth. When Burma was ready for state socialism, the state or people's cooperatives would assume control of all means of production, while allowing private ownership. The Sorrento Villa Conference thus established the economic basis of a truly independent Burma, one that would inform national planning until 1988.[18]

Along these lines, foreign businesses became the first target of the Nu government when it took power in 1948. Nu had argued, more vocally in mid-1947 than ever before, that during the colonial period, a small class of foreign capitalists had dominated the Burmese economy. Foreign businesses in Burma were not surprised when the government began nationalizing their concerns because AFPFL statements over the course of 1947 had foreshadowed this, although foreign businessmen had held on to the hope that London would negotiate with Rangoon on behalf of their interests. The Burmese government would only concede non-interference with British commercial concerns in the country during the interim period between the signing of the treaty and January 1948, when independence was formally declared. Winston Churchill, the leader of the Conservative opposition in the British Parliament, strongly voiced his concern regarding the fate of British businesses. Nevertheless, Labour MPs who wanted to distance themselves from colonialism as quickly as possible overrode his opposition.[19]

The Nu government quickly took steps to control the flight of capital from the country, particularly to India. This first took the form of strict control on the export of precious stones, government control of Sterling Area currency and security transactions, and limits on single normal business remittances to £100. The government also prohibited the transfer of savings-bank accounts out of the country and limited money-order remittances to forty rupees per person per day. Unlike the case in many other newly independent countries that utilized nationalization, Nu did not seek simply a turnover of business elites. He did not want to see the emergence of a new Burmese business class to usurp this position, but rather the creation of state socialism, which he saw as the only way of preventing the same kind of social inequalities Burma had suffered in the colonial period. Later, however, the Nu government wanted Burmese businesspeople to set up effective businesses as a means of putting the country's commerce into Burmese hands. However, by 1955, it complained

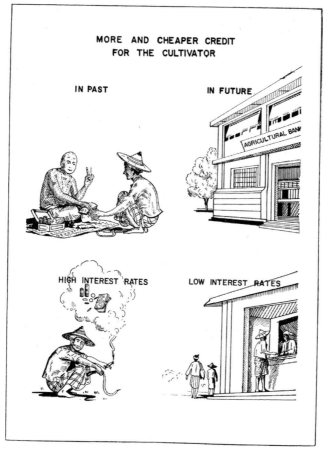

Figure 4.1 Nu-era state propaganda promises a better life for rural cultivators

that Burmese businessmen were trying to make a quick profit by selling their import or export licenses to foreigners and the latter in turn hoarded the goods and profiteered.[20]

By 1950, Nu had developed the Pyidawtha, or "pleasant country," scheme for government-directed economic development and the creation of a welfare state (see Fig. 4.1).[21] The first eight-year plan, whose goal was to increase the country's level of production by 88 percent, was begun in 1952. State investment increased steadily in the first few years and, by the end of 1954–1955, investment had reached 31 percent of the total planned. In terms of real growth Burma's GDP was 30 percent greater at this time than it had been from 1950 to 1951 and thus the government expected to reach its target on time. Despite the grand hopes of the economic development plans, Burma failed to escape from its colonial-era dependence on its main export crop, rice. Thus, the prosperity of the domestic economy was pinned to fluctuations in the world market. When the Korean War broke out in 1950, Burmese rice exports grew, but then fell from 1953 with the collapse of rice prices when that war ended, reducing export earnings. This would later lead the Caretaker Government (1958–1960) to emphasize the diversification of crops so that Burma would not remain so dependent upon rice exports. Dependence on artificial sources of income thus grew as Burmese rice exports slumped. A peace treaty was signed with Japan in November 1954, for example, which included a reparation agreement. Japan agreed to repay Burma 200 million dollars in goods and services over a ten-year period. Another 50 million dollars was allotted for joint enterprises over the course of the same period. In December 1955, Nikita Khrushchev arrived in Rangoon for a one-week visit during which he promised Russian aid for Burmese economic development, including industrial plants and major irrigation works. In exchange, the Burmese would supply the Soviet Union with rice.[22]

By 1957, the Nu government's economic and social initiatives had led to severe problems threatening the stability of the country. Nu had realized that he had made a serious error in emphasizing economic reform and social welfare from 1951 without first having resolved the ongoing civil war. As he explained:

our greatest blunder ... [was] our diversion to economic and social welfare activities as soon as the law and order situation improved slightly, instead of concentrating all our energies on the complete restoration of law and order in the country.[23]

A major financial crisis also resulted from inflation, the failure of the rice crop due to drought, rising costs of living, and falling foreign exchange reserves.[24]

A DIFFICULT DEMOCRACY

Although the first fourteen years of Burmese independence hold the romantic appeal of being Burma's only democratic period, the "Nu years" were difficult for the country. Independence under the Japanese during the war had proved to be a poor training ground for the real independence from 1948. Operating under the observation and manipulation of Japanese military authorities, the kind of bureaucratic and political infighting that would dominate Burmese politics in the years ahead was generally absent. After the war, the solidarity forged by opposition to the return of British rule and the presence of the charismatic Aung San had already begun to fall apart in 1947, the assassination of Aung San and his cabinet serving as the main catalyst. It was already apparent to many even before the British flag was finally lowered that this solidarity had begun to disintegrate and that a new kind of politics would ensue. As early as November 1947, Nu had planned to serve as Prime Minister for only the first six months following his assumption of office. He would then step down, in July 1948, in favor of his deputy prime minister and would then devote himself to strengthening the AFPFL as president of the organization. For Nu, this was necessary because it had become clear that some members of the League had turned away from the "correct path" and had begun to engage in wrongdoing by asking for privileges as a reward for their sacrifice during the independence struggle, competing for personal power and influence, and misusing power.[25] The overwhelming challenges faced by the new government in holding the country together forced Nu to abandon these plans to surrender power to a successor early on. Alongside the outbreak and continuance of the civil war, the corruption and political infighting would emerge as a significant challenge to the Nu administration, leading to its downfall, twice, in 1958 and again in 1962.

The first post-independence national elections held in 1951 were compromised by party politics within the AFPFL and the ongoing civil war. The League had originally been dominated by the Communists and other leftwing groups but after the war had expanded to include a heterogeneous assembly of parties and groups, many of which reflected the interests of the middle class. As mentioned, Communists leaders were expelled or shunned, most of the PVOs had joined the former with the outbreak of the Civil War, and in December 1950, leftwing Socialists who had abandoned the moderate Socialist Party that now controlled the AFPFL to form the BWPP were expelled from the League. This meant, as one scholar has pointed out, that as the original leadership of the AFPFL was overturned and their Marxist ideology was abandoned, the League lost "its initial unifying set of beliefs."[26] In this confusing ideological landscape, the AFPFL relied mainly upon its association with the late Aung San and Nu's personal charisma, the fact that many of its serious rivals were now in arms against the government, and that elections could only be held in government-controlled and thus AFPFL-dominated areas to garner a 1951 electoral victory that amounted to less than 60 percent of the vote cast in an election in which less than 20 percent of qualified voters cast a ballot.[27]

In the April 1956 elections for the House of Deputies, the AFPFL ran on its record and on the continuation of state policies. Its chief opponent was the National United Front (NUF), which ran mainly on the pledge that it would immediately begin peace negotiations with the rebels. The AFPFL won the elections, in part because Nu asked Ne Win for the Army's support in order to keep likely opposition voters away from the polls in some cases and to throw Army votes to weak League candidates in others. The following month, Nu temporarily relinquished the prime ministership for a one-year period during which, in his continuing capacity as President of the AFPFL, he would reorganize the League. Meanwhile, Ba Swe took Nu's place at the helm of state. Ba Swe intended to make the restoration of law and order the first priority of his government. Since reason and liberal amnesty offers had all failed to stop the violence, the government would intensify its efforts to bring matters to a close by increasing the effectiveness of the police, expanding the Army, and intensifying the activities of paramilitary brigades. The government would also take on the nation's moral decay by educating people in administration and politics in the "evils of corruption," by taking severe measures against those guilty of immorality, and by cleaning up the administrative and political system.[28]

Nu resumed the prime ministership in June 1957. A few months earlier, U Win Maung had been unanimously nominated as the President of the Union, a position second only to that of the Prime Minister. Win Maung's selection was due to the AFPFL principle at the time that given Burma's multi-ethnic makeup, the presidency should be rotated among the different ethnic groups. Burma's first president had been a Shan and the outgoing president, Dr. Ba U, was a Burman. Thus, the presidency would now go to a Karen, Win Maung, followed, it was predicted, by an Arakanese, a Chin, a Kayah, and a Mon.[29]

THE PRESS AND PROPAGANDA

Nu's estimation of the importance of print propaganda is hard to gauge. Since the 1930s, he himself had used print literature to spread political ideas. Not only did he write his own plays to convey political messages during the colonial period; he had also helped encourage the influx of foreign ideologies into Burma through the Nagani (Red Dragon) Book Club, which he co-established with Than Tun in Rangoon in 1937. On the other hand, while Nu had suggested in 1947 that the US launch a propaganda counteroffensive against anti-US stories appearing in the Burmese press, he intimated to the US chargé d'affaires that mass propaganda would not really work because most Burmese did not read the papers. Instead, Nu advised that the best way to win over the Burmese masses was to provide solid US assistance in the form of infant and maternal welfare.[30]

Whether or not Nu was misunderstood, when he became Prime Minister, Nu took the press seriously and reacted very harshly to negative coverage of his government's performance. This reaction, perhaps even overreaction, indicated that Nu indeed saw the press as a very powerful propaganda tool. The Soviet Union and later the PRC saw it too. Since publishing houses in these countries were state-owned, they could afford to pump thousands of books into Burma at cheap prices, most of these books having a strong ideological slant. The PRC developed an especially effective approach, having Chinese books translated into Burmese in China, printing them in Burmese script, and then exporting them to Burma. After complaints from the Burmese press, both from political and financial considerations, the Nu government banned the importation of Burmese language books that had been printed abroad.[31]

The first major problem with the domestic press occurred in Rangoon in March 1948, when AFPFL supporters protested against criticism of the AFPFL by certain newspapers. The protest turned violent, leading to damage to the presses of *The Economic Daily*, *The Forum*, and *Oway*. Nu, while stressing the problem of demonstrators taking the law into their own hands and promising legal action against them, agreed with the demonstrators that the press criticism of the AFPFL was "unrestrained and unwarranted." The press was voicing the hostility of the "great land owners" and the "great capitalists." As he admonished, the "workers and peasants should not . . . allow themselves to be tricked by newspapers into losing sight of their real enemies and of being diverted." Nevertheless, Nu explained that instead of violence, he would pursue the "correct course" of beginning legal proceedings against the newspapers. The government tackled the press vigorously during the year that Ba Swe officially served as Prime Minister, although Nu, as AFPFL president, remained influential from behind the scenes. In May 1956, U Pe Thein, the chief editor of the Mandalay daily *Ludu* was arrested for an editorial he had written criticizing Nu's policies, while U Hla, the publisher, was sentenced to nine months' "rigorous" imprisonment. Hla's crime was that his newspaper had mistakenly claimed that a certain monk had died in a riot several years earlier.[32] On 17 August, in his capacity as AFPFL president, Nu told students at the School of Journalism that while democracy needed a free press, journalists needed to remember that the newspaper is a public utility and advised them that when they decided what or what not to write about, "the general test to be applied is whether what you propose to write is in the interests of the people of the country . . . if it is not, you should refrain from writing it."[33]

Nu also mobilized his skills as a playwright to produce favorable propaganda that warned the Burmese about foreign intervention and political manipulation of internal political groups. The best example is the play *The People Win Through* (*Ludu Aung Than*). Written in cooperation with a number of well-known Burmese literati and U Thant, *The People Win Through* is the story of a young Burmese who joins the Communists in the ongoing civil war and soon becomes disenchanted with the rebels. The story emphasizes not so much the evils of Communism but the problems caused when external forces, from any quarter, attempt to interfere in Burma's internal problems. This became one of the most heavily circulated publications of the Nu period, leading to both radio performances and a cartoon strip, and was included in the national school curriculum as required reading. Hollywood and the US Embassy eventually became involved, transforming the play into a specifically anti-Communist story, and produced a Burmese language movie that was by the mid-1950s shown everywhere in Burma, not only in city theaters, but in makeshift cinemas in warehouses and in roadside stalls. Soon after, an English translation of the play was published in New York for an American audience, strengthening yet again the play's anti-Communist message. In this way, Burmese propaganda against the intersection of foreign interests and domestic rebellions was manipulated by Cold War politics into propaganda that served the interests of the West.[34]

BUDDHISM AND THE STATE

While Nu is remembered for having encouraged a strong relationship between Buddhism and the state, prior to 1949 there were few indications in his official speeches, policies, or appointments that he would soon move in this direction, although admittedly in his personal life he was a devoted Buddhist. It has thus been suggested that perhaps the shedding of the Communists and other far left leaders from the AFPFL in the early independence period gave Nu the freedom to explore more traditional means of encouraging national unity, while others have entertained the notion that Nehru may have recommended to Nu that now that leftist unity had failed, he should pursue "Buddhist Unity."[35]

Whatever the reasons for the timing, three main factors encouraged Nu's adoption of this approach. First, throughout his rule and after, Nu was particularly keen to produce meritorious works out of genuine personal religiosity. Second, monks had formed a powerful lobby since the end of World War II. Some monastic leaders pushed in 1947 for the designation of Buddhism as the state religion on the grounds that over 80 percent of Burma's population was Buddhist. The All-Burma Buddhist Association and the All-Burma Pongyi Association had been particularly vocal in their opposition to provisions in the 1947 Constitution that allowed freedom of religion. Third, Nu believed that promoting Buddhism was one way to fight the attraction of Communism among segments of the general population. Nu's Buddhist program began with the passage of the Vinasaya Act of 1949, which required all monks to be registered and established ecclesiastical tribunals to judge cases of monastic misbehavior. The Pali University and Dhammacariya Act of 1950 set up a Pali University that would train monks in the Dhamma and produce Buddhist missionary monks. The same year, the Buddha Sasana Council Act provided the means to enforce the government's policies regarding Buddhism. With Nu's encouragement, Buddhist laymen, many of them wealthy, served on the Council. As a result of large private donations and generous state funding, the Rangoon headquarters of the Buddha Sasana Council (BSC) expanded rapidly to include Buddhist universities and an advanced institute, the Maha Pasana Guha, a large man-made cave, and the World Peace Pagoda. The Pali Education Board Act of 1952 created a body to oversee government-sponsored Pali examinations.[36]

The BSC represented a state-backed body for the promotion of Buddhism. The BSC Executive Committee passed on to the government resolutions it had made on 19 September 1954. These included the resumption of Buddhist religious instruction in state schools and the formation of an Inquiry Committee to study the matter of providing non-Buddhist religious instruction in the schools as well. Nu afterwards announced that both requests were acceptable and took steps to initiate both. Nu began having Buddhism taught in state schools, but also tried to allow the teaching of the Bible and the Koran as well. However, monks tried to block this. Thereupon, Nu, arguing that if the Bible and the Koran could not be taught, then the Buddhist scriptures could not be taught either, suspended the teaching of Buddhism in state schools. Monks and laymen protested. In order to get dissenting monks to withdraw their complaints, Nu broadcast a speech on 25 September in which he called upon the monks to view religion and politics separately. Nonetheless, as would also the military later on, Nu used Buddhism as a means of expelling the Communist-oriented BWPP from the AFPFL and challenging the appeal of the Communist insurgents, on the basis of their adoption of atheistic Marxist-Leninist doctrine.[37]

Arrangements for the Sixth Great Buddhist Council to commemorate the 2,500th anniversary of Gotama Buddha's Enlightenment began in 1951 but were not completed until 1954. The Great Council lasted for two years, from May 1954 until May 1956. At some point toward the close of the proceedings the suggestion was made – rekindling an old dream of Burmese monks – that Buddhism should become the state religion. Nu resolved to work toward the realization of this goal. In March 1956, Nu outlined his three reasons for doing so: to make another deed of merit equal to that of the convening of the Council; the realization that other monks and laymen would share this desire; and that if this was delayed, it would be taken up by fanatical politicians, monks, and laymen. If the issue did fall into the hands of fanatics, Nu argued, then this would not be good for Buddhism as it would bring discrimination against non-Buddhists, and it would work against liberty, equality, and justice. If Nu sponsored the project, however, he would be able to confront the fanatics without being accused of betraying the religion.

The proclamation of Buddhism as the state religion was delayed for a considerable period. Opinion was still strongly influenced by Aung San, who, in 1946, had called for a clear division between politics and religion in an independent Burma. One scholar has even suggested that the influence of Aung San's style of nationalism was so complete that the earlier tradition of Buddhist nationalism promoted by Ottama and San was nearly forgotten until Nu attempted to take the AFPFL back in this direction. As for the Army, which would soon emerge as preeminent on the political scene, it still espoused a kind of secularism that went hand in hand with its perception that this was part of the proper orientation of a modern military force. The Army also had important practical reasons for avoiding the promotion of Buddhism. Chief amongst these was the ongoing civil war, in which many of the opponents the Army sought to pacify were non-Buddhists.[38]

THE AFPFL SPLIT

The AFPFL was about fourteen years old when it finally imploded in 1958. The causes of the split were both institutional and personal. On the one hand, this odd political umbrella for diverse and constantly bickering parties had lasted so long mainly because of the popularity and aura of its late founding father, Aung San. Further, the departure of the CPB in 1946 and the expulsion of the BCP in 1948 – and their subsequent armed insurrections against the government – removed its most extreme wings and encouraged support for a more moderate leadership that appealed broadly to Burmese (especially Burman) nationalists for a number of years. However, as the regime wore on and military successes seemed to have reduced the insurgent threat, internal disagreements over domestic and foreign policy became more severe. These differences were further complicated by personal rivalries among AFPFL leaders that transcended policy issues. Such a rivalry emerged slowly between Kyaw Nyein and Nu. As personal rivalry broadened to include other major party leaders, the AFPFL split in April 1958 into two competing halves: the "Clean" faction led by Nu and Thakin Tin, the latter viewed as an "uneducated" socialist, because he favored developing agriculture as the main goal of the government; and the "Stable" faction led by Kyaw Nyein and Ba Swe, both viewed as "educated" socialists because they favored industrialization.[39]

To shore up support for the Clean AFPFL, Nu released and pardoned numerous political prisoners, including one hundred students detained since the government ban on the organization of student unions in 1956. Nu also softened his opposition to autonomous states and legalized formerly illegal parties, such as the Communists. The Army was worried that the government was falling under Communist influence while Nu worried that the Army supported the Stable AFPFL. Nu then dissolved parliament, announced new elections, and passed the Budget by presidential decree. The Clean faction then pushed for the expulsion of members of the Stable faction from the police and civil government, and then from the Army, to hurt their chances in winning the next election. By mid-September, the political crisis that had been caused by the split had gone beyond Nu's ability to cope. Murders of Clean and Stable AFPFL members were reported to the police. In the middle of the crisis, Nu left on a tour of Upper Burma and only returned on 22 September. In the meantime, the Army had surrounded the capital and prevented many, but not all, of the Union Military Police Units loyal to Nu from entering it. Even so, in the Clean AFPFL strongholds in the Tharrawaddy, Insein, and Prome districts there were over 10,000 militiamen who were ready to come to Nu's aid should he need it. Reportedly, the Army wanted no confrontation between itself and the Nu government, for this would only create an opportunity for the Communists to re-assert themselves. The Army decided to act upon Nu's return and so brought the chief strategic points in Rangoon and Insein under its control, secured the armories of the city police and Union Military Police, and sealed off all road connexions. On 23 September, Colonel Maung Maung visited Nu to warn him that, if Clean AFPFL forces attacked the Army, the Army would defend itself. Maung Maung visited Nu again the following day, this time with Colonel Aung Gyi, and complained of how Nu had manipulated the Constitution for his own ends and that the situation was a powder-keg, although they would try to prevent violence if they could. Ultimately, Nu agreed to resign and hand over power to a "caretaker" government, under the leadership of Ne Win, that would manage the country for a six-month period.[40]

CONCLUSION

Even before independence, the AFPFL had suffered an irreparable blow with the assassination of Aung San, although the full impact would not be realized for years. Without strong central leadership, something the erratic Nu could not offer, there was little to hold an umbrella organization together. The AFPFL was hydra-headed and as it shed its original leadership and shifted toward the political center, it lost its vision. But the AFPFL was not the only problem. The Nu government was under constant pressure to build a socialist economy while fighting an ongoing and very serious civil war, on the one hand, and maintaining an equally challenging neutral position in the Cold War, on the other. Political fragmentation, economic slowdown (after the end of the Korean War), and a careful international balancing act, all played out in the context of a country divided into republican and rebel areas, prevented the Nu government from developing effective state institutions. Nu had no choice but to surrender control to the military, temporarily, in 1958. While his regime was overstretched, underdeveloped, and riddled from within, over the course of the 1950s, the military became larger, better equipped, and better managed.

CHAPTER 5

Dress rehearsals, 1958–1962

The period from 1958 to 1960 is often viewed more or less correctly as a dress rehearsal for the military takeover in 1962. In actuality, there were two. Nu had plans to take Burma in a new direction in the 1960s, including relinquishing his leadership. Preparations for this new Burma were built around Buddhist nationalism, and were less elitist, and economically more socialist than anything seen in the 1950s. Just as the military took Burma along a "revolutionary" course, Nu's vision of the future promised nothing less. There is another reason for considering the period from 1958 to 1962 as one entity. Although the military surrendered its direct involvement in the civil administration, it did not surrender its physical control of territory under the republic's control, probably to avoid the kind of tense situation with regard to the militias that had existed in 1958. The military waited until 1962 to put an end to the Nu regime, but it had the capacity to do this at any time it wished. In the meantime, Burmese watched to see if Nu's Burma between 1960 and 1962 could live up to the heightened economic prosperity and efficiency of the military caretaker government from 1958 to 1960.

THE INTRODUCTION OF THE CARETAKER GOVERNMENT

Nu announced the end of his five-month-old Clean AFPFL government in a brief broadcast on the evening of 24 September 1958. If general elections were held as scheduled in November, he argued, these would be neither free nor fair. Nu then explained that he had invited General Ne Win to make it possible to hold truly free elections within six months (April 1959) and Ne Win had accepted. He now appealed to the entire population to "give their support to General Ne Win in the same way as they have given their support to me." Nu had also written two letters that he postdated to 26 September 1958, the date of the proposed transfer of power. In the first, Nu undertook to resign the prime ministership and promised that the

Chamber of Deputies would elect Ne Win as the new Prime Minister. The second letter was Ne Win's letter of acceptance. Both letters stressed that the Army should not become involved in politics beyond the performance of their new administrative duties, that internal peace should be restored, and that Burma should continue to follow a strictly neutral foreign policy. Burmese soldiers then entered government buildings and police stations, mounted two-inch guns at the airport, and set up roadblocks throughout the city to check automobiles for hidden firearms.[1]

Students protested against the changeover, as did different political groups who had had problems with the military in the past or sympathies with the insurgents who were currently fighting the Army. It took some weeks for Burmese to understand fully that this was not a military coup. Two weeks after the transfer, the NUF was still convinced that members of the Stable AFPFL had joined with the military to seize power. Nu publicly countered claims that he had been forced to surrender power at gunpoint, explaining that he had only done so to prevent internal political disintegration, foreign intervention, and bloodshed.[2]

TRAINING AND MORALITY

One of the targets of the caretaker regime was bureaucratic inefficiency and corruption. Part of their solution was to build up a new spirit of personal and institutional responsibility to the state and to the people. The caretaker regime ran training and reorientation classes for government officials, reeducating 9,000 in the first nine months. The government was also to abandon some administrative practices inherited from the colonial period. In April 1957, the Home Ministry had ordered that all government correspondence, except foreign correspondence, was to be in Burmese, but civil servants continued to rely upon English anyway. However, the Caretaker Government now enforced the order. In November 1958, it created a Screening Committee to investigate the promotions, demotions, dismissals, and transfers of government officials made by the Nu-Tin government during its five months in office. In December, the Council of Ministers formed an Executive Branch Punishment Committee, consisting of heads of departments, to guide ministries in rooting out inefficiency and negligence among civil servants, with the exception of the judicial services. Civilian politicians were also investigated and three months later, 371 civilian politicians had been arrested, including 58 from the Clean AFPFL, 4 from the Stable AFPFL, and 309 from other parties.[3]

The Caretaker Government created social and discussion groups for people of different ages known as the "National Solidarity Associations" (NSAs). The NSAs were organized throughout the country at the ward, village, town, and district levels to make the population aware of their civic responsibilities and mobilize them in carrying them out. Through the NSAs, the Army believed it was creating a new forum for communication between the general population and the government. The NSAs would achieve this in two ways: by allowing democracy to flourish (by helping the authorities to fight and apprehend economic and political insurgents, as well as other criminals, in order to eliminate lawlessness) and by the creation of peaceful conditions necessary for the masses to pursue happiness and economic prosperity. In order to accomplish these goals, the associations were empowered both to aid the government in maintaining public morality and suppressing crime, and to educate the masses concerning their rights and responsibilities in a democracy. Further, the NSA Constitution required collective efforts to counter attempts to "undermine the development of democratic institutions, the maintenance of stable social conditions and the development of trade and progress." The NSA Constitution also stipulated that there would be no central unit or headquarters to control association activities. However, it also arranged for annual conferences of the associations at which a nine-member executive committee served for a one-year term; this council mainly handled applications for membership and discussion of proposals for association activities. NSA members were supposedly drawn from "among prominent non-political citizens" in order to provide the population "with possible alternative leadership to local politicians who formerly were dominant."[4]

The smooth functioning of the associations required the separation of association activities from those of politics. The association was not to become a political organization in any way. Members were allowed to engage in politics and belong to political parties, but, according to the NSA Constitution, they were not allowed to discuss politics, promote political parties, allow the introduction of an "aura of politics" within the association itself, or take sides in any political conflict. The NSAs, armed with crossbows and bamboo spears, were said to act as "the people's sentinels," always watching out for criminals and insurgents. They helped make the courts operate more efficiently, organized supplies of firewood, helped solve sanitation problems, and engaged in a number of other tasks. Simultaneously with the emergence of the NSAs, the Army overhauled the leadership of Burmese labour unions, banning politicians from union leadership. All union leaders were now required to "come from the ranks."[5]

THE SWEAT CAMPAIGNS

The Corporation of Rangoon was declared incompetent on 29 November 1958, leading to the compulsory retirement of all thirty-five of its elected councilors. The former Municipal Commissioner blamed the dismal state of the Corporation on a lack of civic pride among the public and the incompetence of both the councilors and the corporation civil staff. In place of the elected leadership, a highly decorated brigade commander, Colonel Tun Sein, was now appointed simultaneously as Corporation Commissioner of the Rangoon Municipal Corporation and Mayor of Rangoon. The 38-year-old, 240-pound, graduate of the University of Rangoon and the Military Academy, was the son of a schoolmaster and an inspectress of schools, and was known then and a few years later (when he was reassigned to Kengtung) as an efficient administrator who liked to keep things clean and tidy. Like other military men assigned to civil posts during the Caretaker period, he cut through the kind of red tape that had hamstrung the Nu government. Daw Khin Ma Gyi, who opened up the Khant Khant Gyi Photo Studio in Rangoon on the corner of 35th and Mahabandula Streets in 1952, relates how she had erected a huge (and illegal) sign that took up the entire corner; she paid the yearly fines levied by the municipality rather than remove the sign because it was cheaper than paying for legal advertising. When Tun Sein took charge of Rangoon, he explained that there would be no more fines and ordered her to take down the sign immediately; she quickly complied with the order.[6]

Tun Sein's present task was to restore Rangoon to the splendid, smoothly functioning city it had been (or was remembered to have been) prior to World War II. While much had been rebuilt since the devastating Allied air attacks of that war, Rangoon was unprepared for the volume of refugees who would seek shelter there during that conflict and after the outbreak of civil war in Burma from 1948. New homes were not built privately or by the cash-strapped Nu government. Instead, hundreds of thousands lived in fire-prone ramshackle huts scattered about the capital where overcrowding and overburdened sanitation systems led to disease. When Nu promised in 1957 to deport the squatters to new settlements in four months, he retracted his statements in the face of squatter protests. With greater determination and perhaps greater intimidation, the Caretaker Government moved squatters, vagrants, beggars, and lepers out of Rangoon. To house them, army engineers conducted surveys for the creation of three satellite towns on the outskirts of Rangoon, named Okkalapa North, Okkalapa South, and Thaketa. Over 150 miles of new roads soon followed, as did streetlights and piped tap water for each town block. Every squatter family was registered and given a lot in one of the satellite towns and a deadline for evacuation from Rangoon. Within six months, 170,000 people were shipped out, with their belongings, on army trucks. Supplies of lumber, roofing, and bamboo were also shipped in for sale at cost for use in building new homes. Reflecting the lowered population level and perhaps the removal of the threat to public health associated with the former slums, the total number of deaths in Rangoon dropped from 7,603 (1957–1958) to 5,328 (1958–1959).[7]

Simultaneously with resettlement, Tun Sein launched "sweat" campaigns to instill civic pride and an awareness of public responsibilities in keeping Rangoon clean, both physically and morally. The streets and pavements of Rangoon were covered with garbage mainly because of corruption – out of every three trips a garbage truck driver was required to make, he might make only one and sell the remaining gasoline on the black market. The campaigns also were meant to raise respect for the law as all of the measures represented a strict reading of the Corporation of Rangoon's municipal by-laws. They provided 3,000 garbage cans and organized the systematic disposal of their contents. On 7 December 1958, Tun Sein began "Operation Clean-up" to remove dirt and litter from Rangoon's streets with a "mass assault" by over 5,000 members of the government, the armed forces, and the public in four separate areas. A week later, a second "assault" included over 9,000 soldiers, government servants, and members of the public who cleaned another four sections of the city. Thereafter, 2,000 government servants would sweep the streets and clean the pavements every Sunday. Similar "sweat" campaigns were conducted all over the country, in small towns and villages.[8]

Unauthorized stalls were removed from the pavements and from parking spaces. Tun Sein also targeted the problems of water supply and sewerage. To keep people from defecating and urinating in drains, existing latrines were now put under proper maintenance and additional temporary bamboo latrines were erected until underground toilets could be built. Tun Sein contracted with the US International Co-operation Administration to purchase US$700,000 worth of equipment to improve Rangoon's supply of water and its sewerage system. Streets were widened and potholes were filled. Another public blight was the red coating that resulted from spat betel juice. Burmese chew the betel nut, wrapped in a banana leaf, as a mild stimulant, which results in red, bitter saliva. Under the Caretaker Government, betel-chewing became taboo in Rangoon, where the municipality prohibited shopkeepers from selling "pan" which was the "betel leaf concoction," in order to keep the pavements free of ugly red blotches that

looked disturbingly like blood. Noise pollution in the form of the unrestrained use of radio sets was also brought under control and owners were
forced to take out licenses for them. Seventeen revised bus lines helped to
relieve the problem of urban congestion in Rangoon.[9]

The clean-up campaign also targeted crows, flies, mice, and other stray
animals, even moving stray cattle out of the downtown area. Stray dogs
were a particular problem on Rangoon's streets, being a nuisance to both
pedestrians and motorists. On Buddhist grounds, the Nu government
had refused to allow the extermination of the animals and developed an
impractical plan of capturing them, dividing them by gender, and then
resettling them on same-sex islands. Under Tun Sein's administration,
soldiers toured the streets of Rangoon by night, laying pieces of poisoned
meat by the stray dogs they came across. Within six months 50,000 dogs
and 10,000 crows were exterminated in this manner.[10]

Tun Sein emphasized civic responsibility as well. In early December 1958,
he told 1,500 teachers from 250 Rangoon schools to foster greater discipline
among their students. He also pressured bus-drivers and conductors to
adopt good manners and polite language. The Army began giving "practical
lessons" in citizenship and enforced tight moral discipline. It suppressed
vendors of pornographic literature. It now had every household member
above twelve years old in Rangoon photographed for national registration.
Both soldiers and police were ordered to hunt down street toughs and
gangs who were despoiling public buildings. Among them were two gangs
of juvenile delinquents, called the "Eagles" and the "Road Devils," who had
been heavily influenced by Western comic books and Hollywood movies.
They had begun to assault other young people leading the Rangoon Police
Commissioner to order their arrest in February 1959. Crime rates quickly
plummeted.[11]

Aung Gyi was put in charge of the Committee to Combat Economic
Insurgency (CCEI). The Caretaker Government targeted "economic insurgents" in order to limit profiteering, secure fair prices and thus stabilize
the cost of living. The anti-hoarding campaign focussed on Rangoon and
involved the cooperation of the Army, the police, and the Bureau of Special
Investigation. It began in late November 1958 with the sealing up of 300
shops and warehouses in Rangoon in order to check stocks for hoarding. In
official press releases, the fight against economic insurgents was lauded for
putting a number of Indian and Chinese traders out of business. The Civil
Supplies Department also issued orders against the hoarding of canned
fish. The next day, shops and warehouses in Chinatown in Rangoon were
sealed up to check for hoarding. The investigators then hit Mogul Street

to look for smuggled gold and over the course of the following three days they sealed and then investigated safe deposit boxes in Rangoon banks. As fines alone had proven not to work for preventing hoarding, the penalty was raised to three years in prison. In expectation of the courts being over-burdened by a tremendous increase in cases against economic insurgents, the government posted magistrates at police stations so that they could quickly pass judgments as cases emerged.[12]

Aung Gyi also sought to reduce the cost of living. In order to lower the prices of consumer goods, the Army sold beef and distributed firewood. Restrictions were introduced on the retailing of essential commodities. Fish, firewood and other domestic requirements and essential commodities such as textiles were now sold at controlled prices. By mid-December 1958, the government's price control program began limiting importers and wholesalers to 5 percent profit each and retailers to a profit of 10 percent. Nylon was declared an essential consumer item and made a government monopoly. The Civil Supplies Department, cooperatives, joint venture corporations (JVCs), and the Defence Services' Institute (DSI) opened more retail shops. Although the military issued regular statements about their success in lowering the cost of living, this was claimed to be propaganda by the civilian opposition. U Ba Nyein of the NUF claimed in Parliament in August, that in reality many essential items, such as fish, poultry, and fuel, were almost unavailable. If someone wanted any of the few items available, they had to stand in line for hours from early dawn.[13]

THE RETURN TO CIVILIAN RULE

Ba Swe, leader of the Stable AFPFL, announced on 1 January 1959 that he had no objection to adding another six months to the six months already given to the Caretaker Government and in mid-February he tabled a motion to this effect. The Clean AFPFL, with the support of the NUF, then pressured the Caretaker Government to stick to its promise to hold new elections by April. In a shrewd political move, Ne Win and his cabinet resigned in February while simultaneously explaining that it would be impossible to hold fair and free elections in April without putting the anti-insurgency campaign in jeopardy. In order for the Caretaker Government to accomplish its mission, Ne Win demanded that Section 116 of the Union Constitution be amended to remove the six-months limitation on the term of office of non-parliamentary members. The Caretaker Government also released copies of a Communist Party directive regarding its plans to infiltrate the Clean AFPFL. Ne Win was afterwards re-confirmed as prime minister and the Constitution was amended to allow him to remain in this capacity until 1960.[14]

There were strong indications that the caretaker regime would end with an electoral victory by the Stable AFPFL. By February 1959, the Stable AFPFL had gained a majority in the Parliament due to desertions of MPs from the Clean AFPFL. The two AFPFL parties both took stands against the measures adopted by the Caretaker Government, Nu also complaining that the Army was bullying the people. Stable AFPFL President Ba Swe promised that all difficult measures imposed on the people by the Caretaker Government would be removed and that army officers occupying civil administrative posts would resume their military duties. The Stable AFPFL, however, was unable to compete with Nu's appeal among the Buddhist majority, his promise to make Buddhism the state religion, the active aid lent by monastic organizations to his campaign, and his use of the color of monastic robes as his party's campaign color. Further, to the Army's dismay, Nu promised autonomous states to the Arakanese and the Mons. Thus, in the February 1960 elections, Nu's Clean AFPFL won a landslide victory, including all nine Rangoon constituencies. Stable AFPFL morale was particularly hurt as party leaders Ba Swe and Kyaw Nyein both lost their seats.[15]

As Ne Win had promised, he relinquished control and the Nu government commenced on a sounder economic and perhaps political footing than it had enjoyed at any time in the 1950s. Nu immediately sought to cultivate the image of national unity and democratic stability. The All-Burma Conference of the Clean AFPFL now renamed the party the Pyidaungsu Party (the Union Party), while Nu promised that the Party would be completely reorganized around a popular democratic principle. The Party would be rooted in the masses, all leaders in the Party would have to rise from the bottom, and all Party decisions would be made after discussion and consultation with the masses. In doing so, its component organizations were also dissolved and incorporated directly into the new party, with the exception of the All-Burma Peasants' Organization (ABPO) and a few others that would remain separate. In June, the new Pyidaungsu government adopted a two-cabinet system of government, with one cabinet for the Union and the other for the States. To correct problems of inner-party disputes within the Pyidaungsu Party, Nu initiated the practice of "eating together," whereby each Party leader invited colleagues to dinner.[16]

Nu, apparently attempting to compete with the successful administration under Ne Win, also sought to demonstrate that the new government would be more efficient than it had been prior to 1958. In August

1961, the government temporarily suspended the ten-year-old Democratization of Local Administration Scheme on the grounds that three obstacles had emerged over the course of its implementation: "Deficiencies of the legislation, deficiencies of the public servants, deficiencies of the people." To rectify these problems, an advisory committee was set up under Dr. Ba U to hold consultations and report to the government. The New Pyidawtha Scheme, launched in October, reformed local administration. Until then decision-making regarding agriculture, communications, rural economy, education, health and social services had been slowed by bureaucratic red tape, such as financial sanctioning procedures and correspondence, as orders would have to be elicited from central departments. The new scheme would transfer authority to new decision-making bodies organized in rural districts that would be empowered to take "rapid action." The New Pyidawtha Scheme was viewed as a transitional measure, necessary before the democratization of local administration would be recommenced.[17]

By early 1962, however, it was apparent that Nu's return to power promised to rekindle a number of developments inimical to the interests of the military, among others. Nu's Pyidaungsu Party began to split into factions, for example, just as the AFPFL had prior to 1958, which was taken as a sign that democratic institutions would be no more successful in maintaining national political solidarity than they had been prior to caretaker rule. The civil war was on the verge of re-escalation. Worse, from the perspective of field commanders, there were signs that hard-fought victories over ethnic insurgents would be sacrificed to autonomy concessions. In June 1961, at the Conference of States held at Taunggyi, the Shan capital, federalism received a majority of the votes from delegates thus outvoting the official Karen, Chin, and Kachin leaders. While the Burmese press launched a media campaign against the Conference's decision, the Stable AFPFL proclaimed that federalism would threaten national unity. Nu held a press conference at which he said that if the demand was made in a democratic manner, it would be considered. For the Army, Nu's subsequent agreement to formally discuss with Shan leaders the replacement of Burma's unitary with a federal constitution was taken as a sign of unforgivable weakness.[18]

BUDDHISM

When Nu returned to power he was even more vigorous in promoting Buddhism through the means of the state than ever before. There was now even broader popular appeal for this effort than there had been before 1958. Ironically, this was partly the result of military efforts during the Caretaker period. In an effort to whip up popular support for the struggle against the Communist rebels, the military's Psychological Warfare Department began an anti-Communist propaganda effort in 1959 that focussed on the alleged Communist campaign against Buddhism. The centerpiece of this effort was a pamphlet entitled "Buddhism in Danger" that outlined the nature of the Communists' anti-Buddhist program. In response, 800,000 lay Buddhists and monks attended hundreds of mass meetings to mobilize active popular support for the war against the Communists. Although the military was essentially attempting to influence public opinion against the Communists it also fostered greater popular interest in encouraging state promotion of Buddhism. Thus, it also ensured Nu's victory in the 1960 elections.[19]

At the All-Burma Clean AFPFL Conference at the World Peace Pagoda in Rangoon from 31 August to 2 September 1958, Nu promised that if the Clean AFPFL came to power he would implement his 1954 undertaking to make Buddhism the state religion. Nu's efforts eventually led to charges, made by the Stable AFPFL in November and December 1959, that he was exploiting religion "as a stepping stone" and that his plan violated the Constitution. Nevertheless, once returned to power in 1960, Nu recommended his campaign for an officially Buddhist Burma, arguing that if this was not done it might create animosity in Burma against other religions. In March, the United Sanghas Association and the Annual Meeting of the All-Burma Presiding Monks' Association both urged Nu to keep his promise. Under their unrelenting pressure, Nu formed two committees, a Commission of Monks and a Commission of Laymen to solicit from both monks and laymen their views on the prospective establishment of Buddhism as the official religion. After their reports were submitted in 1961, Nu conferred with his Cabinet and then decided to submit the Constitution Amendment Bill to Parliament.[20]

Non-Buddhist opposition was quick to emerge. Kachin protestors stoned one of the committees. On 11 February 1961, the National Religious Minorities Alliance, representing three million non-Buddhist Shans, Chins, Kachins, Karens, Burmans and others held a special meeting on the subject and adopted the position that making Buddhism the state religion would make non-Buddhists second-class citizens. Shortly after, Nu also promised a meeting of Christian bishops that the move would not alter the freedom of religion for non-Buddhists in any way. On 1 August, the Union of Burma National Muslim Affairs Committee wrote to Nu asking him to act as Defender of the Faiths rather than making Buddhism the state religion.[21]

The push to introduce the amendment was intensified as monastic problems grew. In February 1961, young Buddhist monks complained that the Religious Affairs Department was not doing enough to rectify cheating in the religious Patama-byan examination. As the department delayed in deciding who should pass and who should fail, the monks demanded that cheats be identified publicly. On 16 February, monks surrounded the Secretariat building, not letting any high-ranking government servants in or out, for twenty-six hours, immobilizing the government ministries. Nu, on vacation, had to rush back to Rangoon, where he brought the crisis to an end by promising a government inquiry into the matter. Nu feared violent opposition to the constitutional amendment when he introduced it to the Chamber of Deputies in mid-August. That morning, he took the precaution of placing soldiers with fixed bayonets at strategic points in Rangoon and encircling the Old Secretariat building (which housed the Chamber of Deputies) with armored cars, riot cars, and Bren machine-gun carriers. Those members of the public who had applied to the government for permission to demonstrate were denied permission and only allowed to hold private meetings. Nu attempted to placate the opposition by promising that the proposed amendment would avoid any provision that would infringe on the rights of non-Buddhists to practice their religion or that would create classes of Buddhists and non-Buddhists. Non-Buddhist students responded to these developments by marching to Aung San's tomb and calling to him, complaining that Nu was destroying his vision of a united and secular Burma.[22]

Nu urged Burmese monks and lay people to differentiate between restrained and unrestrained monks. Restrained monks, Nu claimed, followed the twelve principles included in the Dhamma Vinaya Order that had been promulgated by the Sixth Great Buddhist Council, including avoiding commerce, prescribing medicines, attending puppet shows and so on. Unrestrained monks were those who did not observe these rules and should be identified and expelled from the monkhood. Nu understood non-Buddhist objections to making Buddhism the state religion. They were afraid, he observed, that it would encourage fanaticism among Buddhists and lead to the end of freedom to practice other faiths and even encroach upon their social and economic rights. However, Nu believed that existing laws could help to protect against these developments and, if not, new protective laws could be promulgated. He also admitted that laws would not be enough and that Buddhist monks and laymen would have to adopt "the right view" and exercise restraint, including avoiding certain kinds of speech, acts, and thoughts. The State Religion Act was promulgated by a vote of 324 to 28 in the Joint Session of the two Houses of Parliament. In adopting Buddhism as the state religion, the government was now responsible for matters relating to maintaining, preserving, and printing the Pali Canon, holding a yearly consultation with leading monks, aiding in the restoration of damaged pagodas, constructing special hospitals throughout the country for monks, the protection of the religion, the promotion of the study and practice of Buddhism, and a minimum state provision of half a percent of the state's annual budget for religious activities.[23]

In the following months, Burma witnessed an upsurge in religious violence. Hindu Tamil demonstrators protested against the screening of an Indian film whose theme centered on a Muslim king who fell in love with a Hindu girl. The government, in response to Muslim protests, had previously banned a film that depicted a Hindu king falling in love with a Muslim girl. The demonstration soon descended into rock throwing and eventually shots were fired, leaving one of the protestors dead. The government then ordered an investigation into why the earlier film had been banned and the new film not. At the end of October 1961, militant monks, complaining of the high number of mosques in North Okkalapa, outside Rangoon, stormed and seized control of a partially finished mosque, promising to leave only if the government sealed up the mosque. The government, arguing that it would not be intimidated, brought in the police. After other monks smashed the streetlighting, the monks inside the mosque set fire to it and other mosques in the area. As rioters began to sack stores and homes, police opened fire, killing five. To resolve the protests, the government agreed to the advice of presiding monks to take the charred mosques under its control. In response to the violence, the Ministry of Religious Affairs issued a call for the building of sand pagodas all over the country "to ward off dangers and bring peace." This call was answered on 9 December, when Burmese throughout the country simultaneously built 60,000 nine-cubit-high pagodas.[24]

Nu also faced a hostile press. Nu's poor relationship with the press in the 1950s was still a recent memory and the caretaker regime had brought the newspeople no relief. Ne Win had personally shunned publicity and only held one press conference, telling reporters to write whatever they wanted. Subsequently, newsmen and newspaper owners frequently found themselves in trouble with the law, either on charges of contempt or sedition, for writing or publishing articles critical of the government, and several newspaper presses were confiscated. The resumption of civilian rule under Nu initially saw a continuity of government suppression of the press rather than the revocation of harsh government controls. Nu asked newsmen to exercise restraint in reporting the news in order to prevent "untoward incidents" and later argued that "irresponsible and wild speaking, writing, and acting as one's thoughts incline is not democracy." Arrests and restrictions on press freedom led to demands for the restoration of civil liberties guaranteed by the Constitution. This was followed by the publication of two protest articles in all major newspapers in late November. Nu responded by finally agreeing to end laws that restrained the press and similar laws that violated personal freedoms in the country, a promise he carried out in February 1962.[25]

THE ECONOMY UNDER THE RETURNED NU GOVERNMENT

The Nu government was unhappy with many of the Caretaker Government's policies. It thus undertook a number of steps to reverse them. First, it suspended the reorganization of the Highways Department. It then reinstated 165 of the more than 2,000 firms that had been deregistered under the caretaker regime. Nu did compromise with the Army over the commercial ventures of the DSI. The Burmese military had initially established the DSI in 1951 to supply consumer goods at inexpensive prices to military personnel. Over the years, its economic activities expanded and became a model of the kind of efficiency that civil branches of the Nu government lacked. It minimized red tape, supposedly had no private profit motive, and employed significant numbers of foreign experts and, by 1958, had become the largest economic enterprise in the country. Nu, however, did not want an "Army-controlled economy." The Burma Economic Development Corporation (BEDC), which was run along the same lines as the DSI, but not under Army control, assumed control of nineteen of the DSI's commercial ventures. Cutting off this avenue of funding meant the Army would have to rely on government funding alone, thus making it more dependent upon civil government.[26]

The government had created the first JVCs from 1956 to 1957 because Burmese nationals proved unable to wrest control of Burma's foreign trade from foreigners. Afterwards, imports increased dramatically. By 1961, the JVC share of imports was still only 8 percent, cooperatives 4 percent, other government agencies and boards (mainly the Civil Supplies Management Board) 55 percent, and private importers 33 percent, 87 percent of whom were Burmese. However, prices rose rather than dropped. Burmese private traders began to make significant earnings by selling import licenses to foreigners at a profit reaching as much as 200 percent of the value of the license. Since the foreigners had to absorb these additional costs, prices were guaranteed not to fall. Further, limited supply of goods and an uncontrolled black market also worked to raise prices further. From October 1961, the government began to reform the system of commodity distribution through the JVCs, Consumers' Cooperatives, and the Parahita shops. Shops and retailers began to be shut down. The government also announced plans, in response to corruption and bureaucratic inefficiency in state agencies and among importers, to put the private import trade into the hands of the JVCs. This move promised to stop Burmese businessmen from selling licenses to Indians, Chinese, and Europeans. Finally, the government extended Burmanization to industry and to bazaar and market stalls.[27]

CONCLUSION

The AFPFL never recovered from the "split" (discussed in Chapter 4) and while Nu sought solutions in a Buddhist revival, the military continued to be held in high regard for its genuinely praiseworthy performance in the period 1958 to 1960. By 1962, the AFPFL was all but dead, Nu even choosing to abandon association with the party name. The AFPFL, to many, had almost become a dirty word. Some, such as the army leadership, had come to associate the AFPFL specifically and democracy, generally, with political infighting and national disorder. As Nu increasingly relied on a cult of personality and the promotion of Buddhist nationalism, in the context of his perceived attempts to sacrifice national unity, the Army wondered if it could now, as it had just a few years before, do a better job at managing the country.

CHAPTER 6

The Revolutionary Council

There is a tendency to treat the Revolutionary Council period, from 1962, and the Burma Socialist Program Party (BSPP) years that followed it, as one entity. This has been partly for reasons of simplicity. The point at which the Revolutionary Council ended and the BSPP Government began is hazy, due to the myriad political steps that were involved in the process, including the opening up of the BSPP for mass membership in 1971 and the promulgation of a new constitution in 1974. The most important change, however, occurred in 1972 when the Revolutionary Council was transformed into a civilian body and a new administrative system was established. Another reason for the presumed continuity was that the main leaders of the Revolutionary Council remained the ruling cohort of the BSPP government. In an arguable sense, then, the establishment of the BSPP government meant no real change in the political leadership of the country. Finally, it is convenient to consider 1962 as the beginning of a single period of military rule as it adds weight to understandable assertions of the overlong tenure of military men at the helm of state and their responsibility for the country's economic woes since the Nu years.

Nevertheless, there are equally sound reasons for considering the Revolutionary Council era separately. One is that it was a period when the final fate of the country remained unclear, when policies remained unfixed in one direction or another, and in which it was not yet clear to anyone, including Ne Win and his friends, if they would continue to hold on to power (in which case the Revolutionary Council would have been viewed merely as a second caretaker regime). A political compromise with Nu and other democratic leaders was still a possibility, though admittedly a distant one. By contrast, Burma under the BSPP government would be without the possibility of alternative paths, so much so that it took a popular revolution to end it.

THE COUP

In a radio broadcast delivered at 8:50 A.M. on 2 March 1962, General Ne Win, Commander-in-Chief of the Armed Forces, informed Burmese throughout the country that he had launched a military coup. Earlier, at dawn, tanks entered Rangoon while soldiers entered the home of every government minister, woke them, and, lined up with leveled rifles, read out Ne Win's instructions that they were now under protective custody. Nu and five government ministers were placed in custody, as were forty others, mostly prominent Shans. The airport was then closed and troops took control of the law courts, the Telegraph Office, and police stations throughout the city. At 1:15 P.M., another radio broadcast announced the creation of a military government headed by the Revolutionary Council under Ne Win's chairmanship. The Council included among others brigadiers Aung Gyi, Tin Pe, San Yu, and Sein Win. The Council dissolved Parliament the following day. As those MPs who represented states also constituted state councils, the state councils, including the Shan, Kachin, Karen, and Kayah, as well as the Chin Affairs Council, were all dissolved and new state supreme councils were created to administer the states.[1]

The Revolutionary Council quickly made it clear that the main reason for the coup was disapproval of ongoing negotiations between the Nu government and Shan State leaders. Shan leaders had demanded that Burma adopt a federal rather than a unitary government or they would secede from the union. As Aung Gyi explained at a news conference on 7 March, the question of federalism was very delicate. The States already had autonomy, but if they were allowed to secede, division in a small country like Burma would cause the same problems as were then being experienced in Laos and Vietnam. In this situation, the Shan *sawbwas*, who wanted a return to feudalism, were pushing matters to a point beyond the control of either the Shan leaders or the Burmese government. Aung Gyi asserted that the states could not even support themselves financially and depended upon Burma proper to subsidize them. Money from taxpayers in the Shan State, for example, had not been used to improve the condition of the people by building schools, farms, or a health system, but rather had been used by the *sawbwas* to build luxury homes and buy automobiles. The Council, he claimed, was also not like other coups because, rather than ban political parties, it sought instead to encourage "healthy politics." Finally, Aung Gyi made an indirect critique of the failures of the Nu regime by stressing three new developments. First, the Council intended to abandon government economic "prestige" projects such as the construction of the Taungup

Road to Arakan, the Parliament Building, and a National Theatre, and focus instead on agriculture, by building water pipes and fertilizer and insecticide plants in order to allow dry areas of the country to grow an extra crop in the dry season, and small industry. Second, the Council believed in freedom of religion and it did not plan to emphasize one religion at the expense of another. Third, the Council supported freedom of the press.[2]

After declaring its adherence to socialism, the Revolutionary Council provided an outline of its guiding principles in *The Burmese Way to Socialism*, signed by the members of the Council on 30 April 1962. Social problems, such as "anxieties over food, security, clothing, and shelter," could not be resolved without removing economic systems that allow the exploitation of man by man. This could only be achieved by establishing a just socialist economy. The new socialist economy would be based on the principle of popular participation and ownership and economic planning for the good of the people. Burma's new society would provide for peace and prosperity by being morally better and more economically secure than the one that preceded it. Self-interest and self-seeking would be removed as motives for participation in society and in the economy. The state, cooperatives, and collective unions would own all means of production. The new system would narrow gaps in income. The new society would foster unity among all the nationalities.[3]

According to the Revolutionary Council, since parliamentary democracy, which was suitable in other countries, had failed in Burma because of abuse, the military government would produce the right kind of democracy for Burma. The new society, however, would not appear overnight. Instead, it would have to undergo a transitional period, in which the Council would rely on organizations based on peasants and industrial workers to build up a suitable political infrastructure. After political organizing, the people would be given democratic education and training to ensure "conscious participation" in the system. The people would also have to be educated to take pride in doing hard work. Simultaneously, the Council would undertake efforts to foster genuine personal morality taught by every religion, while eradicating "bogus acts of charity and social work," for vainglorious and hypocritical religiosity.[4]

From the beginning, the Revolutionary Council favored the eventual establishment of a single-party state that would prevent the kind of political infighting that had weakened the Nu government (twice). It was initially uncertain of how to achieve this goal. Its first strategy was to convince the leading political parties, the AFPFL, the Pyidaungsu Party, and the NUF to merge. While all three agreed in principle with the goal of establishing socialism in the "Burmese way," they disagreed on the means to achieve it. The Council thus adopted the second course of action, to develop the nucleus of an entirely new state party that would eventually develop a civilian mass base.[5]

With the adoption by the Revolutionary Council of a party constitution on 4 July 1962, the Burmese Way to Socialism Party (the BWSP, later known as the BSPP) was formally established. The justification for the creation of the BWSP/BSPP was that the Council was revolutionary in essence, but due to a historical accident, wore "the outward garb" of a military junta. The Council, it was claimed, did not like this situation, arguing that instead the natural leader of the new Burma should be a revolutionary political party. The BSPP was initially a cadre party organized on the principle of centralism, with membership drawn mainly from the armed forces. However, the cadre party was only a transitional stage as it was always intended that the BSPP would grow into a national or state party. As explained in the party constitution, the Council promised that as the BSPP grew into a mass party, it would be reorganized on the principle of democratic centralism, a new party constitution would be written, and party leadership would be popularly elected. For now, the Council, which the party constitution deemed the supreme authority in the party during the cadre phase, would begin to set up the organizational structure of the BSPP. Two of the three major party committees, the Central Organizing Committee and the Disciplinary Committee, were formed in July 1963 (a Socialist Economic Planning Committee would be added in 1967).[6]

The Revolutionary Council approached the dissolution of political parties slowly, indicating that it had not yet decided what to do with them. A year later, this decision had been made. In early August 1963, the Council made sweeping arrests of important civilian politicians and other public figures on charges that they were turning back emissaries and blocking letters sent by insurgents asking for peace talks. In October, when the government arrested more League leaders for allegedly working against the Council and its socialist program, it stressed that it had not taken the last step of dissolving the political parties. In March 1964, Ne Win informed representatives of the Pyidaungsu Party, the AFPFL, and the Burma Workers Unity Party (formerly the National United Front) that the existence of all political parties would be terminated, due to the use by some political organizations of obstructionist tactics. All property of the parties would be confiscated, anyone continuing to work for political parties would be imprisoned for five years, and the only organizations that would be allowed would be religious ones. In July, the Council terminated preexisting local administrative systems and rules and established Security and Administrative Committees (SACs) in local areas, occupied by local military commanders.[7]

CENSORSHIP

In its first year of control from 1962, the Revolutionary Council stepped lightly in dealing with the public media. Even before the coup had been announced on radio, representatives of the Burma Journalists Association had been promised that the new government would "honor the freedom of the press." Shortly after, Aung Gyi had also promised that the government would observe freedom of the press, including criticism of the government, so long as it did not support the cause of the insurgents. The Council first applied soft pressure in an attempt to woo the press over to its side. In its first few months, the Council actually stopped pending legal action by the government against certain newspapers, as in the case of the withdrawal of legal action against the *Red Star* newspaper, for a story it had run in 1958, on 2 April.[8]

The Minister for Information, Colonel Saw Myint, also arranged a short-term course in journalism for 700 correspondents from around the country from 31 August to 5 September 1962 in Rangoon. The lectures given here were far from the poor quality, "diktat" style addresses made by military officers and civilian drones to half-asleep audiences in later decades. Rather, respected and leading editors and journalists spoke on various substantial matters regarding historical, technical, legal, and terminological aspects of journalism and publishing. From all appearances, the course indicated that the Council felt that by improving the professionalism of the press corps and, of course, by effecting positive bonds between the government and the press, the press would treat the new government more kindly than it had the Nu government.[9]

The regime's concern with the press was not just political but stemmed also from a nationalist and puritanical view of Burmese culture that viewed Western influence, both colonial and postcolonial, as damaging to the national spirit. Within a few months of the coup, for example, the Revolutionary Council had clamped down on the nation's moral decay. It banned beauty contests for hurting moral standards among both men and women and doing nothing to support the responsibilities of women in the new socialist economy that the state was creating. Ne Win informed the directors of the Rangoon Turf Club that horse racing in Burma would be banned within a year, which would put 10,000 people connected with racing out of work. "Houses of ill repute," such as dance halls, as well as "superfluous" activities, such as ballet schools, were all banned.[10] While the symptoms of Western influence could be treated, however, its future eradication depended upon the control of the press.

The Council's initial observance of press freedom soon began to break down. It attempted to bring the press firmly under state control in six ways. First, it set up its own periodicals and newspapers, such as the *Loktha Pyithu Nezin* (first issue, 1 October 1963), and its English-language version the *Working People's Daily* (first issue, 12 January 1964), which were to serve as "a beacon of light to the working people" and follow a neutralist foreign policy.[11]

Second, the Revolutionary Council isolated Burmese private newspapers from foreign news sources and vice versa. The government described the foreign press as consisting of "capitalo-rightist newspapers, journals, and magazines." Since "anti-socialist forces guided it" coverage of Burma from abroad was consistently biassed. Thus, on 26 July 1963, the Council inaugurated the News Agency Burma (NAB, the planned creation of which had been announced on 6 June) which assumed control of the distribution of news from private wire services operating in the country after signing agreements with Tass, Agence France Presse, United Press International, Associated Press, and Reuters. The main purpose, according to the Council, was to censor biasses that would favor either of the two power-blocs in the Cold War, in keeping with Burma's strict neutrality in foreign policy. Less emphasis was placed by the government on perhaps its most important function, the dissemination abroad of domestic news, over which it now exerted a monopoly. In July 1963, BEDC subsidiary Ava House assumed a monopoly over imports of foreign books and periodicals.[12]

Third, the Council gradually eliminated the private press, beginning in the second week of March 1963. This mainly took the form of arresting editors and publishers on seemingly minor complaints, followed by the closure or nationalization of one press after another, beginning with *The Nation*. In December 1966, most of the remaining private newspapers were banned explicitly, except for all Chinese and Indian-language newspapers, which were in effect banned due to the cancellation of their annual re-registrations. On 14 March 1969, thirteen presses owned by Burmese were nationalized, while twenty-nine foreign-owned presses were put under closer scrutiny. By the end of December, the government had nationalized both the *Hanthawaddy* and *Myanma Alin* dailies.[13]

The fourth response to journalistic criticism moved from the practical to the ideological. Even prior to February 1963, the Revolutionary Council viewed press criticism as a problem involving pseudo-journalists who had infiltrated the press corps. On 22 September 1962, for example, the Directorate of Information began to consider how it could identify bogus journalists and weed them out from the press corps. It then initiated a plan to issue identity cards to bona fide journalists as determined by the Information Department. The Printers and Publishers Registration Act of 1962 specifically targeted "bogus" journalists. The Act removed the one-time, life registration of journalists and publishers and now required them to re-register within ninety days and thereafter on an annual basis. They would have to do so with a new, single state authority, the Central Registration Committee. This law also affected foreign diplomatic missions and consular offices that also wanted to distribute any publication within Burma. The Press Registration Board and the Press Scrutiny Board were formed to enforce the Act.[14]

The Revolutionary Council, however, eventually decided that biassed journalists were a product of Western imperialism and the press corps was hopelessly riddled with anti-socialist elements. A new breed of journalists would have to be trained in the socialist spirit. At first, aspiring journalists were sent to East Germany for training, but were later trained locally. The School of Journalism was opened in December 1967. In addition to teaching the technical aspects of journalism and newspaper and radio news administration, the curriculum included study of the philosophy of the Burmese Way to Socialism. Special attention was paid to three principles of socialist newspapers:

(1) earning the trust of workers by avoiding sensationalism, promoting patriotism, mobilizing workers to contribute to socialist construction, and only publishing news that benefited the country and the workers;

(2) acting as a bridge between workers and the government by circulating information about government programs, informing the people of the benefits of these programs if they were successful, and presenting the suggestions of the people to the government; and

(3) only making use of the freedom of the press to serve workers. The socialist journalists also had to be wary of saboteurs and opponents of socialism.[15]

Fifth, the Revolutionary Council developed elaborate bureaucratic control mechanisms to guide Burma's new press over the long term. In July 1964, the Council created the Policy Direction Board for Newspapers, Journals, and Publications to direct the modus operandi of the media. In

September, a new Printers and Publishers Registration Board informed 200 printers and publishers that they should not print anything that contradicted the government's policy of strict neutrality in foreign affairs. The Council dissolved the redundant Policy Direction Board the following year.[16]

Sixth and finally, the Revolutionary Council organized journalists into a self-administering body guided by the Burmese Way to Socialism philosophy. This effort began on 3 December 1966, when the Information Ministry announced the creation of a preparatory committee to establish a writers and journalists' federation that would consist of two unions representing both. The purpose would be to mobilize both groups for the good of socialist construction. A week later, the National Literary Association dissolved and its members were told to join the new Writers and Journalists' Association.[17]

As with the press, the Council moved to reduce the autonomy of the cinema. The Council's concerns about the cinema were sometimes political, but were mainly directed, like Singapore's moves against "yellow" culture, at taking leadership in the shaping of a new national culture and eradicating unwanted foreign influences. Films and other visual media were especially important in a multi-lingual country like Burma with significant levels of illiteracy. Among the first moves to bring the cinema under state control was a July 1962 order that local film producers and importers of foreign films cease producing or importing films that adversely affected the national unity, character, or morale of the population. This was followed by a ban on showing films depicting nats (spirits), ghosts, or witchcraft. A more comprehensive law was the Union of Burma Cinematograph Law of 1962. The law expanded the supervisory and control powers of the Information Minister over every aspect of the cinema industry in Burma. The new law established a ten- to twelve-member Film Censor Board, under the Ministry of Information, to replace the Board of Censors. Under the new board, all films, domestic and imported, for private or public exhibition, even films brought in by foreign diplomatic missions, were now subject to state censorship. The law was intended to protect both the domestic film industry and the country's moral fiber, by preventing the exhibition of films detrimental to national culture and foreign films containing propaganda material. Any part of a domestic film censored by the board would be destroyed, while parts of foreign films censored would be impounded and returned only when the film was to leave the country. On the grounds that domestic producers were hurt by competition with foreign films, the dubbing or subtitling in Burmese of any foreign film was also banned. The law also required films imported by foreign diplomatic missions for private or public use to be submitted to the board for censoring. The Committee would also determine the nature and themes of foreign films that could be imported.[18]

In October 1965, the Revolutionary Council explained that the film industry had a major role to play in the social revolution and had been given instructions on how it should behave, but this advice was thus far not heeded. The guiding principles for movie makers should be: plots should be up to date and correspond to contemporary life; costumes should be appropriate to the character being depicted; raw materials should not be wasted (because they had to be imported and thus paid for with foreign exchange); titles should be appropriate to the theme of the film and not antagonize members of different ethnic groups; and Western music in films should preferably be replaced with indigenous music, or at least be selected with greater care. Films should be original, but also not incompatible with the Council's policies and should not portray the Armed Forces irresponsibly. Out of 171 film scripts submitted to the Censor Board in 1964, 97 were banned. In November 1966, the Film Council of Burma restricted actors to involvement in only three films at any one time and limited them to clothing and hair styles that "conformed to the national tradition and culture." Finally, between December 1968 and July 1969, all cinemas and motion picture companies in the country were nationalized and those cinemas with foreign names were given new, Burmese ones.[19]

REINING IN STUDENTS AND MONKS

Among the first targets for government restraint were university students, who had been the vanguard of the anti-colonial movement in the 1930s and had supplied the country with some of its most dynamic political leaders on all sides of the ideological spectrum in the 1950s. This trend persisted in the decades that followed, leading to continual government efforts to rein the students in, including closing the universities from time to time and even breaking them up altogether into smaller more geographically isolated units, as is the case today. The event that is viewed as the beginning of this process took place in July 1962, about five months after the coup.

Ne Win believed that foreign ideologies were interfering with Burmese domestic politics because of the inclusion of politics in education. Thus, the Revolutionary Council dissolved the university councils of both Rangoon and Mandalay universities and assumed their authority in May 1962. Under military supervision, moral reintegration would resolve alleged problems between the students and their teachers. A curfew of 8:00 P.M. was then imposed on university students, campus hostels being closed. After three days of breaking through the locked doors, the RUSU took leadership as it had in the 1930s. While the RUSU led students on a one-hour protest, government security forces raided the Rangoon University campus and took control of the student union. In the ensuing riot, one hundred students were killed. The following morning, the Army blew up the RUSU building on campus. The university was then closed indefinitely, but reopened four months later.[20]

The destruction of the RUSU building dealt a significant blow to Ne Win's chances of developing popular support. It was more than a student union. It was the site of the beginning of Burma's nationalist struggle and was closely associated with the martyred Aung San, the father of Burmese independence. The destruction was also clearly a sign that the military regime now in place, whether it admitted it or not, saw itself as rooted in a tradition other than the Burmese nationalist struggle cherished by most Burmese. It is unclear how early Ne Win realized the gravity of this act, but he eventually did. In the face of widespread Burmese opposition in the streets in 1988, one of the key episodes he referred to in his departure speech was the destruction of the RUSU building. And as on many other occasions in covering up different errors he had made, he attempted to shift blame on to subordinates. On that occasion, after denying personal responsibility, he claimed that there had been confusion in the relaying of orders. There appears to have been little truth in his claims.[21] As the students would demonstrate again in the mid-1970s and late 1980s, the destruction of RUSU was not the end to student political activism.

Although many members of the Revolutionary Council were devout Buddhists, the Burmese military had a long tradition of favoring the separation of politics and religion. It could be argued that the Council's efforts to separate them were inconsistent with the traditional role of the ruler as chief patron and protector of the monastic order. On the other hand, it was consistent with the obligation of the ruler to prevent monastic corruption, which included monks becoming involved in mundane matters such as politics. As one scholar observes, the professional soldiers who now ruled Burma preferred the more conservative monastic sects, such as the Shwegyin Sangha, as opposed to the more politicized Thudhamma Sangha that Nu had favored and who had also pushed for making Buddhism the state religion, for "[t]he ascetic qualities of the fundamentalists complemented the austerity and discipline of the military ideologues."[22]

The Revolutionary Council thus expressed its belief in freedom of religion and promised not to privilege one religion over another. This was demonstrated in 1962 by its abrogation of the closures of government offices on Buddhist Sabbath days, as required by the State Religion Proclamation Act of 1961, and by revoking the ban on slaughtering cattle. While both measures could be ascribed to efficiency and economy, in the latter case because the extra meat would help lower the price of foodstuffs in the market, they were just as clearly strikes against the Nu policy of making Buddhism the state religion. The ban on the sale of alcohol on Buddhist Sabbath days, for example, was also lifted. Other early measures taken by the Council included the freezing of state funds intended for the construction of state nat shrines in Mandalay and Rangoon, the suspension of the printing and distribution by the government of Buddhist texts, drastic reductions in the broadcast of Buddhist sermons on state radio, and the abolition of the Buddha Sasana Council.[23]

Removing religion from the state, however, did not mean ending state interference with religion, particularly when religious issues threatened public order. When monastic complaints about the Revolutionary Council's policies surfaced, the Council gradually found that involvement in religious matters was impossible to avoid in the long term. It is true that the Mandalay monk, U Kethaya, a vocal anti-Communist, had turned his criticism on the Council's socialist policies. Voicing his complaints to audiences as large as ten thousand, he predicted that Ne Win would soon be assassinated just as Aung San had been, goaded the Council to arrest him, and claimed that when he was arrested he would become a martyr to the Buddhist cause. In this case, the Council avoided direct confrontation. It is probably the case that it did not want to move too quickly against Buddhist opposition to its policies before it had time to solidify its control. The Council may also have been at a loss regarding how to deal with monastic opposition at all. Ne Win's response was to grant the *sangha* a limited period of time in which it would be allowed to purge itself of false monks, warning monks generally not to involve themselves in political affairs. In April 1964, Ne Win proposed the creation of a unitary monastic organisation, the Buddha Sasana Sangha Organisation (BSSO). Registration was ordered but, in the face of serious monastic opposition, the Council reversed itself within a month and made an exception for purely religious organizations.[24]

The Revolutionary Council persisted in attempts to interfere with monastic affairs in reaction to, or through, it was alleged, the actions of

Shin Ottama, a monk who had recently converted from Hinduism. Ottama had an advertisement relating to religion, "Warning for the Purification of the Sangha," published in the Mandalay periodical *Bahosi*, criticizing other monks for being "unproductive, religiously ignorant, and full of political intrigues" and calling upon the Council to purify the monastic order. He became the focus of an equally severe smear campaign directed by monastic associations in Mandalay who accused him of being a Hindu pretending to be a Buddhist whose actions would spark violence between the Hindu and Buddhist communities. In mid-August 1964, young monks from these associations caused disturbances, destroyed the *Bahosi* office and damaged the house of its chief editor. A week later, a meeting of monks in Rangoon condemned the monastic violence in Mandalay and asked newspapers and printing presses not to publish anything that would create misunderstandings between the monastic order and the government. Monks had also grown unhappy after the government demonetized 50- and 100-*kyat* notes, costing the monastic order a significant loss of accumulated donations, and a meeting of monks thus also demanded that the government compensate fully the pagoda trust funds and Sangha common funds for the donated and now demonetized currency. On 27 August, the government repeated its commitment to freedom of religion, but denounced both those who tried to portray the Council as being Communist and those who, it asserted, tried every means available to engage in anti-government activities. Over the course of the next three days, Ottama as well as the chief editor and publisher of *Bahosi* were taken into protective custody to testify before the Shin Ottama Enquiry Commission. In December, a Vinicchaya (Ecclesiastical) court excommunicated Ottama for profaning the Religion.[25]

The Revolutionary Council subsequently told the heads of monastic sects to hold sectional meetings to discuss how to carry out their responsibility for maintaining the purity of the monastic order, and then convene an Inter-denominational Sangha Convention to coordinate their discussions into a unanimous decision, which would then be enforced by the monastic order. Ne Win, who was concerned that the monastic order was being used against him, moved against monastic autonomy. On 18 January 1965, the Council repealed the Vinicchaya Tribunal Act, the Pali University and Dhammacariya Act, and the Pali Education Board Act of 1952. The Ministry of Religious Affairs claimed that the repeals had been made because the acts had failed to achieve their intended goals. The state then took control over cases handled by the ecclesiastical courts as well as the administration of Pali examinations. The Revolutionary Council also attempted to nationalize the *sangha* by assuming control and authority over monastic examinations and the selection of the monastic hierarchy. Ne Win now ordered the creation of the BSSO as quickly as possible, prompting the 17 March All-Sangha, All-Sect Convention at Hmawbi, attended by over two thousand monks, to draft the BSSO's constitution. The Hmawbi Convention had two goals. First, it would allow Ne Win to eradicate the potential involvement of the monastic order in political affairs. Second and more symbolically, it allowed him to realize the traditional responsibility of a Burmese ruler to purify the monastic order when necessary. While the BSSO Constitution would establish a single hierarchy controlling the monkhood, what angered monks most was the requirement that all monks would now have to carry BSSO identity cards. The Council would claim that 80 percent of the monks had supported the draft, but monastic critics argued that this referred only to the percentage of the speakers, who were a very small group.[26]

The Revolutionary Council's BSSO plans resulted in an uprising, mainly among monks at Mandalay, characterized by the torching of army trucks and government buildings. On 25 March, the day after the congregation closed, thirty monks attacked and damaged the BSPP unit office at Taungbyin, referring to it as "The Taungbyin Communist Training School," and injured members of staff. Within a few days, monks put up posters for a rally to begin another attack on the Taungbyin office. The violence only receded in late April, when the government arrested ninety-two monks throughout the country on charges of economic insurgency, lawlessness, and engaging in political activities. Within a year, over 900 other monks would be arrested as well, mainly for encouraging monks to engage in anti-government political activity. The government did back down a little. Despite the existence of the BSSO, many monks did not heed intrusive parts of the BSSO constitution, but enforced self-regulation of monastic discipline to stave off state intervention. For its part, the Revolutionary Council did not enforce many parts of the BSSO Constitution after the monks abandoned destructive, public opposition. The Council even repealed the order requiring monastic registration with the government. The following year, the last foreign Baptist missionaries and foreign Catholic priests and nuns left Burma, as the government either refused to renew their stay permits or explicitly ordered them out of the country.[27]

The Revolutionary Council's confrontations with the monastic order were primarily rooted in two state policies. The Council had first attempted to reduce the place of religion in the state and then sought to bring the monastic order under the state's control. This approach reflected the measured steps that the Council took in approaching many other political and social institutions. The Council was not to be a caretaker regime to resolve a short-term emergency, but instead a more commanding force in redeveloping Burma with a view toward fundamental, long-term change. By all appearances, monastic opposition had forced the Council to back away from its intended program for the monastic order. In actuality, the monastic order won only a temporary reprieve, for the Council only delayed a monastic policy that would be recommended once other aspects of state and society were reformed. This was to be an unavoidable collision because an independent monastic order had shown itself to be a threat to the state, especially one, like the Council, possessed of a totalitarian orientation.[28]

FROM AUNG GYI TO TIN PE

While the 1962 coup, the declaration of a new state ideology, the elimination of freedom of the press, moves against monastic autonomy, and the extension of other forms of social control all represented fundamental and massive changes in the country, the most serious internal disagreements and problems faced by the Revolutionary Council were over economic policy, even with the upsurge in the insurgencies after the decline of armed opposition in the late 1950s and early 1960s. Initially, the main force in guiding the Council's economic reforms was Aung Gyi, who had served under Ne Win during the campaign against the Japanese in 1945 and remained a close collaborator thereafter. Aung Gyi was also the economic hero of the Caretaker Government, as he had salvaged the quickly disintegrating economy after 1958 and the economic revival continued to bear fruit even after the return of Nu in 1960. Aung Gyi headed a powerful clique within the Council, known as the Paungde group, which favored industrialization and a moderate approach to nationalization. With the establishment of the Council, he was given the post of Minister of Industries and dominated the Council's economic policies into early 1963. Aung Gyi had supported the continuity of a private sector in industry and limited private import and export trade. Through the BEDC, he had also established semi-official trading companies.[29]

Under Aung Gyi's guidance, the Revolutionary Council's initial industrial policy was to follow a course of Import Substitution Industrialization (ISI) while simultaneously attracting foreign investment. Too much foreign exchange was being wasted on imports of foreign goods. To reverse this,

Aung Gyi advised that traders shift to industry and begin with small industries that would produce domestically items that were otherwise imported. The caretaker regime had initiated ISI, but the Council gave it greater emphasis. Aung Gyi also advised foreigners in the private import trade (they were allowed to remain in the import trade until September 1962) to invest their capital instead in heavy industries. Agriculture would now be mechanized as well along with the construction of water pumps, pipes, and fertilizer plants, and the production of insecticides.[30]

By the end of 1962, the Revolutionary Council had determined on a more thorough restructuring of the economy to parallel its political and social reforms. The major force behind this change was the grumbling and determined Tin Pe, the "Red Brigadier." Tin Pe had been a battalion commander under Ne Win when the BNA turned on the Japanese in 1945 and, on one occasion, Ne Win placed his command in Tin Pe's charge when he had to leave the front. After the war, Tin Pe steadily rose up the ranks to brigadier. During the caretaker period, he was one of the select few army officers Ne Win assigned to ministerial posts, being appointed as Minister for Mines, Labour, Public Works, and National Housing. Although Tin Pe and Aung Gyi had collaborated frequently in the past, as in the Caretaker Government's campaign against the black market, they disagreed strongly on economic policy. By contrast to Aung Gyi's moderate approach to nationalization, Tin Pe led a faction of Communist-oriented officers strongly influenced by the Marxist economist and former Communist U Ba Nyein. This faction was aided by the influx of Marxist theoreticians who had joined the government when members of the National United Front proved to be among the few political groups that responded positively to Ne Win's call for cooperation.[31] While Aung Gyi controlled overall economic policy, he had grown discontented over the role played by Tin Pe. He would publicly characterize Tin Pe and his associates of this period a quarter of a century later, as "people who did not even know the shape of rice and who pointed to the rice they ate when asked about rice products."[32]

Brigadier Tin Pe, in his capacity as Minister for Co-operatives and Supply, Acting Minister for Finance and Revenue, and Minister for Agriculture and Forests, had spent 1962 and early 1963 pushing for his own agricultural program. In June 1962, Tin Pe cited the cooperative movement as a critical part of the Burma Way to Socialism Program, calling it a virtual battlefield and saying that all necessary measures should be undertaken to ensure its success. To improve the agricultural situation, he oversaw changes in the ways in which agricultural loans were handled. In the past, these loans had been made out on the repayment record of the cultivator for previous loans received. This was now forgotten and the new system of granting agricultural loans was based on the crops to be cultivated. District Commissioners and officers of the SACs and, from June, the State Agricultural Bank disbursed the loans. Tin Pe also arranged paddy transplantation competitions among cultivators to boost agricultural production. Cultivators were encouraged to rotate their crops to improve the fertility of the soil and to provide them with high-quality seeds. Land reclamation was another major project directed toward increasing agricultural productivity. In late August, the Burmese government signed an agreement with the US Agency for International Development (USAID) for a US$ 3.4 million loan to begin a program of land reclamation in the Irrawaddy and Pegu Divisions. Two days later, on the recommendation of Tin Pe, the Revolutionary Council signed an agreement with the Soviet Union for the construction of an irrigation dam in the Myingyan district. Under this arrangement, Burma would repay the Soviet Union over a period of twenty years for the employment of the foreign (Russian) engineers, the machinery, and other construction costs related to the dam itself and the twenty-six-mile canal that would feed the reservoir.[33]

More radical steps than those thus far taken were partly justified when the BSPP's ideology was formally laid out in a published declaration entitled *The System of Correlation of Man and His Environment*, on 17 January 1963. This ideology amounted to a mixture of Marxism, historical dialecticism, and Buddhism. Man's needs were both material and spiritual (intellectual and cultural) and he participated in society to fulfill these needs. Man was responsible for cultivating the growth of society's spiritual life and the latter affected the growth of material life and thus the production of material needs. As man was both an egocentric and an altruistic social animal, social and economic systems, which always undergo change, eventually produced people who exploited others. Another aspect of man is that he constantly strives to seek freedom from oppression. He should reject those social and economic systems that permit exploitation of man by man and oppose the classes and strata that perpetuate such systems. The only reliable classes were those who contributed to the material needs of society, such as the peasants and the industrial workers, and those, such as the intelligentsia, who contributed to its spiritual needs. As these productive forces attempted to change the economic and social system, those whose greed was satisfied by the existing system oppressed the material and spiritual producers. This oppression was responsible for class antagonisms. To abolish these class antagonisms, the conditions that created them must first be abolished.

Only then could a socialist society without exploitation be established. As everything was in a constant state of change, greed would linger, a condition that had to be eradicated by the production of physical and spiritual happiness. Further, the conditions and needs of society would change as well. Hence, party members had to understand that the ideology and programs of the party were merely "relative truths," rather than final and without need of amendment or alteration.[34]

As Tin Pe's influence grew, Aung Gyi was pushed out of the way. In February 1963, Aung Gyi resigned from the Revolutionary Council and from his various other posts. In his resignation letter, Aung Gyi maintained his belief in socialism, as he had for twenty years, but explained that he differed in opinion "in some tasks" with his colleagues. Aung Gyi's closest associates were also removed from the Council, the Army, and other government services. In early June 1965, Aung Gyi was arrested.[35]

After Aung Gyi's initial departure, the Revolutionary Council set about launching a quick Marxist transformation of the Burmese economy. The new economy policy adopted many of the measures that had been opposed by Aung Gyi. Whether or how far Ne Win agreed or was pushed to adopt this redirection in the Council's economic reform program is unclear, although three months later there were suggestions that Ne Win was unable to control either Tin Pe or the commerce minister who were determined to turn Burma into a communist state. Tin Pe gradually expanded his already extensive portfolio by becoming chairman of the Finance Committee of the Revolutionary Council in late November 1964.[36]

Under Tin Pe's guidance, Burma saw sweeping nationalization in all areas of the Burmese economy (all twenty-four private banks in Burma had already been nationalized in 1962). The distribution of domestic rice purchases and the import and export trade were totally nationalized, as were all private businesses, regardless of size, including general stores, department stores, brokerages, wholesale shops, and warehouses. In early March 1965, Ne Win promised to launch an "agrarian revolution" that would bring the tenancy system to an immediate end and, a month later, the Council issued "The Tenancy Law Amending Law" freeing tenant-cultivators from paying land-rents to landlords. A new sweep of nationalization hit the factories and mills in December 1968, including textile factories, sawmills, chemical works, and food industries.[37]

In 1965, the Revolutionary Council invited candid opinions from the public on its performance, but was unprepared for the volume or degree of criticism that was subsequently voiced. Popular discontent had grown mainly over the worsening economy and shortages of consumer goods.

Figure 6.1 Present-day Burmese deliver unhusked rice to mill by boat

The Council's first response was to seize more control over the economy. It promulgated "The Law Empowering Actions in Furtherance of the Construction of the Socialist Economic System of 1965," giving the government more power to build a socialist economy in which the state owned all means of production and distribution. On the same day, the government dissolved the People's Stores Corporation, which had controlled commerce after wholesale and retail businesses were nationalized and which was the main object of public complaints. In its place, it formed a nine-member council called the Trade Council under the chairmanship of the Minister for Trade. The Trade Council would decentralize domestic commerce and, it was hoped, lead to better communication between government suppliers and local consumers. Its explicit purpose was to meet the consumer demands of workers, which were currently being met by a swelling black market. At the close of 1965, Ne Win admitted to a BSPP seminar that the economy was a "mess" and that everyone would be starving if Burma were not essentially an agricultural country.[38]

At the heart of the problem was that from 1964, Burma lost its position as the world's biggest exporter of rice (see Fig. 6.1) as its exportable rice surplus steadily declined. That year, the government had lowered the price of rice to help reduce the cost of living, but two years later, Ne Win voiced concern that the agricultural loans made to farmers might not be paid back. The

Revolutionary Council tried everything to boost agricultural productivity, offering farmers goods not available to anyone else, soft and then hard pressure, and confiscation of pounders and husking blocks necessary for polishing rice, but farmers would not stop hoarding rice and burying it underground where much was lost to decay. From the late 1960s, the government advised farmers to adopt modern cultivation techniques. It sought to reduce dependence on expensive, foreign chemical fertilizer by building a fertilizer plant, and by 1969, it had turned to the mechanization of agriculture as "the key to successful socialization of [the] farm." Tractors were now sold on credit to village cooperatives and training was provided in how to operate and maintain the tractors. Nevertheless, the rice surplus continued to shrink.[39]

THE INSURGENCIES

In April 1963, the Revolutionary Council offered amnesty to insurgents who would lay down their arms, and rewards for the capture of leaders of rebel forces were canceled in June. To prevent sabotaging of the peace talks, the government began arresting the central leadership of the AFPFL in early August and its provincial party secretaries in October. Dissatisfied with the terms offered, however, most rebel groups abandoned the talks by the end of the year. The Council responded to the failure of the talks by blaming the National Democratic United Front's strategy of erecting a parallel government in areas under Communist and ethnic insurgent control. It even claimed that Burma was on the verge of a national divide akin to the divisions between North and South Korea and Vietnam.[40]

While the Revolutionary Council returned to an offensive strategy, the Communist insurgents were in the midst of a crisis. The souring relationship between the Soviet Union and the PRC influenced the inner workings of the party through cadres who were separately associated with either Moscow or Beijing. While the split that led to the emergence of the BCP and the CPB had been serious, the forthcoming conflict within the BCP threatened to become much worse.

The PRC had been hesitant to become involved with the two Communist insurgencies in Nu's time. Nu had been careful to develop a very amicable relationship with Burma's gargantuan and seemingly erratic neighbor. After the Bandung Conference in 1955, the PRC, anxious to promote itself as a neutralist force in world affairs, formally renounced any connexions with the Burmese communists. Things changed, however, after the 1962 coup that put the Revolutionary Council into power. The PRC encouraged both the BCP and the CPB to engage in the 1963 amnesty negotiations. Even the volatile CPB leader Soe, who had gone into hiding in Arakan, agreed to do so, but by August he was unhappy with the terms offered, broke off talks and went back underground. The BCP soon followed. The Council reacted harshly, arresting four senior Communists and 400 above-ground leftist politicians. The Council's growing relationship with the Soviet Bloc, especially after Aung Gyi was booted out, further alienated the PRC. The growing rift between Burma and the PRC soon led the latter to label the Ne Win government as reactionary and to engage in active but covert support for the Communist insurgencies. Things picked up steam from 1966 with the beginning of the Cultural Revolution in the PRC and the attack by PRC thinkers on Khrushchev's revisionism of Communist doctrine. For its part, the Council was concerned about signs that the Cultural Revolution was being exported to Burma through the local Chinese community. This concern, along with the decision by some Chinese students in Burma to wear Maoist badges to school, sparked riots in Rangoon that, while essentially rooted in anxieties caused by food shortages, nonetheless mobilized an anti-PRC vocabulary. This was followed by an intense media barrage and mass demonstrations before the Burmese embassy in the PRC.[41]

The BCP had decided in 1964 upon the strategy of concentrating their strength in the Pegu Hills (Pegu Yoma) where they would develop a base area from which to launch offensives against the Burmese Army. While some Party leaders began to voice concern over the wisdom of the new strategy, Than Tun allied himself with a clique of "Beijing returnees" in the Party. They borrowed from the model of the Cultural Revolution's "Red Guards" and established their own Red Guard units drawn from younger members of the Party. Over the course of 1966–1967, the Red Guards increasingly replaced established members of the Party, sometimes accompanied by executions. In December 1967, Than Tun pushed through the Politburo a decision to formally purge the Party of revisionism and rebuild the BCP on the basis of uncorrupted Marxist-Leninist-Maoist thought. The label "revisionist" was cast around liberally and a major purge commenced. This included mass trials of the "Moscow returnees," intellectuals who had joined the BCP after the 1962 coup, and the original leadership of the BCP. At least fifty-seven BCP leaders were executed, including Bo Yan Aung, one of the Thirty Comrades. The "new" BCP also attempted a local pilot scheme of desecrating Buddhist temples and assassinating monks to determine how successful a general campaign against Buddhism in Burma would be. While the BCP was tearing itself up from within and alienating the local population, the Burmese Army launched a new offensive. Than Tun first turned on the Beijing returnees and, after more executions, fled as the Burmese Army overran BCP positions. On 24 September 1968, Than Tun was assassinated by one of his own bodyguards (possibly a government agent). Remnants of the Party regrouped near the Chinese border, rebuilt its strength with mainly Shan and Wa recruits, and allied with the PRC-backed Kachin Independence Army (KIA). In later years, the BCP would reject this period as a freakish occurrence, something that should have never happened.[42]

The Army's successes against the BCP afforded little time for rejoicing, because elsewhere, along the Thai border, another insurgent force was emerging. The 1950s insurgencies had continued to hold much of highland Burma after the 1962 coup, when they were joined by yet more rebel groups, particularly among the Shan. The rapid increase in the number of insurgent groups simultaneously increased the need for unity while making attempts to unify more difficult. Numerous attempts at bringing rebel groups together, such as the United Nationality Front in 1965, the National United Front in 1967, and the National Liberation Council at the end of 1967 all failed, as would 1972's Revolutionary Nationality Liberation Alliance.[43]

Shan insurgents were also finding it difficult to oppose the government in the face of challenges at home from armed groups interested in controlling the opium trade, whose epicenter was in the Golden Triangle. The Golden Triangle is a mountainous area, distant from major political centers, that overlaps the borders of Laos, Thailand, and Burma. The possibility of living off of funds secured by controlling opium trafficking, the area's isolation, the ability to move out of reach across the border in the face of one or another government offensive, and the apparent willingness of local army or police commanders inside the Thai, Lao, or Burmese borders to be bought off, made the zone an ideal home for rebel groups on the mend.[44]

The GMD was one of the first groups to take advantage of the trade, although from the early 1960s, they operated from bases in the Thai area of the Triangle. In 1972, a Chinese general, commanding an organ of the Government of Taiwan called the Intelligence Bureau of the Ministry of National Defence (IBMND), established himself in the Thai section of the Golden Triangle. Here, he set up a base, the Mainland Operation Department, brought the "Chinese irregular forces," as the old GMD remnants were now called, under his command, and occasionally deployed across the border into Burmese territory. The GMD found Thailand a safe home for years, as they served as a vehemently anti-Communist force along its northwestern frontier at a time when Thailand was anxious about the perceived threat posed by Communist insurgents at home, the BCP across the border in Burma, and the Khmer Rouge in Cambodia.[45]

In 1963, the Revolutionary Council encouraged the establishment of independent local militia units, known as the Ka Kwe Ye (KKY), in the Shan State to fight ethnic insurgents. The KKY units were given a free hand to support themselves and administer areas under their control as they wished, so long as they fought insurgents opposed to the Council. Several years later, the Council allowed any rebel group to become KKY under the same terms. Some of the KKY leaders were chameleon-like in their political outlook and easily shifted allegiances with changing circumstances. The main reason was that their primary interest was in enriching themselves through opium smuggling to Thailand and their militias amounted to mainly private armies used to control the trade. Two KKY leaders, Khun Sa and Lo Hsing-han, for example, followed a comparable path as rebel leaders, state prisoners, and agents of the Burmese government (in fomenting problems among the rebels on the government's behalf); eventually they led lives of luxury in Rangoon under government protection.[46]

In response to international pressure at a time when Ne Win was attempting to change the face of his regime, the BSPP government promulgated a narcotics law in 1974 that made drug addiction a notifiable disease and the production, possession, or smuggling of narcotics illegal. Those guilty of these offenses, or even of having contacts with international drug rings, would be sentenced to death. Only about 19,000 acres under poppy cultivation in the Shan State were exempted for a period of five years, for the purposes of the Burma pharmaceutical industry. The following year, Burma cooperated with the US in an effort to halt the illicit trade in opium and was allowed to purchase eighteen helicopters, followed by a further seven as well as four transport planes, for this purpose. Despite promises otherwise, the helicopters and planes were deployed against bona fide ethnic insurgents as well.[47]

THE RETURN OF NU

The flagging strength of the rebels seemingly provided the Revolutionary Council with space to resolve questions about Burma's political future. Before it could move confidently forward, the Council first determined to secure the visible if not sincere support of parliamentary leaders held in detention since 1962 and 1963, including Nu, Ba Swe, and Kyaw Nyein. Between October 1966 and August 1967, they were all released on the condition that they sign a pledge to remain out of politics and not remobilize their political parties. They were soon included in a thirty-three-member Internal Unity Advisory Board (IUAB) established by Ne Win in December 1968 to help promote national unity and prepare for the writing of a constitution. The IUAB recommended the reestablishment of a parliamentary democracy. Nu's personal recommendations were treated separately from those of the other members of the IUAB, who advised the creation of either a socialist state or a democratic socialist system. Nu favored a multi-phase plan, which would lead to the restoration of freedoms of association, speech, and expression. First, Nu would be given the power necessary to establish an interim government with the guidance of the IUAB and this peaceful transfer of power would remove the stigma of the seizure of power by the current government. Second, the old parliament would be reconvened, which would enact legislation legitimizing Ne Win's election as President of the Union. Nu would then resign and Ne Win would form a government drawn from both the armed forces and from different political parties. Ne Win would also convene a representative National Convention to draw up a new constitution. Ne Win, however, rejected Nu's suggestions on the grounds that they lacked a "specific goal." Nu thus abandoned any hope of reforming the Ne Win government.[48]

Since his initial release, Nu had been touring the country giving talks on Buddhism throughout Burma. When he continued to do so after he joined the IUAB, he aroused concerns among the Revolutionary Council leadership that he was rebuilding his popular base. It was probably for this reason that Ne Win gave permission for Nu to go abroad on a Buddhist pilgrimage to India, where there would be some distance between himself and the general Burmese population. In August 1969, Nu announced the formation of the Parliamentary Democracy Party (PDP) under his leadership, based in Bangkok, with himself as chairman. Its goals were to replace Ne Win peacefully or, if this failed, to begin an insurrection. Nu began his campaign against Ne Win with a world tour, including the United Kingdom, the United States, and Japan, to secure international support for the new party. Nu believed he had (and probably did have) the support of much of the monastic order, underground student groups, most rural Burmans, and some sections of the Burmese civil service and military. Popular recognition of Nu as Burma's preeminent lay Buddhist leader was indicated in part by the mass appeal of his lectures on Buddhism prior to his departure from the country.[49]

Nu turned from politicking to plans to topple the Revolutionary Council by force. In 1970, he and a number of prominent men, including former Prime Minister Bo Let Ya and *The Nation* editor Edward Law Yone, who had been prominent in the 1950s and supported his PDP, joined forces in Bangkok. As Nu's record as Prime Minister meant that he was almost as mistrusted by ethnic minority leaders as Ne Win, these men did the hard work of negotiating an alliance with four of the five major ethnic insurgencies who combined as the United National Liberation Front (UNLF). While the Kachins, who fought for complete independence from any Burmese government, refused to join, the Chin National Democratic Party, the KNU, New Mon State Party, and Shan State Army did. The deal worked out for the pact involved the creation, after their success in felling the Revolutionary Council, of a federal system of states and a joint military high command. On paper, at least, the front was a force to be reckoned with. Its combined strength in regular and irregular troops numbered 50,000 and the territory under its control, not counting isolated towns and cities occupied by the Burmese Army, amounted to over half of Burma's total area. Meanwhile, Ne Win would still have to face the seven-thousand-man-strong BCP, which was not included in the Front, and further territory under their control. In April 1970, the UNLF held its annual conference at which it decided it had the military muscle now to begin a full guerrilla campaign, dominated mainly by attacks on infrastructure for which it had trained men in demolition, against the Burmese Army. The UNLF predicted, given reports of Ne Win's chronic poor health, that by the end of the year either Ne Win would be dead or they would have captured Rangoon, but neither materialized.[50]

The Revolutionary Council took the propaganda offensive rather than the defensive. All of the details and activities of the front published in the West were repeated in state-controlled newspapers and magazines. At the same time, the Ministry of Defense challenged the various claims made by the front, which it called the "unholy alliance." The touted strength of the UNLF was attributed to its leaders simply adding zeros to the numbers of troops it actually had. At the same time, it was asserted, the forces of UNLF allies were rapidly disintegrating in the face of army offensives. With some justification, the Council also observed that the UNLF lacked a "systematic political or military organization" and that strong rivalries within the front threatened to pull it apart. The front, in short, was a paper tiger. To counter claims of Nu's mass support, the Council staged its own mass demonstrations against the UNLF.[51]

At first the UNLF campaign consisted of leaflet dropping and, according to the Burmese government, a series of bomb attacks in Moulmein and Pegu, and related attempts in Rangoon. They were even accused of having plotted to dig a tunnel and plant bombs under the Martyrs' Mausoleum, which they planned to detonate when Ne Win and other Revolutionary Council members came to speak on Martyrs' Day on 19 July 1970. If the bomb plots were genuine, they were foiled. In 1972, the UNLF sent in 500 well-armed commandos, bringing with them gold coins minted by the UNLF to pay for supplies and recruits within Burma. In a few weeks, most of these commandos had been killed, captured, or had fled back inside the Thai border. As mentioned above, by the end of 1970, the UNLF claimed a total fighting force of 50,000 men, including both regular and irregular troops. On the one hand, this was hardly sizeable enough to guarantee victory against a Burmese Army of 150,000 men. On the other hand, it was significant enough for Ne Win to be concerned, for, had a popular uprising greeted the rebel army, as the UNLF hoped, this force would have swelled considerably, but this too never materialized. Nu began to downplay his role in the UNLF and then finally ended his relationship with the anti-Ne Win coalition and, after a state visit by Ne Win to Thailand in June 1973, Thailand asked him to leave the country. Nu then headed for exile elsewhere.[52] The UNLF did not outlive the Revolutionary Council. As we shall see, it would not be Nu's last attempt to make a political comeback, but it proved to be his "last best hope."

CONCLUSION

It is sometimes asserted that the Caretaker Government was a dress rehearsal for the Revolutionary Council period. The military may have stood back to watch the restored civilian government fail to match the record of the 1958–1960 period. The military may also have found that controlling the government helped to provide the kind of national unity necessary to fight the civil war effectively. Certainly, the military found it necessary to remove from Nu the means by which he, by all appearances, would sacrifice the territorial gains made by the military since 1949. Nevertheless, the Council went far beyond these interests. It exerted control over all aspects of the state and society within its grasp and transformed the government and society in fundamental ways. With the disappearance of civilian rule came the demise of freedom of expression and an eradication of foreign influences in the country. Moreover, the Council contradicted the economic approach it had followed in the Caretaker period under Aung Gyi. Although Aung Gyi remained at the helm of the government's economic policies for a brief period, the shift of control to Tin Pe marked the beginning of an economic nightmare that destroyed any real possibility for the Council's popularity.

While Ne Win was once rejected out of hand as a dictator by scholars and domestic opponents alike, it seems likely that during his first decade at the helm of the state at least, he and his colleagues believed that what they were doing was in the country's best interests. The Revolutionary Council produced its own ideology, mixing Marxism together with Buddhism, mobilizing leftist intellectuals and left-leaning military officers to attempt to reshape Burma along lines that, they felt, the Nu regime should have done, but never did. It may have been genuine interest in the welfare of the country among at least some members of the Council that helped speed along the transition to at least nominal civilian rule based on at least nominal civilian consensus. If such a motive was there, it would gradually erode in the years of BSPP rule ahead.

CHAPTER 7

The BSPP years

By the mid-1960s, Ne Win had found that the replacement of civilian rule by the Revolutionary Council, more thorough and penetrating than the earlier caretaker regime, had drawn both himself and the Army into a quagmire of problems. The military was unable to both fight a civil war and manage the state with equal success and its performance in the first area was steadily weakening. Moreover, the Army had become popular in the 1950s as defenders of the Union and for the administrative successes of the caretaker regime. Now that the military was permanently in charge of the government, they were held responsible for the country's economic performance, its social ills, its ethnic problems, and a range of other issues. In other words, without a civilian government, there was no one else to blame.

The general thus began to look for ways to mobilize the civilian population in administration, or rather to give the government a civilian face, without sacrificing real power, for otherwise it would probably invite a return to the political factionalism and state fragmentation witnessed in the latter years of the Nu regime. Moreover, the stated goals of the 1962 coup, while intended to legitimate the takeover, bound Ne Win to a particular direction of reform that substantially reduced alternative options. Further constraints would emerge from increasing economic woes, for which the Council was largely responsible, and reorganization among the rebels.

DEVELOPING A CIVILIAN MASS BASE

The Revolutionary Council began to act on its initial plans to make a transition from military to civilian rule, as Ne Win spelled out in his March 1966 speech to a mass peasants' seminar in which he expressed his concern about the possible emergence of a personality cult. A workers' seminar drafted a constitution for a workers' council and the aforementioned peasants' seminar did the same for a peasants' council. The next stage would involve the creation of a people's party on the basis of the "Burmese Way to Socialism."[1]

The considerable length of time it took for the BSPP to make the transition from a small cadre organization to a mass party – about nine years – indicates, as one scholar observes, "the military's perception of the need to have an effective, totally subservient means to mobilize the population for the leadership's perceived ends."[2] In the late 1960s, the Revolutionary Council sped up the development of the political organs on which a future, civilian single-party state would depend. These included the creation of people's workers' councils and people's peasants' councils at the village, township, district and central levels. In November 1969, Brigadier San Yu (Chief of Staff of the Army) told BSPP cadres that the party would be transformed into a mass party and, one year later, the party drafted the People's Party Organizational Plan. Finally, at the First BSPP Congress held in 1971, the BSPP formally opened up for mass membership, promising a true "People's Party."[3]

At the First BSPP Congress, San Yu, now the General Secretary of the party's Central Organization Committee, also announced that a new constitution, replacing the Constitution of 1947, would be drafted and Burma would be returned to civilian rule. Although the Revolutionary Council would still exercise civilian powers until the new constitution had been written, the Council would now reorganize itself, and the BSPP would be put in charge of the country, with a Prime Minister and a cabinet, until a socialist constitution could be drawn up. San Yu was made chairman of the ninety-seven-member New State Constitution Drafting Commission. To grant the new constitution the veneer of legitimacy, the writing process was emphasized as being more democratic than had been the case for the old constitution. Although an elected body had approved the old constitution, for example, lawyers had done the actual writing. By contrast, the new constitution would go through a series of drafts (there were ultimately three), with popular input. The Commission split into fifteen field teams who circulated around the country holding mass meetings, attended in total by 105,000 people, and asking for opinions, of which it received a total of nearly 5,000. After the BSPP Central Committee drew up the first draft, in March 1972, on the basis of the BSPP guidelines and suggestions gathered by the field teams, the draft was explained to the general population in more meetings, attended, it was claimed, by a total of seven million people, and gathered almost 50,000 more suggestions. After the BSPP Central Committee drew up a second draft one year after the first, the process was repeated, with the new constitution explained to eight million people and more suggestions were collected. The third and final version of the constitution was then drawn up.[4]

Ne Win had explained initially that the right conditions had to be set before the constitution could be promulgated. These included the transition of the Revolutionary Council from a military to a civilian body and the establishment of a new administrative system, both of which were achieved in 1972. Ne Win and twenty other senior officers in the government accordingly resigned from the Army and officially became civilians.[5]

At the Second Congress of the BSPP held in October 1973, with Prime Minister Ne Win as Chairman of the Executive Committee and San Yu as General Secretary of the BSPP, an election was held for its central and executive committees. The BSPP also approved a final draft of the new constitution. According to this constitution, Burma would become a one-party socialist democratic republic entitled the Socialist Republic of the Union of Burma. In December, a countrywide referendum on the new constitution was held in which a majority voted in favor of the new government. The new constitution established a unicameral People's Assembly (*Pyithu Hluttaw*), whose members were elected for four-year terms. This body would elect the State Council from among its own members. The members of the State Council would then elect from among themselves a Chairman, who would also automatically become the President of the state, and a Vice Chairman of the State Council. The highest organ of public administration was now the Council of Ministers, whose members would be elected by the Assembly from a list submitted by the State Council.[6]

The second step in the transition to civilian rule took years of preparatory work. In June 1969, a seven-man committee was formed to eliminate "bureaucratism." In theory, the SACs that had been set up in 1962 to replace commissioners, deputy commissioners, sub-divisional officers, and township officers, also became more representative in the new administrative system. Between 1962 and 1972, they had mainly consisted of members of the military and police forces. In the new administrative system, the SACs, at the central, divisional, township, and village levels (wards were now dropped as a unit of administration), would now consist of representatives drawn from the BSPP membership, the people's peasants' councils, and the people's workers' councils.[7] The people, the Revolutionary Council promised, would now "have to participate daily in the work of legislation, administration and judicial process by making decisions, making arrangements, supervising, inspecting, taking necessary action and making necessary changes."[8]

The year 1974 opened with the preparations for a new government system, albeit with no major change in the leadership. In January, elections were held for seats in the 450-member Assembly, although only candidates from the BSPP, the sole officially permitted party, were allowed to run. Officially, military rule ended on the night of 2 March, when Ne Win, in his capacity as Chairman of the Revolutionary Council, handed power over to the Assembly. Upon its inauguration, the Assembly elected the highest authority in the new government, the twenty-eight-member State Council, which in turn named Ne Win as President.[9]

THE POST-TIN PE ECONOMY

In August 1967, Ne Win rehabilitated Aung Gyi, releasing him from custody and asking him to return to the government. The fact that he did so while Tin Pe happened to be out of the country raised speculation that Tin Pe's influence on Revolutionary Council economic policy was quickly coming to an end. In November 1968, as Ne Win prepared to make major changes in Burma's national policy, Tin Pe made final efforts to escalate nationalization before his influence with Ne Win was terminated. Finally, in November 1970, Tin Pe was forced to retire.[10]

Ne Win and the Revolutionary Council had taken significant steps toward changing the face of the regime from a military junta to a one-party socialist state. However, they left unresolved the fundamental economic problems created by twelve years of military rule. The negative impact of Tin Pe's management of the economy not only lingered, but actually grew as the Revolutionary Council found it difficult to reverse the downward slide. In September 1972, Ne Win warned of a possible rice shortage by December. This message led to panic buying and hoarding by Burmese consumers. As prices for rice and cooking oil skyrocketed, the Burmese government launched a campaign against "economic insurgents," such as hoarders and profiteers, who were out to destroy the socialist economy, taking 530 dealers into custody within a week.[11]

In order to encourage increased rice paddy cultivation and its domestic availability, in May 1973 the government both partially decontrolled the rice trade and suspended the export of rice. Anything grown beyond a set quota, to be delivered to the government, could be directed to the free market. As the government purchase price was 25 percent below that available on the free market, farmers hoarded their crop and minimized their delivery to the government. This helped to keep rice prices high in the general economy, doubling the price of rice. With insufficient rice stocks, the government had to reduce the monthly rice ration, forcing workers and others to purchase more rice at substantially higher prices from private traders and encouraging an increase in the price of other basic commodities. By April 1974, the government recognized that the majority of workers were both demoralized and angry as a result of rising prices for rice and other essential commodities.[12]

As rice prices increased to as high as five times the official retail price, the Burmese government faced major labour unrest. This began in early May 1974, when a workers' strike broke out at the state-owned Railway Corporation's central workshop near Mandalay. Strikes soon spread to other state-owned facilities throughout central and Upper Burma, eventually followed by general demonstrations demanding that the government do something about the rising price of rice and other commodities. Some of the demonstrations turned violent and were harshly put down by the Army.[13]

The government attempted to stabilize the situation through various measures until the end of June 1974. It lifted strict controls on the sale, milling, and transportation of rice. It made emergency issues of rice and fish to office and factory workers. A new distribution scheme provided government workers with a monthly ration of rice twice that usually allowed to civilians. In early July, Ne Win attempted to save the government's face by blaming two elements: free traders who speculated on the price of rice and caused the food shortage, and the former Nu government, from which, he claimed, the Revolutionary Council in 1962 had inherited inequalities and unjust practices in different factories and mills. The continuity of labor problems was due to (1) the need to hastily build factories and mills and get them operating in the years that followed, (2) the impossibility of the government being aware of all the numerous problems that continued to exist, (3) the preoccupation of the government in the past two years with the writing of a constitution, and (4) subversive agents, guided by "outside influence," in the factories and mills who coerced otherwise patient and loyal workers into labor action. Government efforts to relieve these problems were delayed in August, when the worst floods in sixty years hit Burma accompanied by an outbreak of cholera.[14]

Retired UN Secretary General U Thant had become a symbol of the old pre-1962 period by the time he died of cancer in New York on 26 November 1974. The return of his body to Rangoon provided a catalyst for the release of frustrations with all the economic problems the Burmese faced. At a public ceremony attended by 50,000 mourners, students seized his body and held it in the RU Convocation Hall. On 8 December, draping the body in the United Nations flag, a procession of students and monks carried it to be entombed in a rough mausoleum they had built close to the site of the student union building (demolished in 1962). After U Thant's body had been seized, the government temporarily closed educational institutions and cut off international communications with the country. On 11 December, 1,000 soldiers and police raided the university campus, forcibly repossessed the body, and carried it to the cantonment gardens where it was re-interred in the mausoleum built by his family. Students, youths, and even Buddhist monks rioted in protest throughout Rangoon, attacking troops and police. Reports claimed that they damaged police stations and markets, destroyed the government's Road Transport Corporation building as well as the Housing Board building, set fire to automobiles, and damaged a train at a local railway station, leading to at least 4,000 arrests. Police had also opened fire on rioters killing nine and wounding seventy-four others. Martial law was declared on the same day over the Rangoon Division, and special tribunals were established to try rioters. After the U Thant riots, the government closed Mandalay and Rangoon universities for five months.[15]

Student protests also forced the government to take further steps to save the economy. On 6 June 1975, after seizing a hall where BSPP members were supposed to meet, students in the Institute of Economics called for a strike and an examinations boycott. They then marched on various campuses, including the Rangoon Institute of Technology (RIT) and RU, and the State Textile Mill, where they gathered more supporters, demanding the release of those students and workers who were still in detention after the December 1974 riots. The following day, 500 of the protestors marched from RU to Sule Pagoda Road and into central Rangoon (see Fig. 7.1), by which time their numbers had grown to 3,000, and burned effigies of Ne Win and San Yu at the Independence Monument. Their demands now included an end to military rule, an end to rising prices and unemployment, and the right to organize a student union. More demonstrations occurred in the capital and demonstrators made camp at the Shwedagon Pagoda. The government responded by deploying tanks and troops, making arrests, and banning further demonstrations. It also established price controls to halt soaring prices for rice and other basic foodstuffs in order to improve production by improving living conditions, easing commodity flow "among producers, traders and consumers," and establishing proper benefits for both traders and producers. As a result of the strong student role

Figure 7.1 Sule Pagoda in Central Rangoon

in the June unrest, the government closed the universities again in June 1975. Shortly after reopening the following January, however, 5,000 RU students held demonstrations demanding political reform. In late March, the government responded by closing all universities and colleges yet again. Martial law over Rangoon, which had commenced in December 1974, was not lifted until September 1976.[16]

Monastic involvement in the riots had raised again the potential threat to the BSPP public order of monastic involvement in mundane affairs. The U Thant riots did not spark an immediate attempt to resolve this situation, perhaps because of the monastic resistance shown on other occasions when the Revolutionary Council and the BSPP had attempted to bring the order under state control. Nonetheless, several years later, in late 1979, Ne Win again attempted to "purify" the order. From December of that year until January 1980, the BSPP held another All-Sangha All-Sect Convention, for the first time since 1965, which succeeded in the monastic acceptance of national registration, an accomplishment that had eluded the 1965 Convention. Consistent with traditional Buddhist rulership, the conclusion of the Convention was accompanied by a general amnesty and the release of 14,000 prisoners, including Ne Win's political opponents. An invitation was also made for the return of those of his opponents who had fled abroad, such as Nu, who would be forgiven if they promised to remain out of politics. Nu was impressed with Ne Win's meritorious behavior, and accepted the offer. The 1979–1980 Convention's success was probably due to the fact that this time, the government depended for leadership in the proceedings not upon the smaller Shwegyin sect, but the giant Thudhamma sect, that included most monks. The religious purification also led to the disbanding of small, heretical sects and the defrocking of individual monks. From June, ecclesiastical courts were set up to try hundreds of monks, including forty senior monks, for violating the monastic code, some on the charge of having sexual intercourse with women.[17]

COMPETITION FOR LEADERSHIP

Another possible reason for Ne Win's softer approach was personal insecurity about his own position in the BSPP government as potential threats within the Army and the BSPP began to emerge. In July 1976, the Burmese government announced that it had uncovered a coup plot leading to the arrest of three army captains and eleven other officers. The conspirators, who planned to assassinate Ne Win, San Yu, and intelligence chief General Tin Oo, sought to liberalize the government. The government claimed the main goal of the plot was to "destroy the socialist economic system." As the trial progressed, however, extensive state press coverage revealed resentment in the ranks concerning corruption within the BSPP, including special purchases of cars by BSPP leaders at about 10 percent of their market value. Stories also began to circulate that BSPP leaders were building up private fortunes and squandering party funds to the point of exhaustion. Ne Win's subsequent call for party leaders to live more economically austere lives appeared to substantiate these beliefs.[18]

Deteriorating political, social, and economic conditions led to the calling of the Third BSPP Congress in February 1977, eight months earlier than scheduled. The Congress saw severe criticism over the failure of Prime Minister Sein Win and Deputy Prime Minister (and minister of National Planning and Finance) U Lwin to adhere to national economic plan guidelines and policies. The Congress also elected a new central committee. Sixteen senior leaders, including Sein Win and Lwin, were left out of the elections in order to allow an infusion of new blood. In a surprising development that suggested that Ne Win was also blamed for the poor economy, San Yu received more votes than Ne Win. The central committee pushed the vote aside and soldiers surrounded party headquarters and seized documents that supposedly linked central committee members with the Soviet KGB. The following purge saw 113 central committee members, the "Gang of 113," forced out of the Party. At the end of March, both Sein Win and Lwin resigned from the government, while U Maung Maung Kha, formerly in charge of the army engineering corps and the defense services industries, became the new Prime Minister.[19]

Another BSPP Congress was then called in November 1977, at which San Yu claimed that corruption and malpractice was hurting the BSPP. Responsibility was attributed to a faction that had formed and acquired positions on leading committees. To resolve this problem, the BSPP was to revise its constitution. In the general election in January 1978, Ne Win was approved to rule for four more years and in March, the People's Assembly re-elected President Ne Win to his second four-year term. At the BSPP Congress held in August 1981, Ne Win finally announced that he would retire as President of the Republic, which he formally did on 9 November. San Yu was unanimously elected by the Assembly to take his place as Chairman of the Council of State and thus, automatically, President of the Republic.[20]

Although Ne Win stepped down as President, he remained in control of the BSPP and thus in firm control of the country, until the collapse of the Party in 1988. With Ne Win's formal departure from the presidency, the government attempted to demonstrate its legitimacy by targeting old problems, especially government corruption and the status of Asian immigrant minorities. From May to June 1983, Ne Win personally led the latest purge of government leadership. Initially, Tin Oo was ousted and confined to his house, accused of building up a private power base outside the official military hierarchy. Ne Win had also complained about Tin Oo's conspicuous spending habits, which had included an expensive wedding and honeymoon abroad for his son and a similarly expensive medical trip to London for his wife. Further, his well-known protégé, Bo Ni, who had been Home and Religious Affairs Minister, was also on trial for misusing private funds after he reportedly used a medical trip to London to purchase luxury goods and smuggle them illegally through Burmese Customs. The following month scores of military men and officials were sacked. While most evaded prison sentences, Tin Oo was sentenced to two life terms and found guilty of misappropriating state funds to finance his property holdings, and Bo Ni was also given a life sentence with hard labour.[21]

The purge of Tin Oo and the resulting disarray in Burma's security and intelligence services was soon blamed for a major intelligence failure of international dimensions. In October 1983, a bomb killed four South

Korean cabinet ministers and fifteen others at a ceremony at the Martyrs' Mausoleum in Rangoon. While the bomb was eventually traced to North Korean agents, just as South Korea's leadership had immediately suspected, other theories held that the bomb was probably planted by the BCP or by dissidents in the Burmese Army in retaliation for the recent purge. Once the North Korean connection was proven, the Burmese government severed diplomatic links with North Korea, ordering North Korean diplomats and their families to leave the country within forty-eight hours, this being the first time that Burma had ever taken such a measure.[22]

In 1981, Ne Win announced BSPP plans to promulgate a new citizenship law within a year. The new law was to include three citizenship classes, including indigenous people, "mixed people" (descendants of intermarriage between Chinese and Indian immigrants and Burmese), and naturalized citizens. Ne Win located the emergence of Burma's foreigner problem in the period between 1824 (the beginning of the First Anglo-Burmese War) and 1948, the period of colonial rule, when the Burmese and indigenous institutions were no longer in control of who could and could not live in the country, nor did the colonial regime restrain the inflow of immigrants. First the British came and they were followed by a multitude of other foreigners, mostly for economic reasons. Thus, when Burma achieved independence in 1948, it found itself with a heterogeneous population of nationals, foreigners, and the descendants of mixed marriages of both, whom Ne Win labeled "thwe hnaw" or mixed blood. In order to determine who were to be citizens in the new republic and who would remain foreigners, the Nu regime passed the Union Citizen Act (4 January 1948), which defined "genuine" citizens and their rights, and the Union Citizenship Election Act (9 May 1948), which gave foreign-born individuals in the country the option of applying for citizenship. One problem was that after the 1948 citizenship laws, many foreigners remained but did not know how to properly apply for citizenship, or indeed, were unclear of what their actual national identity was. These people were categorized as "resident citizens" under the 1948 law, as differentiated from genuine citizens. A second problem was that under Nu, many foreigners who came to Burma after 1948 were improperly given citizenship certificates. Ne Win, using the example of Indians and Chinese in Burma, argued that resident citizens and those post-1948 immigrants who had acquired citizenship certificates should be allowed to remain and work, but should be excluded from involvement in determining the country's future. Some of the Indians and Chinese who left Burma moved to various countries and maintained transnational networks of family members in Burma and abroad for the purposes of black-marketeering. Such people, Ne Win argued, could not be trusted in national organizations and could not be given full citizenship.[23]

The new Burma Citizenship Law established three categories of citizenship. "Genuine citizens" included only "pure blood" nationals. "Resident citizens" included those foreign immigrants who had come to Burma and properly applied for citizenship under the 1948 laws. "Naturalized citizens" included those pre-1948 foreign immigrants who had not applied for citizenship under the 1948 laws, because they either did not know about them or did not understand them, and were found after application and scrutiny by the state to meet the requirements for citizenship. Immigrants who knew about the laws and refused to apply for citizenship, or who did not know or understand the laws and did not qualify after scrutiny, would be denied citizenship. Ne Win also explained that while there were three categories of citizen now, in the future there would only be one, as the third generation descendant of a resident or naturalized citizen would become a "genuine" citizen.[24]

THE CONTINUING CIVIL WAR

After so many failures at unifying themselves into a broad alliance, in 1976, thirteen insurgent groups succeeded in doing so with the establishment of the National Democratic Front (NDF) under the command of KNU General Saw Bo Mya. The NDF based itself at Manerplaw ("Field of Victory"), established as the KNU capital in 1974, on the Thai border. Bo Mya was a pro-Western commander who had rapidly emerged as leader of the KNU. In the 1960s, the KNU was wracked by military reverses, failed negotiations with Rangoon, and two major schisms, the last in 1966, only to be disappointed in the early 1970s by the failure of the UNLF. Bo Mya's predecessor, Mahn Ba Zan, had attempted to graft a leftist ideology onto the KNU and formed an alliance with the BCP. During this period, the KNU's military wing, the KNDO, was renamed the Karen National Liberation Army (KNLA). Under Bo Mya, the KNU would become an anti-Communist force, despite a military alliance with the BCP in the mid-1980s.[25]

Aside from the KNU and four other relatively minor insurgencies, the NDF included the Arakan Liberation Party, the Kachin Independence Organization (KIO), the Karenni Progressive Party, the Kayan New Land Party, the Lahu National Unity Party, the Union Pa-O National Organization, the Palaung State Liberation Organization, and the Shan State Progressive Party. Although the NDF intended to raise an army of

100,000 men, its initial combined strength amounted to only 10,000 fighters. The main weakness was the absence of outside support. Members of the NDF would not cooperate much militarily, but the alliance did cause the various ethnic insurgent groups to abandon their earlier demands for separate sovereign states and accept the establishment of a federal union as a common goal. The NDF frequently lost soldiers to the better-funded BCP. Nonetheless, the NDF rivaled the BCP in numbers of soldiers and territorial control and, unlike previous attempts at non-Communist alliances, the NDF endured.[26]

Despite greater cooperation with other insurgent forces, however, KNU fortunes would rapidly decline from the mid-1980s. The BSPP government launched a massive counter-insurgency campaign in 1984 eventually leading to the capture of the KNU base at Palu in 1986. More importantly, the KNU was cut off from its main source of revenue. Unlike some of its opium-enriched competitors, the KNU depended upon a 10 percent tax it levied on goods passing through transit points it controlled along the Thai border. From 1984, Thailand's improving relationship with Rangoon led it to seal off this trade.[27]

The notorious Khun Sa (Chapter 6) returned to the Triangle after the creation of the NDF to rebuild the Shan United Army (SUA), which gradually grew to 5,000 soldiers. Although he claimed to be fighting for Shan independence, the fact that the Burmese Army was strangely reluctant to attack his bases did not help his reputation. Khun Sa appears to have mainly been intent on rebuilding his opium empire. Establishing control over territory on both sides of the Thai–Burmese border, he ran between ten and twelve heroin refineries. In 1981, the Thai government and the US Drug Enforcement Agency each put out rewards for his capture, dead or alive. The Thai Army began an offensive in 1982 that drove his forces out of their main base at Ban Hin Taek in northwestern Thailand and out of another stronghold at Doi Sanchu, also in Thailand, in August 1983. By 1985, the indefatigable Khun Sa had rebuilt his forces yet again and expanded his army further when he forced the Thailand Revolutionary Council to merge its forces with his own SUA, creating the Mong Tai Army (MTA).[28]

THE CRACKING OF THE ECONOMY

In the mid- to late-1970s, it appeared that international help might resolve Burma's economic woes. In 1976, the World Bank set up an aid consortium, including Britain, the US, Japan, Germany, France, Australia, and

Canada for consultation and the establishment of a common policy regarding aid to Burma. In 1977, San Yu reported to the BSPP Congress that isolationist policies had hurt Burma's social and economic progress and would cease. While it had been hoped that Burma's gross national product would increase by 4 percent, it had only grown by 2.6 percent; productivity among state and cooperative sectors of the economy had been projected to increase at 2 percent per year, but had only achieved a 1.2 percent rate of increase. In order to exploit its natural resources, and establish joint enterprises with other countries, without sacrificing the socialist economic system, Burma would need significant capital investment, foreign technical assistance and equipment. Although Japan and West Germany were the largest of foreign aid donors, the PRC also emerged as a major source of loans to the country from 1979.[29]

The Burmese economy began to crack again by the mid-1980s. Between 1981 and 1986, the national debt doubled to US$ 2.8 billion. By 1986, the net debt burden was 650 percent of foreign exchange earnings, with a debt–service ratio of almost 60 percent of foreign-exchange earnings. During the same period, the World Bank estimated that the value of Burma's export declined by half, having dropped by 15 percent in 1985 alone, while rice ceased to be the major export item, being displaced by teak and hardwood. As a result, Burma's creditworthiness began to slip in international eyes. In early November 1985, the Burmese government attempted to fight the black market by withdrawing, without prior notice, high denomination notes for the second time. The 100-*kyat* note, Burma's principal unit of currency, ceased to be legal tender and would be replaced by a new 75-*kyat* denomination note.[30]

Ne Win announced that steps would be taken to liberalize the rice trade in 1987. Although some parts of private trade were being opened, foreign investment was still blocked. In March, the BSPP government passed a law which limited the sale of land or buildings to or from foreigners and forbade such transfers by gift or mortgage as well, violation of this law being subject to up to five years in prison and confiscation by the government of the property concerned. In September, the government lifted the ban on citizens buying or selling domestically rice paddy, maize, mung beans, butter beans, and a range of other crops. It also announced that peasants cultivating these crops would pay their taxes with a share of the crops rather than by paying cash.[31]

The government's rice procurement program, which supplied much of Burma's urban populace, was severely damaged because government prices could not compete with those on the black market. Shortages of spare parts and petrol also created transport problems that made it difficult to distribute the rice that had been procured. This would be followed on 5 September 1987 with the demonetization of 25-, 35-, and 75-*kyat* notes as well. The following day, students protested the measure, leading to the closure of universities for a month. In August, Ne Win admitted to the BSPP Central Committee that there had been mistakes in the regime's economic policies and announced that it would now experiment, through a short-term program, with allowing the private trade in rice to resume. Like the cultivators, private businessmen would also pay their taxes in the form of crops or commodities rather than cash. The government also gave cooperative societies and private entrepreneurs (Burmese citizens only) permission to begin exporting rice.[32]

The Burmese economy hit rock bottom by late 1987. In November of that year, the UN granted Burma Least Developed Country status, shared by forty other poor countries, which in theory made the country eligible for special technical and development assistance, as well as low or zero interest loans. This new status, however, came too late to save the BSPP government, as revelations made in early 1988 would indicate. In mid-March 1988, the Deputy Prime Minister and Minister for Planning and Finance, U Tun Tin, told a People's Assembly budget session that the GDP growth rate for 1987–1988 was almost half the expected target of 5 percent. He also announced, for the first time, that Burma had a foreign debt of US$4 billion. In the new budget, the GDP growth rate target would only be 2.3 percent.[33]

The deteriorating economic situation raised concerns about unrest. At the end of March, General Saw Maung explained that an unstable world economy had adversely affected Burma and to adapt to this situation, the government had begun to undertake economic reforms. A month later, San Yu observed that Burma's industrial sector suffered from many problems. First, factories were not operating at capacity because they lacked raw materials, oil, and spare parts. As a result, there was a decline in available consumer products. The yearly decline in oil production also meant that the economy could not meet the needs of the production and transport sectors. The government also attempted to speed up the delivery of goods to port for export, by ending the government's monopoly on the transport of private goods. "Unrestricted" private transport would be allowed, with the exception of government department and cooperatives' goods, which would have to continue to rely on government-controlled transport. After a few months, however, Rangoon authorities warned private traders not to escalate prices of basic commodities. The purpose of freeing up trade, they argued, had been to bring prices down "while enabling private traders to enjoy justifiable profits." However, commodity prices were now spiraling out of control as a result of the "greed" of the private sector and amounted to the exploitation of Burmese consumers. The basic problem was that as the *kyat* had become unreliable, rice became the new currency and so was hoarded.[34]

CONCLUSION

Whatever the underlying motives for the transition from Revolutionary Council to BSPP rule, the latter's failure was not so much political as economic. The legacy of Tin Pe's misdirection of the economy, the problems of supplying consumer demands, demonetization, and corruption at the top all contributed to the general malaise and popular dissatisfaction with the regime's performance. Despite the promises of the Revolutionary Council period, the BSPP government had not eliminated greed or economic exploitation, but instead, as in many of the Communist states that collapsed in the 1980s, saw the emergence of a privileged class of military and associated families who thrived. Many of these families would move to prevent democratization in the years after the collapse of the BSPP government in 1988.

CHAPTER 8

Toward democracy, 1988–1990

Although, as we have seen, Burma underwent several major watersheds in its modern historical development, the most crucial and perhaps most surprising, given the scale, the suddenness, and the importance of its impact, is the popular revolution of 1988. While Burmese were clearly unhappy with the BSPP government, the state had successfully managed its international image, convincing the world not that it was a good government, but rather that domestic opposition was largely a problem of ethnic polarization (the ethnic insurgencies) and foreign intervention (the Communists).

Regardless of how much resignation the general population displayed until this point, the BSPP government would fall as a result of the release of popular pent-up frustrations before the year was finished. As one Burmese leader from the period later recalled:

As the years rolled by, we had started to equate lethargy and lack of change with stability; speeches and motions with no progress; excuses with reason; and manipulated statistics with real facts. Our people are not that simple; they saw, they felt, and they knew, but they can be patient, and they can wait. When all the waiting they could do was done, the storm broke.[1]

THE STUDENT DEMONSTRATIONS

The collapse of BSPP rule had surprisingly small beginnings. Indeed, its spark was regarded at the time as almost insignificant. On 12 March, four months after universities and colleges reopened, several RIT students became involved in a brawl with local people at the Sanda Win teashop. The incident began with an argument over a song request and a local hitting one of the students over the head with a stool. Although arrests were made, the offending parties were released the following day, the main culprit being the son of a local party official. In the days that followed, more clashes between locals and outraged RIT students occurred until riot police fired on the students, wounding many, several of whom died

when police forbade doctors to operate. RIT students soon demanded a
report on the killings and compensation for the families of those killed.
On 15 March, soldiers and police raided the RIT campus. The police were
unusually swift and brutal, beating students with batons and arresting them
en masse, state radio later claiming that the students were completely at fault
for the raid. The following day, as student protestors who had collected at
Rangoon University passed the White Bridge on Prome Road, demanding
an end to one-party rule, they were stopped by a barbed wire barricade
and soldiers armed with clubs and automatic weapons. In the ensuing one-
hour carnage, reputedly orchestrated by General Sein Lwin, as many as one
hundred (some say 200) students were beaten to death. Female students
dragged off by the soldiers were gang-raped. Recognizing that the violence
had gotten out of hand even by the standards of the military government,
and in the tense atmosphere of an economy ruined by a quarter of a century
of military rule, on 17 March, the government established a commission to
investigate the initial student death, but refused to acknowledge the White
Bridge incident.[2]

Reacting to the harsh response by the authorities, more protests erupted
in the following few days, broken up by riot police. One of the most serious
episodes occurred when forty-one students died of suffocation after being
packed into a single prison van for two hours on the ten-mile journey to
prison. The bodies were cremated the following day, it was claimed, because
of their poor condition. The government knew about this incident, but,
claiming that the police had been short of prison vans, it would delay
admitting responsibility until mid-July, leading to the resignation of the
Home Minister. In response to the March events, retired Aung Gyi wrote to
Ne Win demanding an immediate inquiry. If the security forces had acted
as rumored, he argued, then they were guilty of human rights violations
and this would hurt Burma's international image.[3]

Little had been resolved by early June. The government blocked a student
attempt to organize a peaceful memorial ceremony on 13 June for the
students who had been killed in the March riots. On 16 June, the students
of Rangoon Arts and Sciences University (RASU) gave the government one
day to meet their demands to release 1,500 imprisoned students and allow
freedom of association. When the government made no response, 5,000
students of the RIT and two medical schools boycotted their classes and
began protests. The protests grew over the course of the following week,
leading to a major confrontation with riot police on 21 June. This time, after
the police killed several children, ordinary citizens lent aid to the students,
killing some of the police at a Rangoon market. In other skirmishes that day

elsewhere in the city, police fired indiscriminately into protesting crowds. The government was outraged and closed the universities and declared curfews over the city. Nevertheless, in the next few days, riots, met by mass arrests and more curfews, spread to Mandalay and Pegu.[4]

The seventy-year-old Aung Gyi, who had criticized the security forces' handling of student protestors in March, wrote a forty-one-page letter to Ne Win and San Yu criticizing the government's handling of the economy. He claimed that Burma had been transformed into a "beggar nation," because of Tin Pe's misunderstandings of socialism in the 1960s. He now urged Ne Win to undertake serious economic reforms such as those then underway in the Soviet Union and China. Aung Gyi was then arrested for leaking his letters criticizing Ne Win to the public.[5]

THE FALL OF NE WIN

The curfew over Rangoon was finally lifted on 30 June, followed by the lifting of curfews in Pegu, Prome, and Moulmein and a week later, the government began releasing hundreds of students detained for the March and June riots. Violence broke out again in the middle of July at Taunggyi and Prome. In view of the deteriorating domestic situation, an extraordinary congress of the BSPP was called for on 23 July and was attended by 1,062 BSPP delegates. There was wide speculation that as the Home Minister and the Rangoon police chief had resigned already, Ne Win would use the session to legitimate a prospective purge of the government. Instead, two major changes were proposed. First, U Aye Ko, the General Secretary of the BSPP, admitted that the BSPP government's approach to the economy had been wrong and said that it would now fully open up the economy.[6]

The key to improving the economic performance of the private, public, and cooperative sectors, he asserted, was in fostering conditions and making guarantees that would mobilize private entrepreneurs to increase investment and provide economic dynamism. The private sector should now be allowed to own land and farm machinery; participate in the fishing and timber industries; establish and operate all industries (apart from munitions) for the construction of homes, roads, and bridges, the operation of air and rail transport, the manufacture of automobiles and trucks, local and foreign trade, and the publication of periodicals. The private sector would not be allowed to operate in certain areas, such as cinemas and the music industry, but the changes now proposed amounted to a sweeping retraction of much of the economic legislation of the Revolutionary Council and BSPP periods.[7]

Second, Ne Win explained that the bloodshed of March and June indicated significant mistrust of the government. To decide whether this reflected a majority or a minority, he called for the congress to approve his proposal that a national referendum be held, as soon as possible but no later than the end of September, to decide whether Burma should maintain a single-party system or revert to a multi-party system. If the latter were voted for, the Constitution would have to be amended to accommodate a multi-party electoral system and the newly elected Parliament would have to write a new Constitution. To prevent chaos, Ne Win asked existing organizations to remain in place until that Parliament could establish new organizations. If the new Parliament no longer wanted the organizations it inherited from the BSPP government, these should, without hesitation, hand over their responsibilities.[8]

If the national referendum were to vote for a continuity of the single-party state, however, Ne Win would clarify his personal position. Accepting indirect responsibility for the March and June events and observing that he was now very old (seventy-seven), he asked the Congress to allow him to resign from his position as BSPP Chairman and from the BSPP altogether. This would require an amendment to the party regulations that denied any full member the right to resign from the Party. Ne Win further explained that he had tried in the past to resign and retire, but his colleagues had stopped him from doing so, thus trapping him in the "whirlpool of politics." This time, however, these colleagues, such as Vice-Chairman San Yu and BSPP General Secretary Sein Lwin, not only agreed, but also submitted their own resignation letters as well. The Congress refused Sein Lwin's resignation and while it accepted those of San Yu and Ne Win, it did not permit them to leave the Party. The Congress also decided not to hold a national referendum, on the grounds that the government should first concern itself with resolving the country's economic problems. Ne Win also denied responsibility for the dynamiting of the RU Student Union in 1962, claiming that there had been confusion in the relaying of orders.[9]

SEIN LWIN

At the Tenth Meeting of the BSPP Central Committee, Sein Lwin was named the new Chairman of the BSPP, and thus became President of Burma. The sixty-four-year-old was a known hardliner and was held to be responsible for the White Bridge incident and for brutally crushing the RU student demonstrations in July 1962. On 27 July 1988, Sein Lwin had claimed that it was not the "Burmese Road to Socialism" that had caused

Burma's economic crisis, but rather "bad officials." After his appointment, Sein Lwin immediately issued dismissal orders for Prime Minister U Maung Maung Kha and the Chairman of the Council of People's Attorneys U Myint Maung (now replaced by Dr. Maung Maung). Saw Maung was also promoted to Minister of Defense.[10]

Upset at Sein Lwin's promotion, students in the capital immediately began to make public speeches, put up anti-government posters, hold protest marches to the Shwedagon Pagoda, and hand out pamphlets referring to Sein Lwin as "The Butcher of Rangoon" and leaflets calling for a general strike in demand for a return to democracy and multi-party elections. This continued from 28 July until 3 August. At one demonstration at the Shwedagon alone, 500 students and monks participated. Rather than attempt dialogue, Sein Lwin took a hard line, responding in the same way that the military had to most civil disobedience since the 1962 coup. The government placed under detention Aung Gyi and ten other former army officers, officials, and businessmen associated with him, followed by the arrest of two of the surviving eleven members of the Thirty Comrades, as a precautionary measure. Two days later, martial law was declared over the Greater Rangoon area. Even so, the protests continued to grow in numbers and frequency, and spread from Rangoon to other major towns in Burma, including Mandalay and Moulmein.[11]

In his resignation speech in July, Ne Win had given a stern warning to protestors. He explained that

when the army shoots, it shoots to hit; it does not fire in the air to scare. Therefore, I warn those causing disturbances that they will not be spared if in the future the army is brought in to control disturbances.[12]

Although the Army fired only warning shots when confronted with 10,000 protestors on 4 August, further confrontations over the course of the following week led to bloodshed at Mandalay, Mergui, Pegu, and Thanpinit, but failed to deter other demonstrations, which by 9 August had broken out in most towns throughout the country.[13]

The government's response to the breakdown in public order was confused and desperate, as it vainly sought ways to stem the growth of the opposition. On 7 August it secured the agreement of the State Sangha Maha Nayaka Committee and Sangha Nayaka committees at the state, divisional, township, ward, and village levels not to allow monks to participate in the "disturbances." The following day, it retroactively raised the pay of the armed forces, pensioners, mill and factory workers, and other government employees. On 9 August, the Ministry of Education closed all primary, middle, and high schools as well as teacher training institutes, reportedly in order to protect the students from the demonstrators. That same day, the government announced a curfew from 8:00 P.M. until 4:00 A.M., and banned groups of five or more from marching, gathering, walking, making speeches, or chanting slogans. As deaths mounted, the State Sangha Maha Nayaka Committee called on the government to "uphold the 10 kingly virtues" and "to concede to the demands of the people" as far as permitted by law. Elements among the demonstrators took the law into their own hands, beheading three policemen, burning buses, and damaging government buildings. On 10 August, tanks and machine-gun carriers were brought in to form barricades to prevent demonstrators from moving through Rangoon. Demonstrators also erected their own barricades and those who had been able to steal guns from ransacked police stations now fired back on the soldiers. The next day, the Air Force began dropping leaflets warning that they would begin bombing if demonstrators did not remove the barricades. The following day, 12 August, Sein Lwin resigned as Chairman of the BSPP, Chairman of the State Council, and as President of Burma, bringing the demonstrations to a halt. By this time, the government claimed that one hundred people had been killed, although hospital staff estimated that 3,000 had died in Rangoon alone.[14]

THE MAUNG MAUNG GOVERNMENT

Ne Win's long-time friend and biographer, Dr. Maung Maung, replaced Sein Lwin, taking office on 19 August 1988. On the same day, the BSPP government began to make a flood of concessions to demonstrators, whether asked for or not, beginning with the declaration that the public, cooperatives, and private sectors were now allowed to publish newspapers, journals, and magazines. Those publications and presses that had been nationalized under the Revolutionary Council in the 1960s were now to be returned to their original owners. All sectors were also now allowed to become involved in public entertainment, to build cinemas, and to show commercial films.[15]

The opposition was generally unsatisfied with the choice of Maung Maung to head the government and his succession to office was rejected by tens of thousands of demonstrators. They associated him with Ne Win and felt he was no better. He had helped draft the 1974 Constitution that established one-party rule. They also claimed that in his role as Chief Justice, the senior legal officer of the BSPP government, he was responsible for illegalities and for the regime's poor record on human rights. There was also significant opposition to Maung Maung's creation of the Public Opinion Soliciting Commission on 19 August 1988. The Commission consisted entirely of government people. Its purpose was to determine authentic popular opinion on the condition of the country and interview members of state organizations and individual citizens, Maung Maung promising that no one would be punished for freely expressing opinions. The Commission's questionnaires asked for views on the direction government reform should take, including whether a one-party system should be continued, whether the judicial system should be maintained as it was, and whether student unions should be permitted. The Commission was then to submit a report to the People's Assembly in October.[16]

The government also took pains to approach the demonstrations in a new way. Regarding numerous demonstrations that took place on 23 August, government radio repeatedly stressed how demonstrators were acting peacefully and that security forces had not shot anyone. The following day, Maung Maung announced that the government had now lifted martial law in Rangoon and Prome. He explained that the Army did not like to confront civilians and that it meant no harm to genuine demonstrators. It only acted as necessary when troublemakers took advantage of the situation in order to loot and cause destruction and in these circumstances it was difficult for the Army to differentiate between them. Maung Maung further announced that the government had decided to call an extraordinary party congress on 12 September to discuss holding a national referendum on whether or not Burma should continue to have a one-party system. If the Congress decided to remain with a one-party system and not hold a national referendum on the matter, Maung Maung promised that he and the entire BSPP Central Executive Committee would immediately resign and end their membership in the Party. The next day, on 25 August, the Maung Maung government released Aung Gyi from prison.[17]

As the number of protesters grew from thousands to tens of thousands and then hundreds of thousands, a unifying force was needed. The most popular emerging figure was the charismatic Aung San Suu Kyi (born in 1945 in Rangoon). She had left Burma with her mother, when the latter was appointed Ambassador to India. Aung San Suu Kyi had lived abroad for most of her adult life. She had no direct claim to leadership, but as the daughter of Aung San, the widely recognized father of Burmese independence (and the Army), she had an aura of legitimacy. She had come to Burma earlier in 1988 to attend her sick mother. Aung San Suu Kyi first entered the fray when she wrote to the Council of State in August, while it was deciding on a new leader following Ne Win's resignation, proposing the establishment of a consultative committee whose members would be independents drawn from outside the ruling BSPP elite. They would oversee the establishment of a multi-party political system. The Council made no comment. By 25 August she was urging that there should be no problems between the Army and the people. Many of the protestors began to recognize her as the leader of the pro-Democracy movement after her speech before a mass audience at the Shwedagon Pagoda on the following day. Aung San Suu Kyi viewed the popular protests as a "second struggle for Burmese independence," for while the Burmese had secured independence from colonialism, they did not now enjoy a political system that fully observed human rights. It was now too late for the BSPP government to hold a referendum, for the popular desire for multi-party elections had already been demonstrated through the protests. By late August, she still foresaw no particular role for herself in a future government, as she was not attracted to a "life in politics," but, for the time being, because of her father's name, she was satisfied to serve merely as a "kind of unifying force."[18]

Demonstrators gave the Maung Maung government a 7 September deadline to resign, or they would launch national strikes and demonstrations. When that deadline arrived, the Maung Maung government instead announced that people in Rangoon could "no longer live in peace and security" and that some people participating in the rallies were only doing so to loot public property. As the demonstrations grew, the government curiously began to release over 10,000 criminals from prison in an apparent attempt to discredit the democracy demonstrators or to encourage the view of a breakdown in national order. It was widely believed that the government wanted an excuse to summon army intervention. Prior to the deadline, a group of students, monks, and others who had formed a vigilante committee and taken over an abandoned police station attempted to maintain order when looters, many recently released from prison, broke into a biscuit factory. Eight were killed, including the deputy abbot of a local monastery. Hundreds of people then stormed the factory and a battle involving axes, knives, and slingshots immediately ensued. Some of the looters who were captured were burned to death, hung from trees or lampposts, or decapitated. After teachers of the Hmawbi Military Academy and several battalions declared that they would not shoot demonstrators, the BSPP government made a special effort to coordinate between departments to withdraw 600 million *kyat* from the Union of Burma Bank to pay its soldiers, presumably to keep them loyal and dissuade them from abandoning their posts.[19]

Despite the protests, 968 out of 1080 (about 90 percent) BSPP delegates attended the emergency congress, which was held two days earlier than originally scheduled, on 10 September. The delegates were to vote for a national referendum to determine whether Burma should continue as a one-party state or change to a multi-party state. At that congress, 75 percent of delegates voted against holding a national referendum and in favor of holding a general election instead. The People's Assembly would now hold a session on the following day to identify respected elders who could form an electoral commission to supervise the holding of free and fair multi-party elections with the help of local elders, monks, and students to observe the polling booths. The Army would not be allowed to support any party in the elections the Congress held, following its tradition of neutrality in politics. These elections would be for the parliamentary level only. This parliament, when constituted, would form a government that it saw fit to run the country and make the necessary changes to the existing Constitution. Finally, in order to hold fair elections, the BSPP government would have to secure law and order, assure food supplies at low prices for the people, and make certain that transportation was operating smoothly. The following day, the Assembly also voted in favor of multi-party general elections and stipulated that these elections would be held within three months.[20] The five-member Multi-Party Democratic General Election Commission was finally formed on 12 September.

Maung Maung had earlier publicly admitted the failings of the BSPP on 1 September 1988. The 1974 Constitution, he explained, was arranged so that there was a diffusion of power from the central government down to the level of wards and villages, so that no one could command absolute power. However, since 1974, these remained only "printed passages on paper," and this denial of power grew into frustration over the fourteen years of BSPP rule. Maung Maung gave another speech following the 10 September vote in which he praised the delegates for having put the interests of the people above those of the BSPP.[21] He argued that the historical development of the BSPP had made it incapable of handling new conditions. As he explained: "the weakness of the party was that it was born as a ruling party and grew up as one. In practice, it lacked the experience of making sacrifices, taking risks, and working hard to overcome difficulties . . ."[22] The BSPP, in short, had failed, just as the AFPFL had failed by 1958, and thus the BSPP provoked the anti-government demonstrations that now challenged the Party's and the government's survival. As Maung Maung continued, "Changes come about once every 10 or 12 years. If they do not come about peacefully, they come about in a violent and torrid way."[23]

Maung Maung was instructing BSPP delegates concerning the legitimacy of the reasons for popular unhappiness with the government and with the Party, but he was in no way supporting the forces that were taking shape to lead the people in their protests. He believed that the protestors represented anarchy:

They – whoever "they" might be – wanted to sweep everything aside, bring everything down, rush in on human waves shouting their war cries to the cheers and applause of outsiders, and establish their occupation.[24]

Thus, while viewing Ne Win's retirement as a "benevolent act," he also viewed the protestors as riddled with opportunists, destructive elements and their "slanderous statements," and foreign influence. These people did not value law and order, which was a violation of Burmese culture and, Maung Maung argued, did not represent genuine democracy. Even so, he warned the BSPP delegates not to "hold grudges" or to retaliate in any way, but rather to change according to the times and conditions at hand and exercise patience with the newly emerging parties.[25]

Nu had returned to Burma under amnesty in 1980, vowing that he would stay out of politics and spend the rest of his life devoted to Buddhism.[26] Nevertheless, in late August 1988, the 81-year-old Nu now re-emerged to make another bid for political leadership. Having entered and removed himself from national leadership so many times before, he now jumped back again into the fray at the head of a motley crew of former ministers and military men. On 9 September, Nu invited local and foreign journalists, foreign embassy staff, and representatives of unions to a press conference at which he announced the creation of a parallel government, and listed the twenty-six members of this new government, among whom many were members of the old government. Nu argued that the only legal constitution Burma had was the 1947 Constitution. According to this constitution, he was the legal prime minister of Burma. As Nu explained: "I have exercised my constitutional right . . . I have taken back the power which General Ne Win has robbed from me . . . sovereign power no longer rests with General Ne Win. It has come back into my hands, and I announce this fact with joy." He explained that although this amounted to high treason in the eyes of the BSPP government and that he had no interest in political office, it was something that had to be done. Nu issued a statement on 19 September repeating his claims as well as explaining that he had the power to dissolve Parliament. Other opposition leaders had already warned Nu that the establishment of his rival government was "a dangerous move."[27]

The future founders of the National League for Democracy (NLD), Aung San Suu Kyi, Tin U and Aung Gyi, also had initially rejected the proposed multi-party elections in mid-September. At a coordination meeting arranged by the Election Commission on 13 September, they and others were told that it would be neutral and the election would be fair; in exchange, those present would have to cooperate sincerely with the commission. After explaining the details of the election process, Aung Gyi, Aung San Suu Kyi, and Tin U argued that while they respected the members of the commission, the fact that the BSPP government had created it meant that it was not legitimate and could not be trusted. Further, if the elections were held in the current circumstances, the elections would not be fair for two reasons. First, the new political parties – without financial resources – would have to face a state-financed BSPP, entrenched for twenty-six years; and second, although the armed forces promised to remain neutral, the fact was that all armed forces personnel and a majority of other state employees were BSPP members, and there would be no possibility of the general population having faith in that guarantee. Instead, a neutral government would have to be established before multi-party elections could be held. Aung San Suu Kyi had stressed the previous day that the creation of such a neutral government could only be achieved if Ne Win were exiled first from the country.[28]

The BSPP Election Commission delayed but eventually relented on some of these demands. On 16 September, the State Council announced that since government servants should "be loyal to the state and only serve the people" and in keeping with the multi-party system that the government now promised to create, all state employees, including the military, could no longer be members of a political party including the BSPP. The BSPP government announced that if government employees took part in the demonstrations to encourage multi-party elections "in the belief that such a national movement would bring about the best system for the state," then the BSPP government would not criticize them for doing so. However, the government argued that now that the demand for holding multi-party elections had been agreed to, the political movement could no longer be viewed as a national movement, but instead as a party movement. In parliamentary democracies abroad, the government asserted, the code of conduct of government employees did not allow them to participate in party movements. Only by observing this apolitical code of conduct would the popular needs of peace, prosperity, food, clothing, shelter, and transport be met. Thus, government employees should abandon strike action and return to work with effect from 19 September and if they had not done so within one week, the government warned, public service rules and regulations would be invoked to take action against them.[29]

At this point, the Army grew more alarmed. It faced three major problems, none of which it would allow to progress any further. First, despite lip service to multi-party elections and the removal of the armed forces and government personnel from the BSPP, large numbers of demonstrators continued their protests while the Army was becoming less potent a force in stopping them. This was underscored on 16 September when 7,000 demonstrators surrounded the Defense Ministry Building and only pulled back on the urging of Aung Gyi. The following day protestors surrounded government buildings, including the City Hall and the Central Bank. When drunken soldiers on top of the Trade Ministry Building taunted another crowd and then fired into it, protestors stormed the building and nearly decapitated the offenders before Aung Gyi and Tin U persuaded them to disperse, but not before they had burned three motor vehicles.[30] After decades of total control, the Army was extremely concerned about the complete breakdown of government authority. Indeed, due to the strike, government machinery had simply evaporated in the capital and in many of Burma's main towns.

Second, foreign diplomats and others in the country grew confident that the BSPP government would give in and allow the formation of an interim government, which would suddenly remove the armed forces' authority as well; there was no guarantee what their authority would be under the BSPP government's interim or permanent successor. Third, the Army was most concerned about its internal disintegration. On the one hand, it faced popular former generals in Aung Gyi, Tin U and others. On the other hand, it was beginning to lose soldiers on a daily basis; individuals crossed the lines to join the demonstrators and whole units mutinied, as in the case of 200 Air Force personnel in Rangoon who ignored army orders and joined the demonstrations as well.[31] The disintegration of the armed forces appeared to go hand in hand with the collapse of the BSPP government.

On 18 September, Ne Win's close associate, Saw Maung, staged a coup (considered by some to have been a fake), toppling Maung Maung and the BSPP government. The new government authority consisted of military officers headed by Saw Maung. He immediately changed Maung Maung's request for government servants to return to work to an order; established a curfew that forbade anyone being on the streets; and explained that during non-curfew hours, walking in procession, chanting slogans, gathering in groups of five or more people, opening a strike center, blocking a road, and interfering with soldiers carrying out their orders were now crimes.

The Army then began breaking up the strike centers and shooting students who resisted.[32]

THE ESTABLISHMENT OF THE SLORC

After seizing power, Saw Maung and his officers initially called themselves the Organization for Building Law and Order in the State. This body immediately declared an end to state institutions, including the State Council, the Council of Ministers, and all councils down to the ward and village levels. All deputy ministers were also suspended from their duties. Saw Maung also announced on 18 September that the coup was unavoidable lest the country fall deeper into anarchy. He explained that the Military Council would restore law and order and rebuild the administrative machinery of the state. It was the responsibility of corporations, cooperatives, and "private concerns" to restore communications in order to deliver goods to the people and to "alleviate the food, clothing and shelter needs of the people." After these tasks were accomplished, Saw Maung assured the country, the multi-party elections would be held and the Military Council would not interfere in any way with the Election Commission. On 20 September, the Military Council announced the new cabinet and the responsibilities they would assume on the following day, at which meeting Council members elected Saw Maung as Burma's new prime minister.[33]

By 26 September the junta had established itself as the State Law and Order Restoration Council (SLORC). Regional and local Law and Order Restoration Councils (LORCs) were also established at the divisional, township, ward, and village levels. The township councils would have a military officer as chairman, the deputy head of the state and divisional general department, the deputy commander of the state and divisional people's police force, and the chairman's choice of secretary. At the ward and village tract level, the LORCs would consist of three local elders, one of whom would be selected by a higher ranking LORC as chairman, and a local council clerk with no history of involvement in political organizations.[34]

After the coup, Saw Maung laid out the SLORC's four immediate tasks:
1. law and order and peace and tranquility
2. secure and smooth transport
3. easing the food, clothing and shelter needs of the people and
4. holding democratic multi-party general elections.[35]

The immediate goal of the junta was to reestablish law and order. On 5 October 1988, Burmese troops killed twelve looters, raising the official death toll to 440 since 18 September. On 19 October, the SLORC announced that while subdued politicking was permitted, it would take strict action against political parties that caused misunderstandings between the military and the people. Suppression associated with the coup led to between 8,000 and 10,000 deaths. The Council then called for the punishment of government workers guilty of corruption, bribes, embezzlement, and self-aggrandizement as these acts were incurring the loss of state funds and hindering the development of the economy.[36]

The SLORC explained that martial law was necessary because unlawful acts had been perpetrated by elements among the protestors and the political parties had done nothing to stop them and even abetted them in some cases. Some members of political parties, it claimed, were even giving training in small arms and the use of hand grenades. The press would be allowed freedom so long as they also took responsibility and acted according to the rules and regulations of publishers. The Army, it claimed, was not guilty of intimidation. Rather, it was those "under internal and external influence," including some political parties, who were making the threats. It also claimed that the release of political prisoners was a moot issue as there had been no political arrests, only the arrest of criminals. The Universal Declaration on Human Rights would only be observed if people were responsible and did not abuse these rights as they did in the demonstrations. The SLORC also complimented those who submitted articles to newspapers contributing to the four tasks of the SLORC and asked the people to take a nationalistic stance and support this kind of writing. Above all, the SLORC urged, "Please do not antagonize, attack and oppose the SLORC."[37]

Saw Maung also announced that the interim government would proceed with Ne Win's earlier proposal of a multi-party political system. The SLORC enacted the Political Parties Registration Law on 27 September 1988, requiring all parties that wished to run for election to register with the Election Commission. By the 28 February deadline, 233 parties had registered. Not all of the new parties were legitimate, for some appear to have been merely fronts for the military. Others were formed simply to take advantage of rationing allotted by the government to political parties, including petrol and four telephones per party. On 3 November 1988, the junta, claiming that certain people had complained that their names had been put forward as patrons or executive committee members of newly registered parties without their consent, required parties to submit, along with their registration, letters of consent from those named as leaders of the party being registered. Two weeks later, SLORC

Figure 8.1 Military propaganda poster

propaganda (see Fig. 8.1) claimed that the majority of the people were unhappy with the "activities of some small groups of people" who were holding demonstrations and engaging in disturbances. Worried that these acts would give their local areas a bad name, they wanted to cooperate with the government by reporting on these activities and those involved in them, and publishing this information on television, radio, and in the newspapers.[38]

THE ALL BURMA STUDENTS' DEMOCRATIC FRONT

After the Saw Maung coup, thousands of students fled to the border areas and to Thailand. Some fled for safety while thousands of others fled to ethnic rebel camps to prepare to launch armed resistance against the government. Bo Mya, the leader of the KNU, promised students who had gone underground military camps, weapons, and training. By late September, Burmese students at a KNU guerrilla camp were being trained in how to use mortars. The BCP's Tenasserim Military Command also gave students an eleven-day course in the use of small arms. These students expected to begin a guerrilla campaign against the Saw Maung regime within three to four months. The goal would be to establish a democratic government in Burma. They had obtained weapons and supplies in Burma's border areas. Some among Burmese communities abroad also offered support. The Burmese students also wanted to be as independent as possible from the ethnic rebels. By 9 October 1988, there were 2,000 students and protestors training in one KNU camp (Thay Baw Bo) alone. A month later, fifty delegates from the estimated 10,000 Burmese students who had fled Rangoon agreed on the creation of the All Burma Students' Democratic Front (ABSDF), an umbrella organization to supervise the student war on Rangoon.[39]

The SLORC announced an amnesty program for those students who returned to government-held areas by a deadline of 18 November. The Council claimed that while it could legitimately view the students in the border areas as insurgents, it still chose to view them as simply "misguided youths." Reception committees and twenty-seven camps in border towns under government control (such as Bhamo, Buthidaung, Kale, and Tavoy) were opened on 14 October to receive the returning students. The SLORC claimed that these camps would provide returning students with the basic necessities, such as medicine, shelter, and food, and then send them back home to their parents as quickly as possible. The government claimed students taking refuge with the rebels had been prevented from listening to anything but British Broadcasting Corporation (BBC) and Voice of America (VOA) broadcasts and so were unaware of either the amnesty offer or the "true stand of the Defence Forces." Thus, it began air-dropping pamphlets indicating the locations of the twenty-seven camps. By 24 October, 380 students had taken advantage of the amnesty. The deadline for the returning students was later extended to 31 January 1989 and even when this day approached, the SLORC explained that the twenty-seven "reception centers" would remain open anyway. By 3 February, the SLORC claimed that 2,401 students had returned.[40]

THE ELECTIONS

Brigadier Khin Nyunt gave a press conference on 20 January 1989, which elaborated on the terms of holding an election as formerly enunciated by Saw Maung and others. Khin Nyunt explained that the right to organize freely and issue press releases would gradually be extended to the political parties. However, the holding of elections would depend on cooperation among the government, the people, and the political parties. The date would not be set until the parties had finished organizing, when the people were ready to cooperate, and when the country "is peaceful and tranquil without disturbances." Khin Nyunt did not make clear what was meant by cooperation or how it would be determined whether the parties were finished organizing. However, the third condition, that of restoring internal peace, was the most worrying requirement. Khin Nyunt explained that the restoration of peace could not be viewed in the context of one area, but as a nationwide situation. This seems to have meant not only the end of looting and demonstrations, but also the end of the ethnic and Communist insurgencies, which previous regimes had failed to bring about since 1948. Khin Nyunt's statement, then, could be interpreted to mean indefinite military rule over the long term. As Khin Nyunt confirmed, the SLORC was trying also to change from one economic and political system to another to provide stability to the next government and this task could not be completed in a hurry.[41]

However, BBC and VOA broadcasts had been airing reports and statements from various political parties that claimed that no elections would really be held, or, if held, would take at least two or three years. In this context, the Election Law Drafting Committee produced an election timetable in February 1989, which scheduled general elections for May 1990, some fourteen months later. The SLORC announced this schedule along with strong denials of reporting by VOA and the BBC, suggesting that the two developments were strongly linked. The exact date of the elections, 27 May, however, was not decided until a meeting of the SLORC and the Election Commission held on 6 November 1989. The draft Election Law barred government servants, members of the military and police, monks, ethnic rebels, foreigners, and anyone funded by foreign organizations from voting, the last indicating again the SLORC's fear of external intervention in Burma's domestic affairs.[42]

The underlying problem was that the SLORC viewed civilian party politics as necessarily chaotic and contributory to national disunity. Khin Nyunt asserted on 20 January 1989 that the government was hesitant to lift the restrictions on political campaigning and remove the curfew because of infighting among the numerous political parties that had emerged since September. If the political parties were given too much freedom too quickly, they would only attack each other, creating additional security problems for the country and for the SLORC. In the meantime, the SLORC made several efforts to develop support among government servants and keep them from supporting the political opposition. In February, the government raised the pay of civil servants and asked teachers not to participate in politics or be influenced by political parties.[43]

THE MAJOR POLITICAL PARTIES

The government began to take steps to officially dissolve, but unofficially to reshape, the BSPP. The big sign that such a change was imminent came on 10 September when the government granted permission to military and civil service members to resign from the Party. Although the government would not officially announce the end of the BSPP Party until 11 October 1988, the date when it began to repossess BSPP property, cars, and funds, its membership flowed from the now defunct BSPP into a new entity, the National Unity Party (NUP), which had been established two weeks earlier on 25 September. The switch fooled few Burmese and the NUP commanded little loyalty from the demonstrators.[44]

On 29 August 1988, Nu had organized the League for Democracy and Peace (LDP) and, in early September, he called for supporters to set up local branches in provincial towns. The LDP, although eventually inconsequential, was the first formal political coalition to emerge from the protests and the first independent political organization in the country in two and a half decades.[45] The major problem for the LDP was Nu, as the old man found it difficult to build alliances with anyone but monks and the politicians from the pre-1962 period. The LDP thus failed to make inroads among the younger generations of voters. Likewise, few took seriously Nu's attempt to form an alternative government, especially when he became embroiled in a futile attempt to force Ne Win to confess to his "wrongs." After Nu was arrested, the LDP lost its center of gravity and posed no real challenge to anyone.

Aung Gyi, Tin U, and Aung San Suu Kyi initially formed the National United Front for Democracy in late September 1988 but soon after changed the name to the National League for Democracy (NLD). Aung San Suu Kyi, the party's General Secretary, headed a group of intellectuals, who were soon joined by writers and lawyers. Party Vice Chairman Tin U had at one point been defense minister and commander-in-chief of the armed forces, during the time of the U Thant funeral crisis in 1975, but resigned from both posts afterwards and was later imprisoned in connection with the 1976 coup plot. In September 1988, Nu had appointed him Defense Minister as part of his alternative government. League Chairman Aung Gyi headed a faction of anti-leftists, including former regional commanders. Among the League's first acts was to call for Burmese to ignore the government's order to return to work.[46]

Unity among the NLD triumvirate soon broke down into rivalry for control of the party. Aung Gyi was immediately identifiable with the protests due to his much-publicized criticism of the BSPP government earlier in 1988. He was also considered to be one of the most capable potential leaders because of his successful economic reforms during the Caretaker period. Aung Gyi, however, was not happy to permit extreme leftist influences to take control over the League and also publicly downplayed the importance of Aung San Suu Kyi in the Democracy movement. In early December, he was removed as League Chairman and replaced by Tin U. Aung Gyi and twelve others then resigned from the League and formed the Union National Democracy Party. However, Aung Gyi later changed tactics and for months claimed that he remained Chairman of the only real NLD and that the Tin U–Aung San Suu Kyi organization was illegal.[47]

The NLD faced the most serious intervention by the SLORC. In January 1989, League campaigners, including Aung San Suu Kyi, were harassed during their campaign tours. During a ten-day tour of the Irrawaddy Delta, a number of incidents occurred, including one case in which soldiers fired guns above spectators. In Bassein, local SLORC officials closed markets and government buildings, cut off electricity and water in the area of town hosting the League office, prevented Aung San Suu Kyi from hiring transport, and arrested fourteen League organizers, with sixty more arrests following in February. The most serious confrontation between Aung San Suu Kyi and the military occurred on 5 April at Danubyu, fifty miles from Rangoon. While she was campaigning in the town, a Burmese captain and a squad of soldiers approached and ordered her to leave the streets. The captain ordered his men to aim and shoot her at the count of three if she did not vacate the area. Instead she walked toward them, reportedly causing the soldiers to shake nervously. Before the captain counted three, a superior officer rushed out of a teashop and countermanded the order.

Aung San Suu Kyi observed that the incident demonstrated that the fact that the captain could give such an order on his own initiative highlighted the Army's inability to manage the country.[48]

Toward the end of June 1989, the SLORC became increasingly vocal regarding its views of the NLD's admitted transgression of martial law and the ban on public assembly. It claimed that Aung San Suu Kyi was deliberately instigating disturbances. Both Aung San Suu Kyi and Tin U were placed under house arrest on 20 July for allegedly attempting to create conditions dangerous for the state and for attempting to get the Burmese to dislike the Army. Upon her own arrest, Aung San Suu Kyi began a hunger strike, not called off until the government assured her that League members would not have to undergo "inhuman interrogation." By that time, between 2,000 and 6,000 League members had been arrested. The SLORC then began a press campaign to associate Aung San Suu Kyi and the League with BCP agents, on the one hand, and with foreign rightist elements, on the other. In either case, it was implied, she threatened the nation by inviting foreign intervention in Burmese affairs.[49]

TOWARD THE ELECTION

The SLORC began to tighten its control from 17 July 1989 by extending the powers of military commanders to try those committing offenses. For general offenses a military commander could choose to submit the case to a law court or to a military tribunal, but in the case of an offense against Council orders, the case could only be tried by a military tribunal. Regardless of existing laws, for such an offense the military tribunal would have to pass one of three sentences: death, life imprisonment, or three years' hard labour, with or without an additional fine. Military tribunals were now allowed to exercise summary trials, waive unnecessary witnesses, indict an offender without witnesses, and change members of the tribunal during the trial. The army commander-in-chief could revise sentences, including increasing them, as he saw fit. On the same day, Rangoon military command delegated its judicial and executive powers to divisional commanders and military region commanders, dividing Rangoon up into military zones. Orders were also given that the names of all guests and strangers in the forty-one townships of Rangoon Division had to be submitted to the local LORCs.[50]

Other steps were taken by the SLORC to bring the elections under tighter control. In August 1989, the SLORC began a six-month campaign to issue citizenship identity cards to every Burmese aged eighteen and over, in order to assist "the holding of the election." In November, it also began scrutinizing the citizenship of political candidates. The issue of citizenship was then used by the NUP as a means of attacking the eligibility of Aung Gyi, on the grounds that he was of partial Chinese ancestry (this was true, however, of former leader Ne Win and future prime minister Khin Nyunt as well), and Aung San Suu Kyi, on the grounds that she was married to a foreigner, to run for election.[51]

The SLORC also took steps to downplay the negative image produced by the large number of former high-ranking officers taking leading roles in the opposition civilian parties. Another concern was probably lingering loyalties within the military to these officers. In October 1989, the SLORC made it a crime for ousted military men to refer to their former military ranks or to their being retired from the military. The new law covered those officers who had been removed from the military or had been convicted of a criminal offense (as many had under earlier regimes) and imposed a prison sentence of up to five years. The overt purpose of the law was to prevent those who had been disgraced from enjoying the normal respect Burmese society paid to members of the armed forces. From March 1990, the SLORC slowly began to lift martial law in various townships, although it remained in many areas until one week before election day and was not lifted in twenty-six townships until 26 May. The SLORC now began disrupting NLD campaigners and detaining NLD officials.[52]

The NLD swept the 16 June elections with over 7.9 million votes, winning 392 of the 447 seats contested. These results must have come as a shock to the SLORC, which was widely believed to have expected a victory for the NUP. The latter immediately claimed that the election was fraudulent. This charge, however, was poorly thought out, and quickly abandoned, for since the SLORC was responsible for the fairness of the election, complaints about the proceedings amounted to a negative critique of their management of the country. Further, although from 15 May the SLORC had banned all foreigners from remaining in Burma to prevent foreign intervention in the electoral process, it partially reversed the decision ten days later and allowed foreign journalists to cover the electoral process. These journalists could easily have countered the NUP charges. The NUP did file an official complaint, but the state-controlled media did not carry the story. Instead, Saw Maung claimed that the results demonstrated the SLORC's fairness.[53]

CONCLUSION

The popular revolution that toppled the BSPP regime in 1988 caught the latter by surprise nearly as much as the 1990 elections results caught the SLORC. While the BSPP government knew that it had problems and Ne Win began to admit these even in 1987, the SLORC leadership exhibited surprising arrogance in allowing the election to go forward. Fourteen years (1974–1988) of success in controlling the country through nominal civilian government had created a political culture wherein civilian politicians reflected and did not direct the military agenda. In retrospect, the SLORC would have had a much easier time in controlling the country after 1990 had they not held an election at all. Ultimately, they produced a martyr whose international prominence has made her virtually untouchable by the military, other than by prolonged house arrest.

On the other hand, the SLORC realized that once it had waded successfully through a sea of political rivals, the NLD had a certain degree of domestic support. This domestic support, however, was associated with the same kinds of opposition that fueled the numerous rural insurgencies in the ongoing civil war. Mass demonstrations, street violence, and calls for the fall of the BSPP government all contributed to the image that the demonstrators, like the ethnic insurgents, represented a threat, the responsibility for suppressing them belonging to the Army. Aung San Suu Kyi's personal connections to the West, general calls for Western-style democratic government, and complaints by the BSPP leadership that the domestic turmoil was being manipulated by Western journalists all added to perceptions that as with the civil war in earlier decades, external intervention was partly – perhaps mostly – at work. The SLORC's solution, to promise preparations for a democratic transition and the eventual holding of elections, was thus paired with efforts to destroy the opposition before things went too far.

The failure of the democratic opposition to prevent the entrenchment of military control, particularly in late 1988, meant that it has lost its best and perhaps only real opportunity to establish a civilian government while confusion in the country still reigned and the government remained bewildered and unable to act. During the year and a half that followed, the military developed a political agenda to retain complete authority for itself and to close off the options for political leadership.

CHAPTER 9

Perpetual delay, 1990 to the present

One of the hallmarks of the military regime has been delay, a process it began in 1988, even before the elections. This seems to have been partly because the new military leaders were at a loss regarding what to do. They knew they did not want to hand over power to the NLD or to any other genuinely popular government. They also knew the ins and outs of keeping a country under martial law, what military regimes are particularly good at, over the course of short periods of time. Something permanent had to be found to provide a state apparatus that could nominally run the country in their name. Another factor was that they remained under the influence of the powerful Ne Win, who remained behind the scenes and for whom, it could be argued, they were nominally in charge. If the SLORC can be viewed as another Ne Win governing entity, then the politics of delay had historical antecedents. Ne Win was equally confused about what to do with the country when he seized control in 1962, other than to provide a more elaborate version of the caretaker regime, albeit with the promise of a more representative regime, as the later BSPP government would be portrayed.

What made the post-1988 delay longer, perhaps, was that Ne Win had run out of ideas. The Revolutionary Council was not a success economically or in putting down the civil war. The BSPP government, as 1988 demonstrated, was a resolute failure on all fronts. What is certain about the post-1988 regime was that it lacked even the rich ideological element that the earlier Ne Win regimes had been able to cultivate. Burma's new leaders were a less creative lot than Ne Win, Aung Gyi, or Tin Pe. Indeed, most "creations" of the post-1988 regime have been rehashed from the Revolutionary Council and BSPP periods.

Another aspect of the post-1988 regime that sets it apart from earlier military regimes is the unabashedly conspicuous carving up of the country's commercial assets by the ruling families. Ne Win and his friends had been keen on preserving the image of austerity in public and more than one erstwhile subordinate was broken down on charges of corruption. Although

Ne Win profited as much as anyone else, he paid lip service to socialism and attempts to improve the lives of the average Burmese. In the years after 1988, however, this changed. The families of the military elite and their friends openly flaunted their wealth, drove expensive cars, loaded themselves with jewels, and took over ownership of new companies that replaced formerly state-run enterprises. As socialism gave way to consumerism, the families of the military elite visibly became Burma's nouveau riche, while the rest of the population continued the long slide into abject poverty

CHANGING NAMES

While the country and the world were transfixed on the forthcoming elections, there were many indications that the military regime was intent on more than reestablishing law and order. One of the most obvious signs was the sudden makeover that the SLORC gave to the naming of the country, its towns, and its population. On 19 October 1988 (with retroactive effect from 18 September), the Council enacted the Law on the Substitution of Terms. This law changed "Socialist Republic of the Union of Burma" to "Union of Burma," "Council of State" to "State Law and Order Restoration Council," "Chairman of the Council of State" or "State President" to "Chairman of the State Law and Order Restoration Council," and a range of other official terms and titles.[1]

The SLORC was also determined to change the way Burmese and foreigners referred to Burmese ethnic groups, cities, and rivers when writing in English. The Council had already begun to use "Myanma" in its own English correspondence and announcements, when it began to refer to the country as the "Union of Myanma." On 26 May 1989, the Council made this official when it held a press conference explaining that the use of Burma in English apparently corresponded to "Bama" which could only refer to the main ethnic group, Burman. The SLORC argued that this usage was incorrect as the word Burma as used in Union of Burma, really referred to all national groups within the country, such as the Kachin, Karen, Mon, and so on. To correct this error, the Council would now require the use of "Union of Myanma" to refer to the country in English. It had even toyed with the idea of changing it again to "Myanma Naingngan" (State of Myanma). On 18 June, the SLORC promulgated the Adaptation of Expressions Law, which was to change English names used for Burmese people and places so that references would conform to Burmese pronunciation. This law officially changed the English term for "Union of Burma" to "Union of Myanma," "Burman" to "Bamar," and "Burmese"

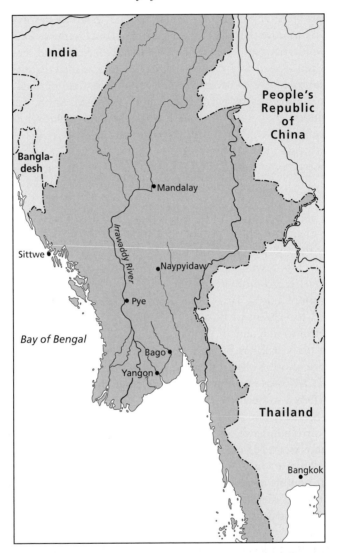

Map 3 Burma today

to "Myanma."[2] Eventually, the spelling of "Myanma" was also changed to "Myanmar."

The Adaptation of Expressions Law also provided for continued changes as the SLORC saw fit, including the change, when necessary, of English terms for "any state, division, townships zone, township, town, ward, village tract or village, or the name of any river, stream, forest, mountain or island." The SLORC also amended the national anthem, as the use of "Bamar" would now suggest that the anthem applied only to the Burmans, even though the anthem referred to all of Burma's "races." Hence, "Bamar" was now replaced with "Myanma."[3] This change was broadly expanded on the same day, when the SLORC issued Notification No 5/89 of the Government of the Union of Myanma Names in Accordance with Myanma Pronunciation, which indigenized place and ethnic names for use in the English language. What these efforts indicated was that the SLORC had a particular view of how the future of the country should be shaped. As events would soon demonstrate, this view was hostile to both foreign interference and democracy, which in the Council's eyes became inextricably linked.

DE-DEMOCRATIZATION

After the NLD victory in the 1990 elections, the Army did not lose composure and Saw Maung ordered it to respect the wishes of the voters. Instead, the SLORC reversed its announcements on the state of the country to legitimize continued military rule over the long term in order to prevent the League from taking power. On 29 April, when the SLORC was assumed to be confident of a victory for the NUP and themselves, Khin Nyunt, in his capacity as Secretary Number 1 of the SLORC, told township and ward-level LORCs in a broadcast speech that the Army had by this time achieved three of its four main tasks. The final task was holding the multi-party democratic elections the following month. At the end of May, however, as the early election results indicated a sweeping NLD victory, Saw Maung changed the SLORC's view of the election in the context of the continuity of its control of the state. The election had been, as SLORC claimed all along, only one task it had to complete before handing over power to a new government. Now, by contrast to what Khin Nyunt had said a month earlier, the tasks of restoring "law and order and regional peace and tranquility . . . facilitating transport" and communications, and meeting people's needs for food, clothes and shelter, all remained to be completed. Regardless of whom government servants had voted for, they were not to bring party politics into the workplace. The fact that Khin Nyunt gave essentially the same speech on 15 June indicated that Saw Maung's comments reflected an official posture regarding the elections and the longevity of the SLORC.[4] A new government would not be established for a considerable period of time.

Saw Maung began to work on de-democratizing the country from the end of June. In a hint at what was to come, Saw Maung warned that the SLORC would not tolerate a repeat of the pro-Democracy demonstrations in 1988 and mentioned the possibility of an "indefinite ban on public political gatherings." As the SLORC made clear that it would not respect its original promises regarding the due recognition of the results of the multi-party elections, popular anger was aroused. Among the most important incidents was the confrontation between army troops and monks at Mandalay on 8 August 1990. A group of 500 monks began moving through the town with their alms bowls, and over time were joined by other monks, students, and others. At one juncture, they began to shout slogans and were asked by soldiers to stop. In the commotion that followed, the Army claimed that the monks and students began to stone the soldiers and attempt to take their weapons from them. Although several were injured, no one was killed, and after the soldiers fired their guns into the air, the crowds dispersed. Other sources, however, indicated that the monks had numbered 5,000 and that the soldiers had fired into the crowd, killing at least four people. The government later blamed the NLD for the disturbances, citing a League directive calling for ceremonies on 8 August to mark the 1988 demonstrations, claiming that the League was attempting to "destroy the country."[5]

Saw Maung had also explained in late June 1990 that before the SLORC handed over power, the 1947 Constitution, which he argued was seriously flawed, would have to be rewritten. Khin Nyunt reaffirmed this two weeks later, when he explained that both the 1947 and the 1974 constitutions were unsuitable because of "changing times and conditions" and that a new constitution would have to be written from scratch. The purpose of the call for a new constitution was to delay or prevent a handover of power to the NLD. In late July, the SLORC announced that the NLD would not be handed state powers until after the SLORC, since it alone "has the right to legislative power," had overseen the drafting of a new constitution by the elected assembly, and its approval by the Burmese (which nearly twenty years later, it nominally did). Although the elected assembly would conduct the drafting, they would have to do so according to guidelines established by the army-appointed special convention.[6]

Another issue was the role of Aung San Suu Kyi. The NLD had insisted that Aung San Suu Kyi should play a leading role in negotiations with the SLORC concerning the Constitution, despite her house arrest. In July 1990, Khin Nyunt argued that he was concerned that this amounted to a personality cult and that this was not the time to insist on a particular individual being allowed to participate in the constitutional process. As he asked of the NLD rhetorically: "Which is more important: obtaining power and the release of Daw Aung San Suu Kyi, or the long-term interests of the country and the people?" Instead, Khin Nyunt demanded, the

Figure 9.1 Burmese democratic protest. Demonstrators hold posters of Aung San Suu Kyi

victorious parties should be striving for unity "in the spirit of patriotism and in the interests of the country" without "attachment to personalities." The SLORC then began to increase its association between Aung San Suu Kyi (see Fig. 9.1) and "foreign elements," in delaying its own pace of constitutional drafting.[7]

The regime created the Convening Commission for the National Convention on 2 October 1992. After establishing the Commission but before the National Convention could take place, the SLORC began to eradicate prospective NLD participation in the constitutional process. It would be difficult to produce a constitution amenable to the SLORC if the overwhelming majority of elected MPs were represented by the NLD. Thus, the SLORC, working through the Election Commission and citing violations of that body's rules and regulations, began nullifying the election of individual NLD MPs. The abolishment of other parties also ensued.[8]

While the National Convention was briefly opened in January 1993 with over 700 delegates, only an initial speech was made before the Convention was adjourned for another month.[9] In the meantime, having significantly weakened the NLD, the SLORC began a campaign that specifically targeted Aung San Suu Kyi. The SLORC asserted that the Nobel Peace Prize Committee had given the award to a "follower they [the West] had raised" and that it would "never accept the leadership of a person under foreign influence who will dance to the tune of a foreign power and who has always opposed the Defence Forces." Aung San Suu Kyi, the SLORC suggested, represented not Burmese, but foreign imperialist powers who "continue their habit of brutally bullying the weak and interfering shamelessly in the internal affairs of other countries." A patriotic Burmese, it argued, should not "be wasting one's time on the narrow personality cult and interests of an organization [the NLD]."[10] Khin Nyunt was even blunter. He argued that the original elections commission had erred when it gave Aung San Suu Kyi hope that she could stand for election, because this was against the law. He then quoted a fifteenth-century Burmese treatise that purportedly instructed readers "There is destruction when the leader is a female." Following this treatise, he argued, it was clear that "a female should never be a leader in Myanmar [if so] the country will be in ruin."[11]

FROM SAW MAUNG TO THAN SHWE

Saw Maung's fortunes began to wane by early 1992. The regime's image as a reforming council had not been secured either at home or abroad. In its early days, Saw Maung had stressed that the small number of the members of the SLORC and the multiple portfolios each held demonstrated that this was not a government meant to last in the long term. However, the expansion of the SLORC by three additional generals and four civilians in late January indicated to many that the SLORC would now remain more or less a permanent government. Saw Maung also began a purge of the government when the SLORC fired 15,000 civil servants. This was the final stage of asserting government control over dissident elements, as students, politicians, and monks had already been dealt with. Simultaneously, Aung San Suu Kyi was also becoming a permanent symbol of popular opposition to the government. To domestic support was added international recognition of her struggle in the form of the Sakharov Prize for Human Rights, awarded to her by the European Union, and, in December 1991, the Nobel Peace Prize. The latter was accepted in her name because the SLORC would refuse her readmission to the country if she left.[12]

Over the course of December 1991 to January 1992, there were signs that Saw Maung was having a nervous breakdown. In addition to the continual stress of running the country since 1988, balancing out competing cliques within the SLORC, and an inability to deal effectively with the continued defiance of the NLD, Saw Maung, a heavy drinker, was also suffering from diabetes. In mid-December, he was hospitalized for two days after he collapsed and was unconscious for a forty-minute period. In a golf tournament attended by other top generals, he reportedly burst out screaming "I am King Kyansittha!" and telling those around them to be careful lest he kill them with his pistol. In January, in a speech broadcast on Burmese television, Saw Maung continued referring to King Kyansittha, assured viewers that he did not practice Black Magic, and asserted that martial law in Burma meant "no law at all."[13]

Two of Saw Maung's most powerful subordinates, Than Shwe and Khin Nyunt, competed to succeed him. Khin Nyunt, head of the intelligence services, was a protégé of Ne Win. Than Shwe, a conservative general, disliked the brash Khin Nyunt and the younger officers who backed him. In March 1992, Than Shwe assumed Saw Maung's positions as defense chief and head of the Army and, in late April, he also replaced Saw Maung as Chairman of the SLORC and assumed the prime ministership. By the end of the year, maneuvering by Khin Nyunt led to four regional commanders, with whom he had difficulties, being "kicked upstairs," that is, reappointed to powerless positions in Rangoon, and replaced by officers connected with himself.[14] This balance of power would carry on beyond the tenure of the SLORC.

As head of the junta, Than Shwe began a number of new initiatives designed to shore up internal security. After exhaustive attempts to capture Karen headquarters, the regime declared a ceasefire. The effectiveness of the military's leadership was also improved through internal reorganization and a restructuring of the state. Several regional military commanders were integrated into the central administration, to keep them closely connected to the SLORC. The cabinet increased in size and specialization as ministries were split (Forestry was divorced from Agriculture and Trade from Planning and Finance).[15]

Teachers, whom the SLORC held responsible for the behavior of their students, were also brought under tighter control. The SLORC's view was that student unrest was the result of teachers having been weak in the guidance and organization of their students. Teachers were also unable to keep politicians, opportunists, and foreign elements from using campuses as base areas for unrest and had failed to cooperate with the government to prevent these "subversive" activities. Hence, teachers now needed to be reeducated to "uphold and implement" the perpetuation of national sovereignty, preservation of national unity, and prevention of national disintegration. The Central Institute of Public Services, a reeducation camp offering "refresher courses," was thus set up for thousands of teachers who now underwent a four-week course of physical exercise and lectures. The camp followed the model of the rural reeducation camps for the Red Guards in the PRC during the Cultural Revolution. Teachers would attend courses on the history of the armed forces and on the national liberation struggle, the emergence of the SLORC, its economic endeavors, and its laws and decrees, so that they would be able to "enlighten their students." Reeducation, and with it the creation of "genuine" students and "responsible" teachers, was to be completed before colleges and universities would reopen. The SLORC also hoped to lessen the potential for student demonstrations by initiating a distance education program.[16]

In an attempt to improve its international standing the SLORC tried on several occasions to soften its approach to the NLD. In April 1992, the regime announced that it would hold a national convention to establish the principles for a new constitution. With this effort in mind, in June and July they met with representatives of the NLD and other opposition parties as well as members of the pro-regime NUP. In September the SLORC lifted the curfew and martial law and released about a quarter of its political prisoners, some 534 people, including Nu and many NLD members. While Aung San Suu Kyi remained under house arrest, the SLORC now allowed her family to visit her. The SLORC also rejoined the Non-Aligned Movement in September, signed four articles of the Geneva Convention (1949) regarding the treatment of civilians and, in December, hosted a meeting of the Colombo Plan in Rangoon.[17]

THE STATE PEACE AND DEVELOPMENT COUNCIL

In November 1997, the SLORC was dissolved and replaced by the State Peace and Development Council (SPDC). Lack of transparency in the inner workings of the government since 1988 has made it difficult for foreign (and domestic) observers to determine the precise reasons for changes within the ruling Council. As a result, analysts necessarily rely on circumstantial evidence to identify the possible factors involved. Generally, these factors are both external and internal. Government changes often occur when there is a pressing need to shore up the government's image abroad. The SPDC, for example, had been set up to replace the SLORC at a time when the regime needed more respectability as it prepared for ASEAN membership in 1997. In this and other turnovers, charges of corruption are usually made to give the move legitimacy, although, given the widespread nature of official corruption, such claims are frequently dubious as main factors in dismissals.

Most foreign observers of Burma view the replacement of the SLORC with the SPDC as merely a cosmetic change. Scholars have followed suit, referring to the SLORC and the SPDC not separately, but as the same government, hence "SLORC/SPDC." While it is true that leadership remained the same, there are fundamental differences that mark the SLORC and the SPDC not as separate governments, but as distinguishable phases of military rule since 1988. The SLORC phase was characterized in part by the absence of Western sanctions, warfare with numerous ethnic insurgencies, problematic relationships with at least some of its Southeast Asian neighbors (especially Thailand), and a continuity of influence from the leaders of the Ne Win period. By contrast, the SPDC period has generally been characterized by severe Western sanctions, ceasefire agreements with most ethnic insurgents, membership in ASEAN, and the elimination of the Ne Win "old guard." The "spirit" of the government had also changed, for during the SLORC period, Burma's leadership were clearly desperate to find ways to deny the establishment of an NLD government, but during the SPDC period the government moved at a more leisurely pace with clear confidence that whatever would be done concerning the NLD, they need not be in any great hurry.

One scholar suggests that the change from the SLORC to the SPDC was partly effected to reduce tensions between the ruling junta and regional military commanders, who had accrued significant wealth and power in outlying commands or in ministerial positions in Rangoon. The SPDC removed some ministers from their posts, replaced them with regional commanders drawn from outside the capital, and in their place appointed junior commanders. Indeed, the chief internal factors in government purges are widely held to be personal political ambitions, disagreements over policy (whether to take seriously dialogue with the NLD), or business rivalries, as the ruling generals have amassed significant commercial portfolios. For any or all of these reasons, government change within the SPDC leadership has consistently favored a concentration of power in the hands of a slimming minority at the top, as purges afforded the most powerful men in the Council the opportunity to replace rivals with less powerful clients. The top four generals, Than Shwe, Maung Aye, Khin Nyunt, and Tin Oo, were reduced to three when Tin Oo was killed in a helicopter crash in 2000 and was not replaced. In 2001, in the biggest purge since 1997, seven generals and ministers were replaced, two on charges of corruption and five on the basis of enforced retirement.[18]

On 7 March 2002, the 92-year-old Ne Win's son-in-law and three grandsons were arrested in a restaurant in Rangoon's Chinatown, while Ne Win and his daughter were placed under house arrest. They were charged with plotting the overthrow of the government. Reportedly, the coup-plotters had planned to enlist support from elements of the Army, kidnap Than Shwe, Maung Aye, and Khin Nyunt, and, having brought them to Ne Win's house, force them to agree to a new government. In the wake of the arrests, four generals were dismissed. Other arrests followed, including Ne Win's personal astrologer. Two separate trials were held for the ringmasters and members of the military connected with the coup plot. In mid-September, eighty-three officers and soldiers were sentenced to fifteen years in prison and by the end of the month Ne Win's son-in-law and three grandsons were sentenced to death. Although they appealed the ruling, the Supreme Court upheld the convictions in late December 2002, Ne Win having died earlier in the month.[19] The Ne Win family lost yet another appeal in August 2003.

The arrests and dismissals may have been used as a means of pleasing ASEAN by removing corrupt senior officers, as those dismissed were initially intimately connected with the Ne Win family's business activities. The ruling triumvirate may also have used the opportunity to continue the replacement of more powerful commanders with younger, more reliable officers. In September 2002, the SPDC announced a flurry of promotions, including Maung Aye who became deputy senior general and Khin Nyunt who became general, and numerous other officers who were promoted to the rank of lieutenant-general.[20]

As potential challenges from within the military declined, rivalry between Khin Nyunt and Maung Aye intensified. This rivalry had serious ramifications for the country as each had come to represent different approaches to dealing with the NLD and the outside world. While the conservative Maung Aye took a hard line, the more flexible Khin Nyunt favored a more pragmatic approach, including international engagement and the paying of at least lip service to the inevitability of a return to democracy. In August 2003, in response to the new US sanctions, another changeover at the top, including the retirement of five ministers and two deputy ministers, appeared to indicate that Khin Nyunt and his approach had gained the upper hand. Than Shwe, who continued as head of state, transferred the office of prime minister to Khin Nyunt, Lieutenant-General Soe Win taking Khin Nyunt's place as SPDC Secretary Number 1. Shortly after, at the end of August, Prime Minister Khin Nyunt announced a seven-point plan. According to this plan, his "roadmap to Democracy," the SPDC would reconvene the National Convention (suspended since 1996), write a new constitution, and hold free elections.[21]

THE FALL OF KHIN NYUNT

The most serious purge since 1988 brought down Khin Nyunt in October 2004. Although clearly the result of Khin Nyunt's long political rivalry with Maung Aye, the purge was characterized as a move by the SPDC to eradicate corruption. As it announced at the time of his dismissal, Khin Nyunt had been allowed to retire "for his violation of Tatmadaw discipline, such as insubordination, for his involvement in the bribery and corrupt practices, and for failure to carry out the duties properly." Khin Nyunt was accused of illegally smuggling 30,000 luxury vehicles from Thailand and China into Burma, circumventing registration laws and thus import duties, which would otherwise have amounted to 400 percent of the price of the vehicle. Such corruption, the government charged, threatened army unity.[22]

Due to Khin Nyunt's extensive connexions and his control of the Military Intelligence Service (MIS), eradicating his base of support meant a massive overhaul of security forces. The purge began with a raid on the MIS Headquarters on 18 October, and the arrest of Khin Nyunt and his two sons the following day. Over the course of the following week, MIS units around the country were dissolved. In November, all of the agents of the SPDC's computer department were fired, relatives of MIS agents were removed from the civil service, the ambassadors to Singapore and Indonesia were dismissed, and Brigadier-Generals Thein Swe and Than Tun were given twenty-two-year prison sentences. Soe Win, who had been head of the Union Solidarity and Development Association (USDA), took Khin Nyunt's place as Prime Minister. Lieutenant-General Than Sein, Chairman of the Convention Convening Committee, then took Soe Win's place as Secretary Number 1.[23]

The SPDC moved quickly to offset criticism that these moves represented anything more than an anti-corruption campaign. It attempted to do so by declaring that no change had taken place in SPDC policies. Thein Sein declared that the roadmap to democracy would continue as it had under Khin Nyunt. In November 2004, the SPDC demonstrated that it was serious about reform by releasing nearly 4,000 prisoners it claimed had been wrongfully imprisoned as a result of Khin Nyunt's intelligence services. The purge continued into the middle of 2005, as individual trials and confessions yielded more information on the extent of corruption and Khin Nyunt's connexions. Beginning in January, hundreds of new arrests were made among border officials, while the Mayor of Mandalay and four ambassadors were all sacked. Khin Nyunt was not put on trial until 12 June and, the following day, was delivered a suspended sentence of forty-four years, his two sons also receiving suspended sentences.[24]

FOREIGN INVESTMENT AND THE BOYCOTTS

From the beginning, the SLORC badly needed foreign aid and investment to help pay off its external debt, which amounted to US$4–5 billion by 1990. The biggest foreign aid donor was Japan, which, in 1987, had furnished over half of Burma's foreign aid, equal to roughly 10 percent of its GNP. A major factor that had helped to push the SLORC in 1988 and early 1989 to keep its commitments on eventually holding elections was the suspension of aid after the Saw Maung coup by West Germany, the US, and Japan. These countries pinned the resumption of aid on the restoration of democracy and respect for human rights. Britain also froze aid to Burma in early November 1988.[25]

With the abrogation of the socialist economic system in October 1988, however, the SLORC now also had access to foreign investment. Among the SLORC's early acts was the liberalizing of trade, domestic and foreign, declaring that Burma would now have a market-oriented economy. The following day, Colonel Abel, the Minister of Trade, announced that laws were being planned that would open up to the private sector trade in

Figure 9.2 A symbol of the "new" Rangoon, the refurbished Strand Hotel

most commodities, with the exception of teak, petroleum, natural gas, and gems. To entice foreign investors, the SLORC would provide tax relief and exemptions and agreements with foreign companies would include guarantees that for the duration of the contract, the company would not be nationalized. At the end of November, the SLORC promulgated the Union of Burma Foreign Investment Law that established the Union of Burma Foreign Investment Commission with the authority to approve investment proposals that promoted the interests of the state, determine the financial credibility of an investor, the "economic justification of the business enterprise, and appropriateness of technology," issue foreign investment permits, and grant tax exemptions or relief. The law also set up basic regulations covering insurance, foreign currency and *kyat* bank accounts, guarantees against nationalization, and related matters. The justification of the law was that it would help the SLORC meet one of its avowed goals of "easing the people's needs for food, clothing, and shelter." It claimed the new foreign investment would provide employment opportunities and technical training and help develop and expand Burma's weak economic infrastructure.[26]

From early 1989, a figurative gold rush began when foreign companies raced for access to the new Burmese economy (see Fig. 9.2). Japan was the first, after it recognized the SLORC government in February. Others quickly followed. A cheap labor supply and cooperative government made Burma a profitable place for Western, South Korean, and Taiwanese clothing companies to make inexpensive clothing that could be sold abroad under designer labels. US soft drink makers found a new untapped market for their products, while Thai companies made logging and fishery deals.[27] Oil was another big area for investment.

Foreign investment handed the SLORC an economic lifeline while it eradicated the democratic opposition. But Burmese campaigners for democracy were not idle. Among the most vocal was the NLD leader Aung San Suu Kyi. In April 1989, Aung San Suu Kyi admonished foreign businessmen for doing business in Burma when the situation was so grave for the Burmese people and, in June 1989, called on foreign countries to boycott trade and aid with Burma until the government stopped reneging on its promises regarding the elections. While foreign governments underwent cycles of economic sanctions regarding aid to the SLORC, they were initially hesitant to restrict private investment in the country. A boycott of the products of Western companies doing business in Burma, however, eventually gained momentum in the mid-1990s and began to show clear signs of success. One major international company after another pulled out. In 1995, three foreign apparel manufacturers succumbed to the boycott campaign and agreed not to contract the manufacture of clothing in Burma any longer. In 1996, a soft drink company and two foreign brewing firms announced they were pulling out. Having successfully dented Western beverages sales and apparel manufacturing in Burma, activists next directed boycotts at the big oil companies. The intended impact of the boycotts, however, was offset by the willingness of companies within the Association of South East Asian Nations (ASEAN) to step in to buy the equity of fleeing Western companies.[28] Ultimately, the boycotts only changed the face of investment and reduced potential Western leverage in the country.

ASEAN, while paying lip service to a policy of constructive engagement, generally followed a hands-off approach to problems in Burma for fear that it would force the SLORC to be even more resistant to change. In July 1991, ASEAN foreign ministers even rejected urgings from the West to cooperate on pressuring Burma to undertake democratic and human rights reforms. Two main issues, treatment of the Rohingyas (Muslim Arakanese) in Arakan State and Burmese border incursions into Thailand, however, have plagued relations. In 1989, the SLORC began settling Burmese Buddhists in new towns it was building in the Rohingya-dominated areas of northern Arakan, while simultaneously doubling the number of Burmese troops in the area to over 20,000. In some areas, the new settlers displaced the Rohingyas and took over their lands and homes. Burma's relations with Bangladesh eroded further from December 1991, when the Army drove 145,000 Muslims out of Arakan in western Burma. In pursuit of fleeing Rohingyas, the Burmese Army also attacked Bangladeshi border posts. Under the old BSPP citizenship laws, the SLORC asserted that the Rohingyas were foreigners who did not have the right to live in Burma nor to own land or the property they held. Refugees complained that the Burmese had taken their identity papers and property and killed or raped resisters.[29]

For several years after 1989, the Thais were willing to overlook incursions by the Burmese army across the Thai border because of the substantial concessions given the Thais over teak reserves in Karen-held areas. This ended in March 1992 with a major Burmese incursion intended to end with an attack on Manerplaw from the rear. Thai aircraft now fired rockets, while Thai artillery bombarded the Burmese, and drove them back across the border.[30]

As the SLORC's actions regarding the Rohingyas and the KNU were potentially destabilizing factors in the region, ASEAN slowly began to change its approach. Malaysia officially protested the SLORC's treatment of Rohingyas on 10 March 1992. Singapore and Indonesia then called on Burma to resolve the situation peacefully. Malaysia then called for the Association to develop a unified front to persuade Burma against these activities using diplomacy. However, it announced that sanctions were not yet necessary at this stage.[31]

Burma's inclusion in ASEAN was partly responsible for the changeover from the SLORC to the SPDC. By January 1997, consensus had grown among ASEAN members that Burma (along with Laos and Cambodia) should be allowed into the Association later in that year. Although efforts by the US and the European Union to prevent Burma's inclusion were thwarted, the West found other ways to isolate the SPDC. In March, the European Union suspended preferential trade benefits to Burma. The Clinton administration, under pressure from anti-government groups, also declared in April that it would impose a formal ban on new US investment in the country on the grounds that the regime's human rights violations had increased. These were the first sanctions imposed by the US, which by then was Burma's fourth most important investor, since 1988. According to the 20 May presidential order, the government suppression in Burma represented a national emergency for the US, on the grounds that the

"Government of Burma has committed large-scale repression of the democratic opposition in Burma . . . and further . . . the actions and policies of the Government of Burma constitute an unusual and extraordinary threat to the national security and foreign policy of the United States."[32]

Following the renewed house arrest of Aung San Suu Kyi in May 2003, President George W. Bush signed into law the Freedom and Democracy Act, which imposed new sanctions on Burma, including a ban on important exports to the US, a ban on visas to SPDC officials, and the freezing of Burmese assets in US banks. Some analysts criticized these sanctions since Burmese exports to the US were dominated by textiles, and the sanctions would thus mainly hurt textile workers and not the SPDC. Over one hundred small factories closed as a result of the new sanctions, putting between 40,000 and 80,000 textile workers and others in the industry out of work. Since the textile industry mainly employed young women whose families had become dependent on their regular income, many of these women were forced into Rangoon's thriving sex and entertainment industry. In August 2006, Bush signed an extension of the Freedom and Democracy Act, citing the continued failure of the regime to engage in meaningful democratic reform and its continued detention of Aung San Suu Kyi.[33]

The results of Western sanctions imposed on the SPDC in order to provoke dialogue with the NLD and meaningful political change have been controversial. Whatever their short-term impact, the government was able to adjust to isolation from the West by turning to the East. This was possible because of its admission to ASEAN, which has historically frowned upon foreign intervention in the region and generally refuses to take a stand on domestic issues in member states; the cooperation of the People's Republic of China, which has been unsympathetic to Western challenges of its own human rights record; and the efforts of Russia and India to build links with Burma in the context of their individual geopolitical strategies.

Under the SPDC, Burma has been able to develop strong links with its two most powerful neighbors, India and China. In the PRC's case, this cooperation has been on the basis of resolving border problems and suppressing the production of drugs in Burma that would largely be destined for the PRC, and in the case of India, in fighting ethnic insurgents fighting New Delhi. International rivalry has also played a role as India sought to offset increasing Chinese influence in the country. India's relationship with Burma improved from about 2000. India represents an alternative source of military training and supply, Burma purchasing its ammunition and tanks. India also engaged with Burma in the construction of a joint high-way connecting India with Mandalay and a second highway connexion between Mandalay and the Thai border.[34]

The PRC established the strongest economic and military linkages with Burma from 1988, supplying most of its military hardware, including jet fighters and tanks. The People's Liberation Army began to provide special-ist training for Burma's army and air force, which soon became so depen-dent upon China for military supply that by the SPDC years Burma's military leadership began to look for other potential sources of supply. The PRC also granted to Burma low-interest loans and technical advi-sors to help build new airports, roads, and a deep-sea port at Mergui. In exchange for its support, the PRC has likely been given a free hand in intelligence gathering regarding the Indian Ocean, but the chief gains for China have been economic. By 2001, the PRC was Burma's third most important trading partner, while access to Burma's Indian Ocean ports now gives the PRC better access to markets in South Asia and the Middle East. More recently, in 2006, the SPDC has turned to the PRC for help in reforming its failing banking system, in recognition of the fact that the PRC has had ten years' experience in successful banking reform.[35]

Russia's relationship with Burma, which had been very strong before the collapse of the Soviet Union, grew stronger after 2000. This began with the government's purchase of Russian MIG fighters, to the great displeasure of the PRC. In February 2001, the Russian Atomic Energy Ministry announced that it would make a proposal to build a nuclear reactor in Burma for research purposes. The SPDC accepted the plan and dispatched over 200 technicians for nuclear training in Russia. There were also unconfirmed reports that the SPDC had given sanctuary in the coun-try to two Pakistani nuclear scientists. The avowed purpose of the reactor was initially to produce isotopes for medical research, but the scope of the nuclear program grew to include the provision of nuclear power, cru-cial for a country suffering under a severe energy crisis. An International Atomic Energy Commission inspection team sent to the country in late 2001, however, concluded that Burma's safety measures were not up to international standards and opposition to the program was voiced not only by the US, but by the PRC as well. A formal agreement was signed in May 2002, in which the scope of the program was expanded to include, in addition to a low-powered reactor, the construction of a nuclear study center, a nuclear waste site, and two nuclear laboratories. Fuel would be supplied by Russia.[36]

THE CEASEFIRES

Unlike earlier Ne Win-led regimes, the SLORC now faced a non-violent, internationally backed Democracy movement that threatened its survival from within. This was a more dangerous and immediate threat than the widespread, but divided, insurgencies it faced along its borders.

In order to shore up its strength, the SLORC sought to end the insurgencies. The BCP collapse in 1989 presented new political possibilities in the border areas. Various armed units in the BCP had mutinied against the Party leadership and transformed themselves into ethnic armies. The most important of these armies and one that soon outgrew in strength the forces of the KNU was the United Wa State Army. Like many of the other ex-BCP insurgent groups, it entered the 1990s with increasing interest in participating in the new business opportunities available in the border area and proved more than willing to consider cooling down the civil war. The Burmese government thus began a determined campaign between 1989 and 1990 to create ceasefire arrangements that permitted the insurgents to keep their weapons, and to control (and exploit economically) areas under their sway, political questions being laid aside until a new constitution had been written. Other ethnic groups were also offered ceasefires on the same terms, but these offers were coupled with military attacks in order to pressure these groups into acceptance. A new counter-insurgency strategy was invoked to isolate ethnic insurgents from their base of support, by forcibly relocating ethnic minority civilians to new camps located near Burmese Army camps. The KIO was the first non-BCP group to agree to a ceasefire in 1993, while most others agreed to ceasefires by 1995.[37]

Although the KNU refused to sign a ceasefire, it was removed as a major threat to the regime by other developments. A group of Buddhist Karen soldiers mutinied against the KNU's Christian leadership and formed the Democratic Karen Buddhist Army (DKBA) in December 1994. Although DKBA numbers were small, this proved to be a devastating blow to the KNU. The DKBA allied itself with the Burmese Army and provided it with intelligence on KNU defenses and the government, seeing an opportunity in the division among the Karens, moved quickly to exploit it. Unable to resist a government offensive of 15,000 men, the KNU torched Manerplaw as they withdrew on 26 January 1995, two days before the Burmese Army overran the Karen capital. Also ousted were the NDF and the Democratic Alliance of Burma that had been based there as well.[38]

The MTA situation was more complicated because of the chameleon-like nature of Khun Sa. After the fall of Manerplaw in January 1995, one of the few significant areas of Burma not in government hands (aside from territory under the control of the United Wa State Army and several Kokang rebel splinter groups) was controlled by Khun Sa's MTA, which consisted of GMD holdovers from the 1950s and local Shan recruits and now numbered some 15,000 well-armed troops. As Khun Sa was wanted in the US on charges relating to heroin trafficking, in 1994, the SLORC tried to use him as a bargaining chip. It offered to crush Khun Sa, who supplied most of the heroin sold in the US, if the US would lift its embargo on arms sales to Burma. The deal was not accepted. For the first time, Khun Sa launched a major offensive against Burma, attacking Tachilek. The MTA's position was made untenable, however, by both counter-attacks by the Burmese Army and by an anti-trafficking campaign by the Thai government, with the support of the US Drug Enforcement Agency which destroyed his supply network in March 1995. As with the KNU, the SLORC also encouraged an ethnic rift within the MTA. Unhappy with reported anti-Shan discrimination within the MTA, for example, one commander defected and raised a new, anti-MTA force. As his position became more vulnerable, Khun Sa even toyed with the idea of relinquishing his place as head of the MTA and having his realm turned into a drug-free zone under UN control. Ceasefire arrangements made by the SLORC with his narcotics rivals who could now operate openly within the country made a similar arrangement with the SLORC look very attractive. In January 1996, Khun Sa allowed his headquarters to be "taken" after he made a deal with the SLORC. He then took up residence in an exclusive Rangoon residential area.[39]

The turning tide of the civil war and the ceasefire arrangements of the mid-1990s, as well as the mobilization of certain groups such as the Buddhist Karens as pro-regime forces (in the Karen case as the Democratic Karen Buddhist Army) altered the SLORC/SPDC's approach to the ethnic insurgents. A new strategy re-divided Burma's twelve or more ethnic groups into 135 races, smaller groups that could be played off against each other more successfully. Further, by allowing significant local autonomy in exchange for the ceasefire agreements, the SLORC/SPDC had surrendered more government control over Burmese territory than any previous government since independence.[40]

Nevertheless, after the 2004 purge of Khin Nyunt and his supporters, Than Shwe and Maung Aye have taken Burma in a different direction from the more moderate engagement of the insurgents encouraged by Khin Nyunt. Ethnic minority insurgents were told that under ceasefire agreements they could keep their arms until a new constitution was in place.

After Khin Nyunt, the SPDC demanded that demobilization take place before the constitutional process reached fruition and some insurgents are considering recommencing their armed conflict with the Burmese state. The Army has also intensified its attacks on the KNU, which never signed a ceasefire agreement despite talks in 2004, and the Karenni, who broke theirs.[41] It remains to be seen how the latest twist in the ever-changing military approach to the ethnic minorities will be reflected in future national politics.

CONTROLLING THE POPULATION

The military regime eventually realized, as Ne Win had in the 1960s, that it could not control the country indefinitely by manufacturing consent. Added to this realization was the equally important challenge presented by international boycotts. As Burma's domestic situation intersected with international boycotts, the government sought a means of transferring power to a nominally civilian government, while simultaneously rejecting the 1990 election results. The solution found echoes in the spirit of the creation of the BSPP government in 1974 and the constitutional and organizational efforts that preceded it since the 1960s. This has been the creation and expansion of the now gargantuan USDA.

The USDA was originally established by the SLORC in 1993. Although it is always used for the domestic political purposes of the regime, it remains officially a non-governmental social organization. The reason for this seeming anomaly is that the SLORC prohibition on members of the armed forces and civil bureaucrats becoming members of political parties would have otherwise prevented the latter from joining the USDA. Guiding the organization is a Central Executive Committee made up of high-ranking government officials, including ministers, who are also frequently high-ranking generals as well. The organization has a regional structure, paralleling that of government territorial divisions. The USDA is a means of generating popular support for the regime through the sponsorship and organization of mass rallies and the participation of Association members in rural development projects in order to gain the general population's trust and support. By early 2002, there was a new push, marked by town rallies, to persuade the general population to accept USDA guiding principles, the same as those of the SPDC, in preparation for the expected transfer of power from the junta to the Association.[42]

The USDA has also been involved in violent confrontations with the political opposition. An attack by Association members on NLD supporters rallying during Aung San Suu Kyi's visit to Dipeyin on 30 May 2003 led to unwanted international attention at a time when the SPDC was attempting to improve its image. As a result, Than Shwe ordered the closing of the offices of the Association a month later, on 29 June, leading to rumors that the organization was going to be disbanded. Speculation at the time held that the regime used the pro-regime Association attack and the closure of its offices to demonstrate its even-handedness after having closed down NLD offices earlier.[43] The Association, however, was not disbanded and survived the crisis.

Under the leadership of its secretary and government minister, Aung Thaung, the scope of the USDA role in daily life has expanded rapidly to control all significant social activities in the regions. In addition to attempting to assert control over all non-government organizations in the country, the Association's Central Office directs members to recruit those expelled from the NLD (and persuade others to quit the League), to support them in public protests before the League's offices, and to produce and circulate anti-NLD leaflets. Association members are also to report on local NLD activities both to the Association's central organ and to military intelligence, although its performance of this function was far from effective.[44]

Today, the USDA appears poised to replace the military when it steps down from power after the implementation of the new constitution. It held 633 seats (58 percent of the total number) in the National Convention and the SPDC claims that the organization has 28 million members. Although critics claim that most members have been forced into the Association through intimidation and harassment, it nonetheless represents a large civilian body that will be useful, in a future government, in downplaying international complaints about military rule.[45] At such a time, recognition of the 1990 election results will be a moot point. The parallels between this model of transition to civilian rule and the change from the Revolutionary Council to the BSPP government are very strong indeed.

In order to prepare the USDA for future leadership in the country, in every sphere of national life, the SPDC runs training courses at the central, state, and divisional levels. At the USDA Central Training School in Rangoon, a small cadre of Association members study Burma Affairs and International Studies; Public Relations and Information Management Courses; a Diploma Course on Leadership; and a Basic Journalism Course. At the state and divisional levels, SPDC members receive training in national development, organizational skills, management, national culture and morality, efficiency, sports, music and art, among other subjects. Consensus is built up through annual general meetings at the state and divisional levels so that the Association will be able to implement their intended tasks.[46]

A NEW CAPITAL

Rangoon, the former capital, was always a problem for the SLORC/SPDC. As the center for government and the country's largest urban area since the nineteenth century, it was only natural that it should be the main location of governance. To do otherwise would have entailed substantial costs that the cash-strapped regime could not afford to cover. On the other hand, fears of the mob have always worried dictators. The most serious of the 1988 popular protests in Burma were in Rangoon. The military could take some comfort in the barbed wire and soldiers stationed around government buildings, the machine gun nest located on the crossover near the Traders Hotel, soldiers stationed on the ground floors of housing complexes near RU, and squads in dozens of other locations, but this was not a permanent solution to security.

Not all concerns regarding Rangoon were directly related to security. Rangoon was an aging city and investment in new buildings, save for some socialist architecture in the 1950s and a number of hotels built in the 1990s, did not keep pace with population growth or the new commercial or technological demands placed on the city. In a repeat of the Caretaker Government's resettlement of squatters in Rangoon between 1958 and 1959, for example, the SLORC began a massive resettlement program in the city from October 1988. On 23 October, the Rangoon Division LORC announced that "squatters" in the Rangoon city development area had been moved to the new towns, one of which was Hlaing Thaya across the river from Insein, Padamya, and Okpo. In January 1989, the SLORC announced, just as the Caretaker Government had almost thirty years earlier, that the government was cleaning up the cities so that they would now look like proper cities and to improve sanitation and avoid fire hazards. To do so, they had to "systematically" remove densely populated squatter areas. Soldiers then put the squatters into army trucks and removed them. The SLORC also emphatically denied that people within proper buildings were being removed as well. Resettlement accelerated in March and April 1990. Over half a million people were moved to new, hastily constructed towns, such as Dagon town, in outlying areas. The new towns were to have hospitals, electricity, water, schools, and markets. In many cases, however, people were simply dropped off into areas that still needed to be reclaimed from the jungle and lacked access to transport, with no local means of employment, and even without shelter. There was some speculation that the resettlement merely amounted to deportations to eradicate centers of opposition within the capital.[47]

Some towns, such as Dagon, were intended to house public servants so that they would own their own homes by the time they retired. However, the government also began to move the homeless and those living on government, factory, and religious lands out of Rangoon. The plan was to reconstruct Rangoon in blocks following a square pattern, fringed by new satellite towns, but the government failed to meet the end of March deadline for the completion of the project. The SLORC blamed government departments for lending only minimal aid to the project and not fulfilling their obligations regarding land allocation, the building of homes, and the movement of new settlers. The SLORC also announced, in mid-April, plans to construct a super-city to the south of Rangoon. The 1,600-square-kilometer city, to be completed by 2005, was to be a four-million-person metropolis, a new center for economic growth in the entire Indian Ocean area. Building the city would cost the government US$1 billion per year for fifteen years, and it would be constructed by a consortium of up to 200 Japanese companies. The city would include twenty-five zones according to function, linked by advanced telecommunications and transport, and an "emphasis on flow of information, rather than materials," as well as 4,000 man-made lakes, highways, and offices built to give it an "atmosphere of a resort."[48]

It was partly a combination of the dream of building a modern super-city, the demand for greater security, and profits from growing Chinese investment that eventually led to the realization of plans to create a new capital city. On 13 June 2005, the SPDC issued orders to key ministries to prepare for relocation to Pyinmana. It was not until November, however, that the government publicly announced that the capital would be shifted from Rangoon and specified a location about 26 kilometers from Pyinmana and 600 kilometers north of Rangoon. The new site was named Naypyidaw Myodaw in March 2006. It was in reality a military compound, occupying ten kilometers, which had been planned for years, although construction had really only been underway over the course of the preceding year.[49] Civil servants were given little warning before they were told to pack their belongings, pile into military trucks, and resettled in a site plagued by malaria and sparse accommodation.

The official reasons for the shift were never satisfactorily explained and popular imagination ran wild in attempting to fill the information gap. One rumor was that Than Shwe, deeply superstitious, made the decision for the move on the basis of the claim by an astrologer that Rangoon (see Fig. 9.3) would soon collapse. Two reasonable observations, however, are convincing. First, in terms of domestic security, the administrative chaos

Figure 9.3 Present-day Rangoon

produced by the demonstrations of 1988 has encouraged a shift of the government away from a major population center to a new, more easily managed site. The latter concern appears to have been confirmed by the SPDC Information and Propaganda Minister, who argued that the move was due to the better communication lines at Pyinmana, which is more centrally located than Rangoon. Second, in terms of international security, the regime appeared concerned about the vulnerability of Rangoon, close to the coast, to a seaborne invasion, if foreign powers were determined to intervene. Some foreign scholars have argued that the move represents a return to a long-term historical norm of having a capital based in Upper Burma, but this argument explains neither the timing nor the fact that the new capital has been located far outside the zone that hosts the major precolonial capitals of Amarapura, Sagaing, Ava, and Mandalay. This does not mean that Pyinmana is without historical precedent. During World War II, the town had been the headquarters for the BDA and Aung San had launched his independence movement from it.[50]

The shift of the capital also indicated that the military was centralizing authority over the country at a time when the drawing up of a new constitution was reaching its final stage. The National Convention, without the participation of the political opposition, met in May 2004, for the first time since 1996, and reconvened on 17 February 2005, in order to draw up the new constitution. However, the result of the Convention, announced in September 2007, was merely a set of guidelines for drafting a new constitution. Predictably and in keeping with the regime's policy of delay, the guidelines required six more steps on what is termed the "road map to democracy." Even then, the guidelines were arranged to establish military dominance in any new government, including control of all major ministries, substantial numbers of reserved seats for the military in legislative bodies, and legal "national security" constraints regarding respect for human rights. The guidelines also established limitations that would prevent Aung San Suu Kyi from holding political office. As a guarantee of meeting the goals of these guidelines, the government announced in December 2007 that the new constitution would be written by a 54-member constitution-drafting commission nominated by the SPDC. Although the completed constitution was subject to a national referendum, held in May 2008, like other steps in the constitution-drafting process, this proved to be a carefully orchestrated sham and merely another step in the long process of delay in the handing over of power to a popularly elected government.[51]

THE SLOW BOIL

As promises and continual preparations with no clear end in sight regarding the economy, the transfer of power, and other matters appeared to be no more than delaying tactics, frustrations among the Burmese population simmered for years. Perhaps just as important as the issue of democracy has been the failing economy. International sanctions and other efforts to isolate the regime have hurt the general Burmese population, pushing most further into poverty and sending many now unemployed female textile workers and others into prostitution.

By contrast, Burma's elite military families have shown incredible resourcefulness in maintaining and expanding their personal wealth. This was demonstrated most recently by the opulent wedding of Than Shwe's daughter, who, in a video leaked to the outside world, was shown sporting jewelry worth many millions of dollars.[52] Subordinate officers also benefited from patronage, extensively used by the junta to maintain officer corps solidarity, in the form of business loans, the purchase of land far below its real value, and opportunities to forge highly rewarding connexions with private businesspeople.[53] The growing disparity in wealth between the general population and military families became very difficult to ignore.

From late 2006, prices of daily necessities, such as cooking oil, began to increase by up to 40 percent, pushing family economies almost to a breaking point. Although life became almost unaffordable, Burmese tolerance of hardship, built up from experience of other long-term hardships that have plagued the country since the early 1960s, proved resilient. Quiet resentment of misrule changed to open protest, however, after 15 August 2007, when the government, apparently taking to the extreme International Monetary Fund advice to take the population off subsidized fuel, issued an overnight increase in fuel prices of between 100 and 500 percent. The sudden increase meant it was now impossible for the average Burmese to afford transport to work, especially as the bus lines immediately stopped running. Increased fuel prices meant that already inflated prices of other basic commodities began to increase further. The protests that broke out on 19 August and carried on into September highlighted the desperation to which the general population has been driven. From 22 August, the government began crushing local demonstrations and arresting protestors.[54]

While the regime remained confident of its ability to suppress the resistance of ordinary citizens, it faced a different kind of opponent in mid-September 2007. In what has become known as the "Saffron Revolution," after the garb of its leaders, monks (numbering some 400,000 in Burma), outraged at what the military has done to the country, began protests in northwestern Burma in support of general protests against the government's new economic policies. When the government physically beat protesting monks on 5 September at Pakokku, where monastic opposition began, monastic protests spread through the country. Ultimately, monasteries at Mandalay, the most important monastic center in the country, called on all monks to refuse donations from the families of the military elite, which effectively meant that they could not earn merit in Buddhist belief.[55] Soon, monks led peaceful protest marches in the capital (see Fig. 9.4). While monks are not supposed to engage in mundane politics according to the monastic code, they have become involved in politics at numerous historical junctures in the past. Indeed, some of the leading anti-colonial activists, including Shin Ottama and others, were monks, and monks participated to some degree in the popular revolution of 1988. At the same time, the fact that harming a monk earns one bad merit and thus rebirth as a lesser being in Buddhist thinking meant that the military was hesitant to stop the protests.[56]

Nevertheless, as the world watched through short video clips or viewed photographs sent out of the country by ordinary Burmese, the military was concerned that years of state media and regime apologists telling the country and the outside world that the Burmese were happy with military rule were being revealed as state propaganda. As the United States and the European Union talked of more sanctions, the military struck on 26 September, beating, shooting, and arresting monastic and other protestors. Early the following morning, several monasteries were raided; monks were forcibly (and illegally under Buddhist law) defrocked, beaten, and interrogated, many being killed in the process. Soldiers fired on street protests that ensued. The violence with which the regime suppressed peaceful monastic protests represents, it has been asserted, a historical watershed in the relationship between the Burmese state and the monastic order. The United Nations responded by forcing the government to accept two visits by a special envoy, Ibrahim Gambari, to evaluate the situation. Gambari would press the government to begin talks with detained NLD leader, Aung San Suu Kyi.[57]

The government tried once more to gain control by spinning a different account of events, outlawing cell phones, blocking email and internet access, and cutting communication posts. Nevertheless, footage already leaked out showed soldiers calmly walking up to a wounded Japanese cameraman and shooting him point-blank to death. Reports have since

Figure 9.4 Monks march in protest against the military junta

emerged that the Army burned bodies shortly after these events to hide evidence of the atrocities. The All-Burma Monks Alliance is currently pressuring the UN to ascertain how many monks were killed.[58]

The Burmese monastic order is under close government surveillance, while the chief monastic council, the Supreme Council of Abbots, has been dissolved by Than Shwe for refusing to defrock monks involved in the protests. Monks were also sent out of Rangoon back to their villages in an effort to prevent a re-congregation of this now potent, political force. This has not been completely successful, as indicated on 31 October by a monastic demonstration at Pakokku, where the monastic opposition had originally begun.[59]

CONCLUSION

Burma has now experienced an unbroken two-decade period of post-BSPP military rule. The SLORC/SPDC has managed to retain power by force rather than consent. Although the promulgation of a new constitution was a constant promise, it was made and broken repeatedly. Even when such a constitution was realized, it has proven not to be truly representative of the desires of most Burmese. At the same time, the NLD, once the focus of so many hopes and dreams among the general population, has only survived in emaciated form. For long, the regime appeared to have successfully stymied, with occasional slip-ups, Aung San Suu Kyi's attempts to reactivate the forces that spawned the 1988 popular revolution. Even so, recent events, especially the extension of monastic support to Burmese opposition to the government and popular unhappiness with the regime's dismal response to Cyclone Nargis (May 2008), indicate that these forces may actually be growing stronger than at any time before.

Bunkered in Naypyidaw, backed by diplomatic and material help from powerful neighbors such as China and India competing with each other for privileged access to Burma's natural resources, and having just crushed the most serious challenge to its rule in two decades, the country's military rulers proceeded with the constitutional referendum in two rounds in May 2008. This confidence was shattered by Cyclone Nargis that struck the Burmese coasts with winds of over 190 kilometers an hour on 2–3 May, sending a 6-meters-high wall of water across the delta. Nargis left behind an estimated 150,000 people dead and missing and another 2.5 million homeless and in desperate need of care. Hundreds of thousands of livestock were lost and much of the country's rice stocks were ruined. The regime delayed for three weeks in admitting most international aid, refusing visas to aid workers and storing in warehouses the few supplies it allowed to be flown in, while it proceeded with the constitutional referendum and informed the world that there was no crisis. An international stand-off ensued leading to the gathering of Western naval vessels, including a US aircraft carrier, off the coast and frantic efforts by the UN Secretary General to gain permission for the introduction of international rescue and care workers. When Western countries threatened to bring the generals up before the International Court at The Hague on charges of Crimes Against Humanity and as even China became concerned about the regime's neglect of the wellbeing of its own people, Than Shwe caved in. How far the millions of dollars in promised aid will go in rebuilding the lives of those living in the devastated areas and not into the bank accounts of the generals remains unclear, but Cyclone Nargis has, like the Saffron Revolution eight months earlier, drawn the world's attention to the plight of one of Asia's most oppressed populations.[60]

Conclusion

In its modern history, Burma has been shaped and reshaped over again by different governments in the context of significant pressures emanating from both within and without the country. Despite its diverse and challenging historical experience, one is often struck by how little Burma appears to have changed, especially in relation to its more politically dynamic and economically more prosperous neighbors in the region. The Burmese today are just as unhappy with their government as earlier generations; economic poverty continues to figure as prominently among Burmese concerns as it has at any time in the past. Basic civil liberties are denied today as they were almost a half-century ago. Continuity has characterized some of the basic themes of modern Burmese history that have transcended the phases of the Burmese experience outlined in this book and contribute to something that might be called the rhythm of Burmese history.

Among the most vexing issues that have plagued the country since the colonial period has been the relationship between the Burman-dominated lowlands and the ethnic minority-dominated highlands. What, after all, is Burma and who are the Burmese? Before colonial rule, the Burmese throne considered the highlands to be part of the royal kingdom, but not of the Burman "country." Under the last Burmese dynasty, highland states were ruled by autonomous, tributary chiefs (in the Shan case, *sawbwas*), separated from lowland centers under the control of direct appointees of the Burmese court. Political anxieties rather than ethnic ones dominated conflicts, although cultural, linguistic, and other differences among the diverse peoples that made up the kingdom were indeed recognized.

The highlands retained their autonomy when, over the course of the nineteenth century, the British first carved up and then welded back together the lowlands into direct-rule districts of British Burma. After the grant of diarchy, as the Scheduled Areas, they were constitutionally separated from parliamentary (lowland) Burma. This typical colonial strategy of "divide and rule" encompassed more than regional autonomy, for it also represented a more visible separation of ethnic groups. Despite the claims of the current regime, the British did not create Burma's "ethnic" minorities, but colonial rule did exacerbate them.[1] Colonial administrators and writers essentialized ethnic identifications, thus creating perceptions of cohesiveness and homogeneity within ethnic groups, and clarified what had been vague boundaries between them and other groups, especially in separating Burmans from non-Burmans, both in terms of ethnicity and geography.[2] The British also exacerbated problems between these groups and the Burmans by both favoring and "protecting" ethnic minorities from what the British portrayed, and ethnic minority leaders eventually accepted, as the threat of Burman domination, not just political, but cultural, linguistic and religious as well. Their separation from Rangoon's control continued under the Japanese, the war working also to put Burmans and the ethnic minorities on opposite sides, and after the war as the Frontier Areas.

Ethnic insurgencies that followed independence maintained de facto separation for decades. The 1962 coup sought to undermine attempts to negotiate constitutional recognition of ethnic (highland) autonomy, but by the late BSPP period, Burma's new citizenship laws made it clear that as members of the privileged "indigenous races," highland minorities were officially considered along with the Burmans as part of the same ethnic family, despite the fabricated differences, the government claimed, introduced by the British.[3] The official view has not eroded ethnic minorities' concerns about integration into a Burman-dominated state although it did make it easier for the SLORC/SPDC to go ahead with ceasefire arrangements with many insurgent groups that left the latter in control of their base areas. However, this has left open the question of federalism in the promised constitution. Even if significant political concessions are made in the direction of highland autonomy once the constitution is promulgated, it is likely that the lowland–highland, and thus Burman–minority, bifurcation of the country will remain an important determining factor in the trajectory of Burmese history in the twenty-first century.

Another continual theme of Burma's modern history has been poverty for the general Burmese population. While colonial economic development marginally improved the economic lot of many Burmese, true economic prosperity was enjoyed by very few, mainly among the colonial elite. Even then, the connexion of the Burmese economy to the world capitalist system and the failure to sufficiently diversify the economy left it vulnerable to the whims of Western markets and the World Depression. The major blow to Burma's economic growth came with the outbreak of World War II, in the form of British destruction of Burma's economic and transportation infrastructure in 1942, the separation of Burma from world markets thereafter, and fighting between the Allies and the Japanese, especially in the last months of the war. British efforts to reestablish the colonial economy after the war for the benefit of colonial interests did too little to help most Burmese. Burma after independence had to cope with the devastation and costs of a civil war that dragged on longer than any other conflict anywhere else in the world. What has also hurt post-independence regimes, aside from the more market-oriented reforms of the Caretaker period, were Burma's confused attempts to promote socialism, the chronic corruption that has continued despite regime facelifts, and, in more recent decades, the impact of Western sanctions.

Although the avowed purpose of establishing the socialist economy was to promote the welfare and economic prosperity of the nation, most of the post-independence regimes sacrificed the wellbeing of the country for the economic benefit of the ruling minority. One of the main underlying reasons for this is the association of wealth with political power, perhaps inherited from precolonial times, but certainly strengthened by the colonial period, in that there is an expectation that political power should bring with it personal wealth. Complaints during the colonial period that Burmese politicians were enriching themselves through their offices at the expense of the general population appear no less relevant when one views the control over the economy exerted by the families of prominent SPDC officers today. Whether this would be different under a democratic government is of course unclear, but the current regime has by no means contributed to changing this association, which would be a helpful step toward the fostering of general economic prosperity.

Another long-term theme of modern Burmese history is the struggle between civilian politicians bent on representative, democratic rule and civil liberties and authoritarian control, whether under British colonialists or indigenous military officers. Although colonial-era Burmese nationalists won their struggle against the British, the latter's absence after independence removed from the political scene a singular, visible opponent that could help maintain political solidarity. The AFPFL was an umbrella group of political parties that was held together by both their shared opposition to colonial rule and the personal charisma and political skills of Aung San. When Aung San was assassinated in 1947, it left Nu in charge. Although Nu is admirable for many reasons and his commitment to the country is unquestioned, his behavior was both too quixotic and often too erratic to hold the political coalition together. Moreover, the push for independence had temporarily pushed aside many political questions that now had to be resolved with too many and too diverse political forces in the field. Military officers viewed civilian politics of the time as inimical to the promotion of national unity and developed notions, strengthened by the caretaker regime's admittedly effective performance, that the military could do a better job at running the country. In other words, in the context of Burma's civil war, its economic woes, and the factious democratic politics, Burma could only be preserved and national unity found through authoritarian military rule. Divided democratic forces could do very little to oppose the 1962 coup.

One tool used by post-1962 regimes in attempts to legitimize their control was inherited from the colonial period. The British had successfully prolonged colonial rule in Burma in part by permitting minor constitutional concessions while retaining control of the real centers of power in the colonial administration. This put Burmese into visible positions within the administration, usually over areas of governance the British were not really interested in anyway, but did not lessen overall colonial authority. Ne Win was especially adept at using similar tactics to the degree that one might view the Revolutionary Council period and its BSPP successor as ideologically rich compared to the SLORC/SPDC. Despite Tin Pe's adventurous Marxist-oriented reforms, lip service to mass participation in governance, and the structures of a civilian, one-party state, Ne Win and the military remained in full control of the country. As one scholar has observed, those most committed to the principles of the Burmese Way to Socialism ideology were squeezed out of the BSPP government, senior leadership positions being determined by personal loyalty to Ne Win.[4] Ne Win had even tried in the late 1960s to bring cowed former Nu-era politicians into a committee to legitimize his proposals, but realizing that these offered no real democratic concessions, they turned to armed rebellion instead, indicating that the struggle between civilian politicians and the military was by no means resolved.

The SLORC/SPDC borrowed significantly from the Ne Win era, particularly the formation of the BSPP as a civilian mass base to seemingly legitimate the preservation of the military's interests. The USDA is perhaps the best example of this attempt. But there are important differences. By contrast with the ideology-rich Revolutionary Council and BSPP governments, the slow pace of reform after 1990 is partly due to the intellectual and ideological hollowness of the current regime. Beyond slogans and bullet points, couched in calls to resist foreign intervention, no systematic ideology has emerged to make government policies meaningful, even understandable to the general population (or even to themselves). Certainly, the end of the Cold War and the collapse of Communism in most of the world has reduced the availability of powerful ideologies that can be used as models for states, such as Burma, that are desperately in search of identities. The fact that the Communists disappeared so quickly from the civil war landscape, in 1989, deprived the military of one of its main justifications for continued control. In the place of ideology, the SLORC/SPDC has utilized what could be called "sustained delay," whereby military control remains always temporary, always on the eve of transfer of the state to civilian control, and continually vigilant about so-called technical problems in the drafting of the Constitution, requiring more committee meetings and more preliminary decision-making. If the country is always kept on the verge of the transfer of power, there is no compelling reason to legitimate present government policies to any significant degree. The democracy issue has thus been "lost in committee" and has been so for nearly two decades.

Another theme of modern Burmese history that the SLORC/SPDC has attempted to mobilize in its favor was sparked under colonial rule, that is, the fear of foreign domination. Anti-colonialism and early Burmese nationalism justifiably saw colonial rule as inimical to the interests of the Burmese population. Such sentiments were certainly strengthened during World War II when Burmese nationalists such as Aung San realized that Japanese "liberation" really meant continued foreign control. After the war, when the British returned to Burma, they made it clear if any doubts still lingered, through the activities of the CASB, that if Burma were to be developed in the interests of the Burmese, then foreign involvement meant commercial exploitation and, necessarily, domination by foreign minorities within the country. The outbreak of the Cold War, which roughly accompanied the grant of independence, deluged Burma with both Western and Communist propaganda but it also brought exposure to leaders in other newly independent countries, such as India and Indonesia, who argued that participation in the Cold War offered nothing for countries like Burma and, indeed, threatened the extension of a new kind of foreign domination, neocolonialism. Moreover, Nu believed that the US, through its support of the GMD, and the Soviet Union, through its perceived backing of the Communists, were exacerbating the civil war that broke out after independence. Indeed, the fundamental message of his play, *The People Win Through*, is that Burmese should not fall under the spell of foreign powers and invite external intervention in Burma's domestic problems. Nu's attempts to placate the PRC were likewise directed at preventing PRC intervention in the country rather than developing any sort of alliance.

Burma's post-1962 regimes maintained the official international neutrality promoted under Nu and although the Revolutionary Council and the BSPP governments associated closely with the Soviet Union and were indeed estranged from the PRC, no official alignment was considered. Whether this was intended to allow the government to use the Cold War to its advantage, by gaining aid from both sides, or to maintain the principle of isolating Burma from external intervention is unclear. In either case, the SLORC took the fears of external intervention to new levels, in a very public way, in 1988. Aung San Suu Kyi's close personal connexions with the West and her support within it have helped to make the appeal, among Burma's military rulers, of rejecting Western interference all the more powerful. This is also partly due to the continued presence of Aung San Suu Kyi and the fact that the denial of recognition of the 1990 election results continues to ride mainly upon foreign intervention. International sanctions strengthened the government's resolve to reshape the external threat to include the West in general.

One more major theme of Burmese history has been monastic participation in politics. According to the monastic code, monks are not supposed to involve themselves in mundane politics, but historically this involvement has been very real, both before colonialism and after. As we have seen, monks such as Ottama and the political monks of 1920s rural Burma played leading roles in Burmese anti-colonialism. Monastic organizations played a fundamental role in pushing for state recognition of Buddhism as the national religion and mobilized against the Communist insurgency during the Caretaker period and after. As under colonial rule, the monastic order fought vigorously Ne Win's attempts to exert control over the monastic order in order to silence monastic criticism of his rule, during both the Revolutionary Council and the BSPP governments. Many monks also took to the streets in 1988 to help bring down the BSPP regime and restore democracy to the country.

The basic problem facing the SPDC in relation to monks is that in Burmese society they are potentially very powerful. In the Burmese Buddhist system of belief, donations to monks are an important way to accrue merit in order to experience a better rebirth on the path to Enlightenment and should these donations be refused, then one faces the prospects of an inferior rebirth. On another level, Burmese monks have been, since precolonial days, the keepers of Burmese tradition and the core of Burmese intellectual life. When Burmese Buddhist boys, even those who grow up to be soldiers, become novices they are taught in the monasteries and learn to recognize the unquestionable authority monks have in determining what is and what is not proper Burmese Buddhist behavior. This is easily extended to politics and if monks disapprove of the regime's claims to represent the "real" Burma, it has an importance greater than any other voice of dissent.

When the monks refused donations from the families of the military elite and complained of the directions in which the country was headed, the government lost whatever gains, if any, it had made in attempting to foster domestic political legitimacy. This was guaranteed when soldiers and police arrested, defrocked, and beat monks in a desperate attempt to suppress what may prove to have been a mortal blow to the regime. Certainly, all indications are, at the time of writing, that monastic opposition has not been cowed. Monks will continue to play an important role in shaping the country's political future, especially since the monastic role in the demonstrations clearly showed that legitimacy rested with the opposition.

Notes

I BURMA UNDER COLONIAL RULE

1. James C. Scott, *The Moral Economy of the Peasant: Rebellion and Subsistence in Southeast Asia* (New Haven, CT: Yale University Press, 1976).
2. Ian Brown, *A Colonial Economy in Crisis: Burma's Rice Cultivators and the World Depression of the 1930s* (London: RoutledgeCurzon, 2005): 9, 11.
3. *Forward* 9.7 (15 November 1970): 18.
4. "Durbar at Mandalay," 28 November 1901, in *Lord Curzon in India* (London: MacMillan, 1906): 215; *Times*, 30 November 1901, 7.
5. Kazuto Ikeda, "The Myaungmya Incident during the Japanese Occupation in Burma: Karens and Shwe Tun Kya," in Kei Nemoto (ed.), *Reconsidering the Japanese Military Occupation in Burma (1942–45)* (Tokyo: Tokyo University of Foreign Studies, 2007): 60–61; Ito Toshikatsu, "Karens and the Kon-baung Polity in Myanmar," *Acta Asiatica* 92 (2007): 105.
6. The problems of the colonial census are tackled by the late Judith L. Richell in *Disease and Demography in Colonial Burma* (Copenhagen: NIAS Press, 2006).
7. Atsuko Naono, *The State of Vaccination*, forthcoming.
8. Michael Adas, *The Burma Delta: Economic Development and Social Change on an Asian Rice Frontier, 1852–1941* (Madison, WI: University of Wisconsin Press, 1974): 118–119; Cheng Siok-Hwa, *The Rice Industry of Burma*, 186–188.
9. "Land Alienation," *World of Books* 23 (November 1937): 448.
10. *Forward* 9.7 (15 November 1970): 18; *Times*, 24 May 1921, supplement, xiv; *Times*, 17 October 1924, 13; *Memorandum Submitted by the Government of Burma to the Indian Statutory Commission* (1930), 25–26; Maurice Collis, *Into Hidden Burma: An Autobiography* (London: Faber, 1953): 162; PBLC 4.5, 25 September 1925: 107, 116, 117, 120.
11. *Forward* 9.7 (15 November 1970): 18; Collis, *Into Hidden Burma*, 164; PBLC 4.5, 25 September 1925: 107, 113–114, 116–117; *Times*, 24 May 1921, supplement, xiv; *Times*, 20 September 1924, 9; 7 October 1924, 13; 17 October 1924, 13; 9 April 1928, 9.
12. *Times*, 20 September 1924, 9; 7 October 1924, 13; 17 October 1924, 13; PBLC 4.5, 25 September 1925: 107, 114; PDC, 5th Series, volume 213, 13 February 1928, 496.

13. *Times*, 9 November 1910, 5; 12 November 1910, 7; 3 December 1910, 7; PDC, 5th Series, volume 28, 11 July 1911, 181; APCLGB 6 April 1914, 346–347; 13 March 1913, 277; 13 March 1914, 311–313; *Memorandum Submitted by the Government of Burma to the Indian Statutory Commission* (1930), 26.
14. Khin Maung Nyunt, "Supannaka Galuna Raja," GMR 15.4 (April 1968): 11.
15. Brown, *A Colonial Economy in Crisis*, 101–108.
16. Maitrii V. Aung-Thwin, "British Counter-Insurgency Narratives and the Construction of a Twentieth Century Burmese Rebel," PhD dissertation, University of Michigan, 2001.
17. Kyaw Htun, "Of Such Stuff Are Heroes Made," GMR 14.4 (April 1967): 22; U Tin Maung, "A Short History of Newspapers," *Burma Digest* 1.14 (1 October 1946): 29.
18. Khin Maung Nyunt, "Supannaka Galuna Raja," 11–12.
19. U Htin Fatt, "Sidelights on Burma's Struggle for Freedom," GMR 16.5 (May 1969): 32; Khin Maung Nyunt, "Supannaka Galuna Raja," 12; Tin Maung, "A Short History of Newspapers," 29–30.
20. Khin Maung Nyunt, "Supannaka Galuna Raja," 12–13; Tin Maung, "A Short History of Newspapers," 30; Zeya Maung, "Saya Lun and the Galon Rebellion of Saya San," GMR 22.2 (March 1975): 21–22; Htin Fatt, "Sidelights on Burma's Struggle for Freedom," 32.
21. GMR 5.8 (August 1958): 42; Htin Fatt, "Sidelights on Burma's Struggle for Freedom," 33; Tin Maung, "A Short History of Newspapers," 30, 32.

2 THE COLONIAL CENTER

1. John L. Christian, "Burma Divorces India," *Current History* 46.1 (April 1937): 82.
2. B. R. Pearn, *History of Rangoon* (Rangoon: American Baptist Mission Press, 1939): 264–266, 283.
3. "The Rangoon Electric Tramway & Supply Company Limited," *BBAQB* 8 (April 1938): 42–44; Pearn, *History of Rangoon*, 266, 278.
4. "The Rangoon Electric Tramway & Supply Company Limited," 45; Pearn, *History of Rangoon*, 279; APCLGB, 9 March 1907, 118.
5. Pearn, *History of Rangoon*, 280; PDC, 4th Series, volume 179, 6 August 1907, 1819.
6. APCLGB 2 January 1920, 628–629.
7. Pearn, *History of Rangoon*, 280–281, 283, 284; U Tun Shein, *Yangon Yazawin Thamaing* (Yangon, Zwe-sape-yeibmyoun, 1962): 152.
8. *Census for 1872*, 17; appendix II, 4; BBAQB 7 (July 1937): 12.
9. GMR 19.6 (June 1972): 17; Richell, *Disease and Demography in Colonial Burma*, 266, 272.
10. J. S. Furnivall, "Burma Fifty Years Ago: Little Picture of Progress," GMR 5.10 (October 1958): 29–30.
11. Alister McCrae, *Scots in Burma: Golden Times in a Golden Land* (Edinburgh: Kiscadale, 1990): 70–71; GMR 19.6 (June 1972): 17.

12. *Who's Who in Burma: under the distinguished patronage of HE Sir Harcourt Butler* (Calcutta: Indo-Burma Publishing Agency, 1927): 54; H. A. Cartwright and O. Breakspear (eds.), *Twentieth Century Impressions of Burma: Its History, People, Commerce, Industries, and Resources* (London: Lloyd's Greater Britain Publishing Co., 1910): 309, 312.

13. GMR 19.6 (June 1972): 17, 19.

14. Ba Maw, *Breakthrough in Burma: Memoirs of a Revolution* (New Haven, CT: Yale University Press, 1968): 13; Pearn, *History of Rangoon*, 290–291.

15. U Nu, *U Nu Saturday's Son*, translated by U Law Yone (New Haven, CT: Yale University Press, 1975): 19.

16. APCLGB 8 December 1903, 3.

17. Emma Larkin, "The Self-Conscious Censor: Censorship Under the British, 1900–1939," *Journal of Burma Studies* 8 (2003): 71.

18. Richell, *Disease and Demography in Colonial Burma*, 266; GMR 19.6 (June 1972): 17.

19. APCLGB 19 December 1901, 3–4; Nu, *Saturday's Son*, 22.

20. APCLGB 19 December 1901, 3–4; 8 December 1903, 3; 29 February 1908, 132; 26 February 1921, 761–765; *Rangoon Municipality Handbook*, 459.

21. Larkin, "The Self-Conscious Censor," 71–72; George Orwell, *Burmese Days* (San Diego: Harcourt Brace, n.d.).

22. APCLGB 26 February 1921, 761–765; *Times*, 24 November 1925, 13; PDC, 4th Series, volume 113, 21 October 1902, 352.

23. *Forward* 9.7 (15 November 1970): 17.

24. Ibid., 18.

25. *Who's Who in Burma*, 154; *Who's Who in Burma, 1961* (Rangoon: People's Literature Committee, 1962): 104–105.

26. U Shwe Mra, "A Civil Servant in Thayetmyo 1935–36," GMR 13.4 (April 1966): 46–47.

27. *Forward* 9.7 (15 November 1970): 18.

28. Christian, "Burma Divorces India," 85; U Htin Fatt, "Burma's Constitutional Developments Before the Second World War," GMR 17.2 (February 1970): 40; *Forward* 9.7 (15 November 1970): 18.

29. *Forward* 9.7 (15 November 1970): 17.

30. Tun Shein, *Yangon Yazawin Thamaing*, 209; Khin Maung Nyunt, "The 'Shoe' Question," GMR 17.2 (February 1970): 26–27.

31. Michael Aung-Thwin, "The British 'Pacification' of Burma: Order Without Meaning," *Journal of Southeast Asian Studies* 16 (1985): 247; Christian, "Burma Divorces India," 85; Htin Fatt, "Burma's Constitutional Developments," 40; Tetkatho Minwaethan, "Burmese Movies in Retrospect," GMR 16.9 (September 1969): 45.

32. GMR 10.1 (January 1963): 29; *Forward* 9.7 (15 November 1970): 18; Htin Fatt, "Sidelights on Burma's Struggle for Freedom," 30–31; Mya Han, *Koloniket, Myanma Thamaing Abhidan* (Yangon: Universities Historical Research Center, 2000): 209–210.

33. Htin Fatt, "Sidelights on Burma's Struggle for Freedom," 31; George E. R. Grant Brown, *Burma as I Saw It, 1889–1917, With a Chapter on Recent Events* (New York: Frederick A. Stokes and Company, 1925): 171; Albert D. Moscotti, *British Policy and the Nationalist Movement in Burma, 1917–1937* (Honolulu, HI: University of Hawaii Press, 1937): 48; Donald Eugene Smith, *Religion and Politics in Burma* (Princeton, NJ: Princeton University Press, 1965): 121; *Times,* 19 August 1924, 10; 6 October 1924, 11; 9 October 1924, 13; 10 October 1924, 11; 11 October 1924, 9.

34. Harvey Adamson, "Burma," *The Asiatic Review* 16.46 (April 1920): 286; Christian, "Burma Divorces India," 84.

35. APCLGB 17 April 1920, 701–702; Spencer Harcourt Butler, "Burma and Its Problems," *Foreign Affairs* 10 (1932): 655; Htin Fatt, "Burma's Constitutional Developments," 41; Henti, "A Scheme of Reform for Burma," 21–22, 42–43.

36. *Forward* 9.8 (1 December 1970): 20; *Times,* 24 May 1921, supplement, xiv.

37. *Forward* 9.8 (1 December 1970): 21; U Lu Pe Win, *History of the 1920 University Boycott* (Rangoon: U Lu Pe Win, 1970): 243–244.

38. Maung Maung, "Mr. Justice Chan Htoon," GMR 2.2 (December 1954): 34; ibid., "Dr. Htin Aung, The Fourth Brother," GMR 5.8 (August 1958): 25; *Forward* 9.8 (1 December 1970): 21.

39. Robert H. Taylor, "British Policy Toward Burma (Myanmar) in the 1920's and 1930's: Separation and Responsible Self-Government," in *Essays in Commemoration of the Golden Jubilee of the Myanmar Historical Commission* (Yangon: UHRC, 2005): 149; Htin Fatt, "Burma's Constitutional Developments," 41; Christian, "Burma Divorces India," 84; *Times,* 2 January 1923, 9; 29 April 1924, 11.

40. Sai Kham Mong, "The Shan in Myanmar," in N. Ganesan and Kyaw Yin Hlaing (eds.), *Myanmar: State, Society and Ethnicity* (Singapore: Institute of Southeast Asian Studies, 2007): 259–260.

41. John F. Cady, *A History of Modern Burma* (Ithaca, NY: Cornell University Press, 1958): 295.

42. *Forward* 9.7 (15 November 1970): 17; *Memorandum Submitted by the Government of Burma to the Indian Statutory Commission* (1930), 25; Moscotti, *British Policy and the Nationalist Movement in Burma, 1917–1937,* 48; Cady, *History of Modern Burma,* 250; *Times,* 6 August 1925, 11; 22 August 1925, 9; 30 July 1925, 13.

43. Zeya Maung, "The Khway Tike of Mr. Maung Hmine," GMR 22.2 (February 1975): 15; *Times,* 30 July 1925, 13; 31 July 1925, 9.

44. Cheryll Baron, "Burma: Feminist Utopia?" *Prospect* 139 (October 2007).

45. PBLC, 9 August 1929, 282.

46. PBLC, 3 February 1927, 201.

47. Unpublished translation by L. E. Bagshawe of Yaw Mingyi U Po Hlaing, *Rajadhammasangaha,* 167–170.

48. Htin Fatt, "Burma's Constitutional Developments," 41; Christian, "Burma Divorces India," 84–85.

49. Christian, "Burma Divorces India," 85–86.

50. Htin Fatt, "Burma's Constitutional Developments," 42.
51. M. B. K., "U Ba Sein, Attorney-General," GMR 6.1 (January 1959): 41; Maung Maung, "Mr. Justice Chan Htoon," 35; Thakin Lay Maung, "A Short History of the Dhobama Asiayone (Thakin Party) and its Policy," *Burma Digest* 1.8 (1 July 1946): 31–32.
52. Nu, *Saturday's Son*, 61–63, 74, 77–78.
53. Maung Tha Hla, "The 1936 Rangoon University Strike [I]," *NBW* 1.4 (21 June 1958): 8; Maung Maung, "U Nyo Mya, Or Maung Thumana," GMR 5.10 (October 1958); 24.
54. Maung Tha Hla, "The 1936 Rangoon University Strike [I]," 9–10, 13.
55. Maung Tha Hla, "The 1936 Rangoon University Strike [II]," *NBW* 1.6 (5 July 1958): 12–14; Maung Maung, "U Nyo Mya," 24.
56. Maung Tha Hla, "The 1936 Rangoon University Strike [III]," *NBW* 1.9 (26 July 1958): 7, 11, 13, 14.

3 SELF-GOVERNMENT WITHOUT INDEPENDENCE, 1937–1947

1. [31 March 1937] *LAD* 3 (1937): 2417; BBAQB 7 (July 1937): 11–12; A. J. S. White, *The Burma of "AJ"* (London: BACSA, 1991): 211, 214–215.
2. *BBAQB* 6 (April 1937): 3–5; Htin Fatt, "Sidelights on Burma's Struggle for Freedom," 33; GMR 9.5 (May 1962): 13–14.
3. Ba Maw, *Breakthrough in Burma*, 35, 69, 87; Lay Maung, "A Short History of the Dhobama Asiayone," 33–34; GMR 9.5 (May 1962): 15; Htin Fatt, "Sidelights on Burma's Struggle for Freedom," 33.
4. *Time Magazine* 3 November 1941; 17 November 1941; Ba Maw, *Breakthrough in Burma*, 52, 61; PDC 443, 5 November 1947, 1849; *Times*, 2 November 1945, 3; 4 September 1946, 5.
5. Maung Khin Maung, "Nagoya Bya-bwe-gyi," *Sun Magazine* 21.1 (March 1937): 83–87.
6. Robert H. Taylor, *The State in Burma* (Honolulu, HI: The University of Hawaii Press, 1987): 232; Cady, *A History of Modern Burma*, 428–429; 14 August has also been given as the date for Aung San's departure for Amoy. See Thant Myint-U, *The River of Lost Footsteps: Histories of Burma* (New York: Farrar, Straus and Giroux, 2006): 228.
7. GMR 7.1 (January 1960): 13; 9.5 (May 1962): 16; 9.6 (June 1962): 14; 11.5 (May 1964): 36; Maung Maung, "General Ne Win," GMR 1.12 (October 1954): 57; Thant Myint-U, *The River of Lost Footsteps*, 229–230.
8. [19 March 1937] *LAD* 3 (1937): 2181; [30 March 1937] *LAD* 3 (1937): 2328; John F. Cady, *Contacts with Burma, 1935–1949: A Personal Account* (Athens, OH: Ohio University Center for International Studies, 1983): 25.
9. GMR 11.5 (May 1964): 36–38; Thant Myint-U, *The River of Lost Footsteps*, 230.
10. Kazuo Tamayama, *Railwaymen in the War: Tales by Japanese Railway Soldiers in Burma and Thailand 1941–1947* (Houndmills: Palgrave MacMillan, 2005): 12–13.

11. M. B. K. "U Ba Sein, Attorney-General," 43; GMR 11.5 (May 1964): 39–40; Maung Maung, "General Ne Win," 57; GMR 10.1 (January 1963): 30; *Burma Today* 1.5 (March 1944): 3; 1.11 (September 1944): 9; 1.12 (October 1944): 1.

12. *Burma Today* 1.12 (October 1944): 2; Maung Maung, "General Ne Win," 57; *Times*, 14 December 1943, 5.

13. GMR 10.1 (January 1963): 30; 11.6 (June 1964): 17; Ba U, "My Burma: Under the Japanese Occupation," GMR 5.1 (January 1958): 20.

14. Tun Shein, *Yangon Yazawin Thamaing*, 249, 254; GMR 10.1 (January 1963): 31; *Burma Today* 1.12 (October 1944): 2; Ba U, "My Burma," 20; Maung Maung, "General Ne Win," 57; GMR 11.6 (June 1964): 17.

15. David I. Steinberg, *Burma: A Socialist Nation of Southeast Asia* (Boulder, CO: Westview Press, 1982): 48.

16. Ibid., 60.

17. Taylor, *The State in Burma*, 233; Steinberg, *Burma: A Socialist Nation of Southeast Asia*, 48; Thant Myint-U, *The River of Lost Footsteps*, 231, 236; Ikeda, "The Myaungmya Incident during the Japanese Occupation in Burma: Karens and Shwe Tun Kya," 64–67.

18. Steinberg, *Burma: A Socialist Nation of Southeast Asia*, 48.

19. U Thaung, *A Journalist, a General and an Army in Burma* (Bangkok: White Lotus, 1995): 58; *Burma Today* 1.5 (March 1944): 3; 2.1 (November 1944): 2; GMR 11.9 (September 1964): 17; Takahiro Iwaki, "Heiho Mobilization and Local Administration in the Japanese Occupation Period: The Case of Pyapon District," in Kei Nemoto, *Reconsidering the Japanese Military Occupation in Burma (1942–45)*, 101–106.

20. *Burma Today* 1.4 (February 1944): 4, 12; 1.5 (March 1944): 4; 1.7 (May 1944): 1, 4, 10, 12; 1.8 (June 1944): 2; 1.9 (July 1944): 4.

21. GMR 11.11 (November 1964): 20; Clarence Hendershot, "Burma Compromise," *Far Eastern Survey* 16.12 (18 June 1947): 134; GMR 9.6 (June 1962): 16–17; *Times*, 31 May 1945, 5.

22. GMR 9.6 (June 1962): 18; 11.11 (November 1964): 20–21; Christopher Bayly and Tim Harper, *Forgotten Armies: The Fall of British Asia 1941–1945* (London: Allen Lane, 2004): 434.

23. *Times*, 16 August 1945, 3; 17 August 1945, 4; 29 August 1945, 4; 25 October 1945, 3.

24. PDC, 2 May 1947, 2357.

25. GMR 10.1 (January 1963): 30; 11.5 (May 1964): 37–38; 11.11 (November 1964): 18; *Burma Digest* 1.15 (15 October 1946): 10.

26. G. Appleton, "Burma Two Years After Liberation," *International Affairs* 23.4 (October 1947): 510–511; PDC 406, 12 December 1944, 1088; 421, 3 April 1946, 1536–1537; 2 May 1947, 2357, 2313; *Times*, 8 March 1946, 5.

27. Frank Gubb, "The Burmese People's Anti-Fascist Freedom League," *Burma Digest* 1.3 (March 1946): 19; Virginia Thompson, "The New Nation of Burma," *Far Eastern Survey* 17.7 (7 April 1948): 81; PDC 425, 8 July 1946, 19; *Times*, 22 May 1945, 4, 8.

28. Appleton, "Burma Two Years After Liberation," 514; Emile C. Foucar, *I lived in Burma* (London: DuFour, 1956): 187, 189.

29. Hendershot, "Burma Compromise," 133–134; Appleton, "Burma Two Years After Liberation," 512; Harold Roper, "Current Affairs in Burma," *Asiatic Review* 42.150 (April 1946): 115; Gubb, "The Burmese People's Anti-Fascist Freedom League," 18; U Set Kya, "Burma's Projects," *Burma Digest* 1.15 (15 October 1946): 7; *Times*, 15 May 1946, 3; Foucar, *I Lived in Burma*, 191–192; *Burma Today* 2.11 (October 1945): 7.

30. *Foreign Relations, 1946*, VIII, 2; Set Kya, "Burma's Projects," 6–7; Appleton, "Burma Two Years After Liberation," 514.

31. Sydney D. Bailey, "The Transfer of Power," GMR 1.12 (October 1954): 53; Hendershot, "Burma Compromise," 134; PDC 421, 5 April 1946, 1529–1530; *Times*, 24 October 1945, 4; 29 October 1945, 3.

32. *Foreign Affairs*, 1946, VIII, 3.

33. GMR 9.6 (June 1962): 18; Bailey, "The Transfer of Power," 53; Hendershot, "Burma Compromise," 134–135; *Times*, 3 June 1946, 4.

34. Hendershot, "Burma Compromise," 135–136; *Foreign Relations, 1946*, VIII, 4.

35. Thompson, "The New Nation of Burma," 81; Bailey, "The Transfer of Power," 53; Hendershot, "Burma Compromise," 136; GMR 9.6 (June 1962): 19; Cecil Hobbs, "Nationalism in British Colonial Burma," *Far Eastern Quarterly* 6.2 (February 1947): 119; *Times*, 2 January 1947, 5; 20 February 1947, 3.

36. Alice Thorner, "White Paper on Burma," *Far Eastern Survey* 14.11 (6 June 1945): 145.

37. Hendershot, "Burma Compromise," 136; *Times*, 2 January 1947, 5.

38. PDC 431, 20 December 1946, 2342; *Times*, 2 January 1947, 5; Bailey, "The Transfer of Power," 53; *Foreign Relations*, 1947, VI, 2; *Conclusions Reached in the Conversations Between His Majesty's Government and the Delegation from the Executive Council of the Governor of Burma* (London: HMSO, 1947): 2.

39. *Foreign Relations, 1947*, VI, 7–8, 13; Bailey, "The Transfer of Power," 53; *Times*, 20 February 1947, 3; PDC, 2 May 1947, 2335.

40. GMR 9.7 (July 1962): 13–14; Vum Ko Hau, "Nu–Attlee Treaty Was Signed," GMR 12 (October 1954): 49–50; *Times*, 9 April 1947, 5; 12 April 1947, 3.

41. *Times*, 28 March 1946, 3; 3 April 1946, 3; 10 February 1947, 4.

42. *Times*, 13 February 1947, 3; PDC, 2 May 1947, 2306–2307; Vum Ko Hau, "Nu–Attlee Treaty Was Signed," 49.

43. PDC 434, 3 March 1947, 18; PRDC, 2 May 1947, 2308; *Times*, 16 August 1947, 3.

44. *Foreign Relations, 1947*, VI, 46; PDC, 2 May 1947, 2308–2309; *Times*, 13 April 1947, 3; Taylor, *The State in Burma*, 243; Cady, *A History of Modern Burma*, 592.

45. *Foreign Relations, 1947*, VI, 44, 47.

46. Thompson, "The New Nation of Burma," 81; *Times*, 23 September 1946, 3; 12 April 1947, 3; *Foreign Relations*, 1947, VI, 3–4, 14.

47. *Times*, 31 October 1947, 3; PDC 443, 5 November 1947, 1848.

48. *Times*, 17 October 1947, 3; 18 October 1947, 3; Foucar, *I Lived in Burma*, 201; Vum Ko Hau, "The July Murders," GMR 1.9 (July 1954): 41; GMR 9.7 (July 1962): 14; GMR 24.10 (1 July 1986): 8–17; GMR 17 (August 1970): 32, 34; *Forward* 6.23 (15 July 1968): 7–8; *Time Magazine* 28 July 1947.

49. *Times*, 18 October 1947, 3; 31 October 1947, 3; Foucar, *I Lived in Burma*, 201–202; GMR 17 (August 1970): 32; *Foreign Relations, 1947*, VI, 38.

50. GMR 10.1 (January 1963): 31–32; *Times*, 26 July 1947, 3; 12 December 1947, 3; PDC 440, 867.

51. *Foreign Relations, 1947*, VI, 44; Vum Ko Hau, "Nu–Attlee Treaty Was Signed," 49–50; *Times*, 25 September 1947, 3; 18 October 1947, 3; Bailey, "The Transfer of Power," 53.

4 THE DEMOCRATIC EXPERIMENT, 1948–1958

1. Thant Myint-U, *The River of Lost Footsteps*, 259.
2. Taylor, *The State in Burma*, 238–239; Martin Smith, *Burma: Insurgency and the Politics of Ethnicity* (London: Zed Books, 1999): 61, 67–68.
3. *Foreign Relations*, 1947, VI, 47; *Times*, 19 November 1947, 3; Taylor, *The State in Burma*, 241; Klaus Fleischmann, *Documents on Communism in Burma 1945–1977* (Hamburg: Institut für Asienkunde, 1989): 69.
4. Thompson, "The New Nation of Burma," 81; *FEER* 5.8 (25 August 1948): 173; *Times*, 25 November 1947, 3; Cady, *A History of Modern Burma*, 584, 588–589.
5. Taylor, *The State in Burma*, 236, 243; Cady, *A History of Modern Burma*, 592.
6. Thaung, *A Journalist, a General and an Army in Burma*, 15.
7. *Times*, 25 April 1961, 13.
8. GMR 5.8 (August 1958): 7, 9; John Hail, "A Blow to the Heartland," *FEER* 108.20 (9 May 1980): 39.
9. *Foreign Relations, 1951*, VI, 281; *IHT*, 15 February 1950.
10. Ba Chan, "A Women's Auxiliary Corps," GMR 1.2 (December 1953): 28; GMR 5.7 (July 1958): 37.
11. Taylor, *The State in Burma*, 268–270; James Dalton, "Babes in the Wood," *FEER* 69.34 (20 August 1970): 31.
12. *BWB* 5.48 (7 March 1957): 389.
13. Thant Myint-U, *The River of Lost Footsteps*, 275; Daniel Wolfstone, "The Burmese Army Experiment," *FEER* 28.7 (18 February 1960): 352.
14. Brian Crozier, "What Now for the Kuomintang?" *Times*, 10 October 1973, 18.
15. *Foreign Relations, 1952–1954*, XII, 367–376.
16. Ibid., 471–472.
17. Thant Myint-U, *The River of Lost Footsteps*, 269–270.
18. *Times*, 21 May 1947, 3; GMR 9.7 (July 1962): 14.
19. Foucar, *I Lived in Burma*, 204; *Times*, 3 November 1947, 4; PDC 443, 5 November 1947, 1851.
20. *FEER* 6.13 (30 March 1949): 399; *Times*, 24 September 1947, 3; *BWB* 4.35 (1 December 1955): 276.
21. Thant Myint-U, *The River of Lost Footsteps*, 272–273.

22. U Kyaw Nyein, "Burma's Eight Year Plan," GMR 3.1 (November 1955): 41; *Times*, 5 February 1960, 11; GMR 10.2 (January 1963): 29; *BWB* 4.36 (8 December 1955): 282; 4.37 (15 December 1955): 295.
23. *BWB* 6.9 (13 June 1957): 64.
24. *NBW* 1.2 (7 June 1958): 2.
25. *Foreign Relations*, 1947, VI, 47; Nu, "Consolidation of the AFPFL," 25 May 1948 broadcast, in *Toward Peace & Democracy* (Rangoon: Ministry of Information, 1949): 98–101.
26. Taylor, *The State in Burma*, 245, 247.
27. Ibid., 245, 247.
28. Maung Maung, *The 1988 Uprising in Burma* (New Haven, CT: Yale University Southeast Asia Studies, 1999): 17; *FEER* 20.21 (24 May 1956): 643; *BWB* 5.14 (12 July 1956): 97, 99.
29. *BWB* 5.20 (21 March 1957): 402.
30. *Foreign Relations*, 1947, VI, 47; Smith, *Burma: Insurgency and the Politics of Ethnicity*, 55.
31. Thaung, *A Journalist, a General and an Army in Burma*, 24–25.
32. Nu, "Acts of Lawlessness," 12 March 1948 broadcast and "The Newspapers and the Law," in *Toward Peace & Democracy*, 46–49; GMR 3.8 (June 1956): 40.
33. *BWB* 5.20 (23 August 1956): 145.
34. Michael W. Charney, "Ludu Aung Than: Nu's Burma and the Cold War," in Christopher Goscha and Christian Ostermann (eds.), *Imperial Retreat and the Cold War in South and Southeast Asia (1945–1962)*, forthcoming.
35. E. Michael Mendelson, *Sangha and State in Burma: A Study of Monastic Sectarianism and Leadership* (Ithaca, NY: Cornell University Press, 1975): 263.
36. Smith, *Religion and Politics in Burma*, 117; James Joseph Dalton, "The 1,000-Year Struggle," *FEER* 67.10 (5 March 1970): 19; *Foreign Relations*, 1947, VI, 24, 26.
37. *BWB* 3.26 (29 September 1954): 200; 10.19 (7 September 1961): 148.
38. *BWB* 10.18 (31 August 1961): 137; Smith, *Religion and Politics in Burma*, 117–119, 121, 127.
39. GMR 5.6 (June 1958): 9; *Times*, 5 February 1960, 11.
40. U Sein Win, *The Split Story: An Account of Recent Political Upheaval in Burma* (Rangoon: The Guardian Press, 1959): 79–83; Wolfstone, "The Burmese Army Experiment," 356; Taylor, *The State in Burma*, 248; *NBW* 4.6 (7 February 1959): 190; GMR 5.8 (August 1958): 7, 10; 5.10 (October 1958): 10; 6.3 (March 1959): 6; 7.8 (August 1958): 10; *Times*, 5 February 1960, 11.

5 DRESS REHEARSALS, 1958–1962

1. *NBW* 2.7 (4 October 1958): 214; *Times*, 5 February 1960, 11; *Time Magazine* (6 October 1958).
2. *NBW* 2.8 (11 October 1958): 242.

3. Wolfstone, "The Burmese Army Experiment," 357; GMR 5.12 (December 1958): 10; *NBW* 3.6 (20 December 1958): 165; 4.1 (3 January 1959): 4; 4.7 (14 February 1959): 228.

4. *Times*, 5 February 1960, 11; GMR 6.10 (October 1959): 8; 7.7 (July 1960): 12; *BWB* 8.6 (4 June 1959): 49–50; 8.8 (18 June 1959): 67; 8.14 (30 July 1959): 119.

5. Wolfstone, "The Burmese Army Experiment," 357; GMR 6.5 (May 1959): 6; 6.10 (October 1959): 8; GNR, 21 August 1959; *BWB* 8.6 (4 June 1959): 49; 8.8 (18 June 1959): 67; 8.14 (30 July 1959): 119.

6. Keith Dahlberg, "Remembering the Coup," *Irrawaddy* (July–August 2002); *Myanmar Times* 4.70 (2–8 July 2001); *NBW* 3.4 (6 December 1958): 1001; GMR 6.1 (January 1959): 7; *Who's Who in Burma 1961*, 150.

7. GMR 6.1 (January 1959): 7; 6.5 (May 1959): 6; 6.10 (October 1959): 8; *NBW* 1.6 (20 December 1958): 166; *Times*, 5 February 1960, 11; Albert Ravenholt, "Burma Army Gives Rangoon New Face," *BWB* 8.14 (30 July 1959): 118.

8. Ravenholt, "Burma Army Gives Rangoon New Face," 118; GMR 6.1 (January 1959): 7, 9–11; *NBW* 1.6 (20 December 1958): 166; 4.1 (3 January 1959): 4–5.

9. GMR 6.1 (January 1959): 7, 10; *NBW* 1.6 (20 December 1958): 166; 4.1 (3 January 1959): 4.

10. *NBW* 4.1 (3 January 1959): 4; GMR 6.1 (January 1959): 7; 6.10 (October 1959): 8; Ravenholt, "Burma Army Gives Rangoon New Face," 119; Wolfstone, "The Burmese Army Experiment," 357.

11. GMR 6.1 (January 1959): 10; 6.10 (October 1959): 8; *NBW* 1.6 (20 December 1958): 166; 4.8 (21 February 1959): 263.

12. *Times*, 5 February 1960, 11; GMR 6.1 (January 1959): 7, 9, 10; *BWB* 8.8 (18 June 1959): 66; 8.14 (30 July 1959): 119; *NBW* 3.4 (6 December 1958): 100; 3.5 (13 December 1958): 134.

13. *NBW* 4.1 (3 January 1959): 5; GMR 6.1 (January 1959): 10–12; Wolfstone, "The Burmese Army Experiment," 357–358; *BWB* 8.8 (18 June 1959): 66; *Nation* 21 August 1959.

14. *NBW* 4.8 (21 February 1959): 262; 4.9 (28 February 1959): 294; GMR 6.12 (February 1959): 9; *Times*, 5 February 1960, 11.

15. *Times*, 5 February 1960, 11; *NBW* 4.8 (21 February 1959): 262; GMR 7.2 (February 1960): 15; 7.3 (March 1960): 12; Steinberg, *Burma: A Socialist Nation of Southeast Asia*, 71–72.

16. GMR 7.5 (May 1960): 18; 7.7 (July 1960): 11; 7.8 (August 1960): 10; 8.1 (January 1961): 11; *BWB* 8.50 (7 April 1960): 456; *Times*, 8 February 1960, 9.

17. *BWB* 10.18 (31 August 1961): 144; 10.19 (7 September 1961): 147.

18. Daniel Wolfstone, "The Phongyis and the Soldiers," *FEER* 33.7 (17 August 1961): 322; *FEER* 35.10 (8 March 1962): 539; Steinberg, *Burma: A Socialist Nation of Southeast Asia*, 72; GMR 8.8 (August 1961): 6.

19. Smith, *Religion and Politics in Burma*, 133, 135.

20. *BWB* 8.50 (7 April 1960): 456; 10.18 (31 August 1961): 138; GMR 7.1 (January 1960): 10–12; 7.5 (May 1960): 18–19; *Times*, 5 February 1960, 11.

21. GMR 8.5 (May 1961): 10; 8.10 (October 1961): 11; Wolfstone, "The Phongyis and the Soldiers," 323.

22. GMR 8.3 (March 1961): 6; 8.9 (September 1961): 6; *BWB* 10.18 (31 August 1961): 138.
23. Smith, *Religion and Politics in Burma*, 275; *BWB* 10.18 (31 August 1961): 139, 140, 144; 10.19 (7 September 1961): 149; GMR 8.12 (December 1961): 9.
24. Smith, *Religion and Politics in Burma*, 171, 278–279; GMR 8.12 (December 1961): 6; 9.2 (February 1962): 9.
25. *BWB* 10.14 (3 August 1961): 105; 10.20 (14 September 1961): 160; GMR 9.1 (January 1962): 6, 10; 5.10 (October 1958): 10; 5.12 (December 1958): 10; 7.2 (February 1960): 14; *NBW* 3.6 (20 December 1958): 161; *GNR*, 20 August 1959; *Time Magazine* (15 February 1960).
26. GMR 7.7 (July 1960): 11; 8.1 (January 1961): 11; 8.12 (December 1961): 10–11; Daniel Wolfstone, "Colonels in the Economy," *FEER* 33.7 (17 August 1961): 296; Taylor, *The State in Burma*, 257.
27. GMR 8.12 (December 1961): 11; 9.1 (January 1962): 9; *FEER* 35.10 (8 March 1962): 539; S. C. Banerji, "Nationalising Import Trade," *FEER* 35.10 (8 March 1962): 547–550; *Forward* 1.4 (22 September 1962): 14.

6 THE REVOLUTIONARY COUNCIL

1. James L. Dalton, "One Man's Tears," *FEER* 65.38 (18 September 1969): 733; *BWB* 10.42 (8 March 1962): 386–387, 391; *Times*, 3 March 1962, 8; 5 March 1962, 8.
2. *Times*, 3 March 1962, 8; *BWB* 10.46 (15 March 1962): 395, 398.
3. GMR 9.7 (July 1962): 29–31.
4. Ibid.
5. S. C. Banerji, "The Burmese Way," *FEER* 37.6 (9 August 1962): 248.
6. *Forward* 1.1 (7 August 1962): 6.
7. GMR 9.7 (July 1962): 8; 10.11 (November 1963): 6; 11.3 (March 1964): 8; *Times*, 10 August 1963, 5; 30 March 1964, 11; *Forward* 2.17 (7 April 1964): 2; 3.10 (1 January 1965): 29; James Dalton, "Babes in the Wood," *FEER* 69.34 (20 August 1970): 31.
8. Thaung, *A Journalist, a General and an Army in Burma*, 51; *BWB* 10.52 (12 April 1962): 427.
9. Smith, *Religion and Politics in Burma*, 295; *Forward* 1.4 (22 September 1962): 2.
10. *BWB* 10.47 (22 March 1962): 407; *Times*, 16 March 1962, 9; GMR 9.7 (July 1962): 6.
11. *Forward* 2.5 (7 October 1963): 7.
12. Smith, *Religion and Politics in Burma*, 294; *Forward* 1.16 (22 March 1963): 3; 1.22 (22 June 1963): 6; 2.1 (7 August 1963): 23; 2.11 (7 January 1964): 17; GMR 10.7 (July 1963): 9.
13. GMR 10.5 (May 1963): 9; 11.3 (March 1964): 8; *Times*, 10 August 1963, 5; Bertil Lintner, "Proud Past, Sad Present," *FEER* 127.12 (28 March 1985): 38–39; *Forward* 7.13 (15 February 1969): 6; 7.16 (1 April 1969): 3.

14. *Forward* 1.5 (7 October 1962): 22, 23; GMR 9.12 (December 1962): 9; Thaung, *A Journalist, a General and an Army in Burma*, 57.

15. Lintner, "Proud Past," 38–39; Maung Wun Tha, "Journalists Go to School," *Forward* 7.6 (1 November 1968): 13; *Forward* 6.10 (1 January 1968): 2; GMR 15.8 (August 1968): 4–5.

16. GMR 11.9 (September 1964): 6; 11.10 (October 1964): 6; 12.2 (February 1965): 6; 14.6 (June 1967): 6; *Forward* 3.8 (1 December 1964): 4.

17. *Forward* 5.9 (15 December 1966): 3; 5.10 (1 January 1967): 23–24.

18. *Forward* 1.9 (7 December 1962): 22; 2.11 (7 January 1964): 18; GMR 9.9 (September 1962): 9, 10; 9.12 (December 1962): 7; 11.3 (March 1964): 9.

19. GMR 13.1 (January 1966): 6; *Forward* 1.9 (7 December 1962): 22; 4.7 (15 November 1965): 2–3; 6.23 (15 July 1968): 4; 7.10 (1 January 1969): 2; 7.17 (15 April 1969): 9; 7.24 (1 August 1969): 7.

20. Christina Fink, *Living Silence: Burma Under Military Rule* (Bangkok: White Lotus, 2001): 31; *Times*, 12 May 1962, 6; 9 July 1962, 8.

21. RHS, 23, 25, 26 July 1988, BBCSWB.

22. Jon Wiant, "Tradition in the Service of Revolution: The Political Symbolism of the Taw-hlan-ye-khit," in F. K. Lehman (ed.), *Military Rule in Burma Since 1962: Kaleidoscope of Views* (Singapore: Maruzen Asia, 1991): 63.

23. Smith, *Religion and Politics in Burma*, 283–286; James Joseph Dalton, "The 1,000-Year Struggle," 19; *BWB* 10.46 (15 March 1962): 395, 398; GMR 9.7 (July 1962): 6.

24. Smith, *Religion and Politics in Burma*, 301–302; *Forward* 3.3 (15 September 1964): 2–3; Dalton, "The 1,000-Year Struggle," 19; John Ashdown, "Burma's Political Puzzle," *FEER* 44.12 (17 September 1964): 516.

25. *Asian Recorder* 10.38 (16–22 September 1964): 6039; GMR 11.10 (October 1964): 7; 12.2 (February 1965): 6; *Forward* 3.3 (15 September 1964): 3; P. H. M. Jones, "Burmese Deadlock," *FEER* 47.12 (25 March 1965): 561; Smith, *Religion and Politics in Burma*, 303–304; Dalton, "The 1,000-Year Struggle," 19–20.

26. *Forward* 3.3 (15 September 1964): 2; 3.12 (1 February 1965): 2; Smith, *Religion and Politics in Burma*, 305; Dalton, "The 1,000-Year Struggle," 45; Sterling Seagrave, "The Minorities Unite," *FEER* 70.45 (7 November 1970): 39; GMR 12.4 (April 1965): 4; Wiant, "Tradition in the Service of Revolution," 63.

27. Seagrave, "The Minorities Unite," 39; Dalton, "The 1,000-Year Struggle," 20; Jones, "Burmese Deadlock," 561; GMR 12.5 (May 1965): 6; *Forward* 3.19 (15 May 1965): 2; *Time Magazine* 3 June 1966.

28. Smith, *Religion and Politics in Burma*, 306.

29. *FEER* 57.5 (3 August 1967): 227; Maung Maung, *Burma and General Ne Win* (London: Asia Publishing House, 1969) 149; *Times*, 16 February 1963, 6.

30. S. C. Banerji, "Industrial Plans," *FEER* 36.4 (26 April 1962): 74; *Forward* 1.1 (7 August 1962): 3–4, 15–17; 1.2 (22 August 1962): 3–4; 1.3 (7 September 1962): 3; 1.5 (7 October 1962): 9, 11; GMR 9.10 (October 1962): 9.

31. Maung Maung, *Burma and General Ne Win*, 145, 149, 155, 166, 255, 260; John F. Cady, *The United States and Burma* (Cambridge, MA: Harvard University Press): 239; Jones, "Burmese Deadlock," 561.

32. RHS, 22 April 1990, BBCSWB.

33. *Forward* 1.1 (7 August 1962): 3–4; 1.2 (22 August 1962): 4; 1.3 (7 September 1962): 2; GMR 9.8 (August 1962): 8; 9.10 (October 1962): 10.

34. *The System of Correlation of Man and His Environment* (Rangoon: Union of Burma, 1963).

35. *Times*, 11 February 1963, 9; GMR 11.6 (June 1964): 8; *FEER* 48.11 (10 June 1965): 495; 57.5 (3 August 1967): 227; Jones, "Burmese Deadlock," 561; *Forward* 3.22 (1 July 1969): 22.

36. Jones, "Burmese Deadlock," 561; *Times*, 16 February 1963, 6; 16 March 1963, 9; Kennedy Library, National Security Files, Countries Series, India, "Krishnamachari Visit." *Foreign Relations* 1961–1963, XIX, 601; *Forward* 3.10 (1 January 1965): 27.

37. *FEER* 81.27 (9 July 1973): 18; Jones, "Burmese Deadlock," 561; *Forward* 3.18 (1 May 1965): 2; 7.10 (1 January 1969): 2; 10.14 (1 March 1972): 7; GMR 13.2 (February 1966): 4; *Times*, 16 February 1963, 6; 3 March 1965, 10.

38. GMR 12.11 (November 1965): 8; *FEER* 50.5 (4 November 1965): 194; *Time Magazine* 24 December 1966.

39. *Forward* 2.24 (1 August 1964): 22; 8.24 (1 August 1970): 2; 8.10 (1 January 1979): 2; *Times*, 3 March 1966, 11; *FEER* 81.27 (9 July 1973): 18; "A Political Alert," *FEER* 63.3 (16 January 1969): 106; Than Win Naing, "Spearheading Agricultural Mechanization," *Forward* 8.19 (15 May 1970): 15; Maung Yin New, "Of Growing More Rice," *Forward* 8.10 (1 January 1970): 19–21.

40. *Times*, 2 April 1963, 9; 28 June 1963, 11; 8 October 1963, 13; 25 November 1963, 8.

41. Robert A. Holmes, "Burmese Domestic Policy: The Politics of Burmanization," *Asian Survey* 7.3 (March 1967): 193–194, 196; Taylor, *The State in Burma*, 335; Frank N. Trager, "Burma: 1967 – A Better Ending Than a Beginning," *Asian Survey* 8.2 (February 1968): 112–113; *Times*, 28 June 1963, 11; 21 August 1963, 6; 8 October 1963, 13.

42. Smith, *Burma: Insurgency and the Politics of Ethnicity*, 231–234; VOPB, 15 June 1986, BBCSWB; Bertil Lintner, *The Rise and Fall of the Communist Party of Burma (CPB)* (Ithaca, NY: Cornell University Press Southeast Asia Program, 1990): 23; S. C. Banerji, "Buddha Awakes," *FEER* 69.35 (27 August 1970): 15; Silverstein, "Minority Problems Since 1962," 57; *FEER* 57.5 (3 August 1967): 227; *Financial Times*, 17 February 1987, 3; *Times*, 19 January 1968, 3; Frank N. Trager, "Burma: 1968 – A New Beginning?" *Asian Survey* 9.2 (February 1969): 106.

43. *FEER* 57.5 (3 August 1967): 227.

44. Neil Kelly, "Thais Put Price on Head of Drugs Chief," *Times*, 30 June 1981, 5.

45. Kelly, "Thais Put Price on Head of Drugs Chief," 5; Melinda Yu, "Warlords, Rebels, and Smugglers," *FEER* 105.35 (31 August 1979): 13; *FEER* 81.27 (9 July 1973): 19; Smith, *Burma: Insurgency and the Politics of Ethnicity*, 297.

46. Kelly, "Thais Put Price on Head of Drugs Chief," 5; Smith, *Burma: Insurgency and the Politics of Ethnicity*, 95–96, 221, 335.
47. *Times*, 23 February 1974, 6; Silverstein, "Minority Problems in Burma Since 1962," 58; Henry Kamm, "Burmese Fighting Rebels on Four Fronts," *Times*, 15 August 1980, 5.
48. *Times*, 28 October 1966, 14; *FEER* 57.5 (3 August 1967): 227; 63.3 (16 January 1969): 105; S. C. Banerji, "The Nu Burmese Way," *FEER* 64.26 (26 June 1969): 698; *FEER* 65.29 (17 July 1969): 151; Richard Harris, "U Nu Says Burmese Regime Must Go," *Times*, 30 August 1969, 4.
49. *FEER* 64.20 (15 May 1969): 374; *Times*, 28 April 1971, 9; Seagrave, "The Minorities Unite," 38.
50. *Times*, 28 April 1971, 9; Seagrave, "The Minorities Unite," 38–39.
51. *Forward* 9.7 (15 November 1970): 3.
52. Seagrave, "The Minorities Unite," 37; M. C. Tun, "Trouble at Home," *FEER* 78.46 (11 November 1972): 17; *FEER* 81.27 (9 July 1973): 18.

7 THE BSPP YEARS

1. *Times*, 3 March 1966, 11; *Forward* 8.12 (1 February 1970): 2; GMR 17.2 (February 1970): 12.
2. David I. Steinberg, *Burma: The State of Myanmar* (Washington, D.C.: Georgetown University Press, 2001): 100.
3. Maung Lu Law, "A Historic Decade," GMR 19.5 (May 1972): 42; GMR 17.2 (February 1970): 12; *Forward* 8.10 (1 January 1979): 2; 8.12 (1 February 1970): 2; 10.14 (1 March 1972): 6.
4. Richard Harris, "Burma on a Slow Road to Progress," *Times*, 30 April 1974, 16; *Times*, 30 June 1971, 8; M. C. Tun, "Change of Status," *FEER* 81.36 (10 September 1973): 24–25.
5. Jon A. Wiant, "Burma: Loosening Up on the Tiger's Tail," *Asian Survey* 13.2 (February 1973): 180; Harris, "Burma on a Slow Road to Progress," 16; John McBeth and M. C. Tun, "Goodbye to the Good Life," *FEER* 120.22 (2 June 1983): 15.
6. Harris, "Burma on a Slow Road to Progress," 16; *Times*, 24 October 1973, 6; 24 December 1973, 4; *Forward* 10.19 (15 May 1972): 7–10.
7. GMR 19.4 (April 1972): 4–5; *PWG* 26.9 (September 1973): 2.
8. *PWG* 26.9 (September 1973): 2.
9. *Times*, 24 October 1973, 6; 24 December 1973, 4; 4 March 1974, 7.
10. *FEER* 57.5 (3 August 1967): 227; 63.3 (16 January 1969): 105; Cady, *United States and Burma*, 265, 272.
11. *Forward* 11.11 (5 January 1971): 1; 11.12 (1 February 1973): 6; M. C. Tun, "Out of the Frying Pan," *FEER* 79.3 (22 January 1973).
12. S. C. Banerji, "Lack of Cooperation," *FEER* 83.6 (11 February 1974): 40; M. C. Tun, "Turning Against the Socialist Way," *FEER* 85.26 (1 July 1974): 30; M. C. Tun, "Feeding Unrest in Burma," *FEER* 85.31 (9 August 1974): 36; *Times*, 21 December 1974, 4.

13. Tun, "Turning Against the Socialist Way," 30; Denzil Peiris, "Socialism Without Commitment," *FEER* 85.36 (13 September 1974): 27–28; *Times*, 10 June 1974, 8.

14. *Times*, 1 July 1974, 5; *Forward* 12.11 (1 August 1974): 4–6; *FEER* 85.36 (13 September 1974): 47.

15. *Times*, 9 December 1974, 7; 12 December 1974, 6; 13 December 1974, 10; 4 January 1975, 4; 14 May 1975, 5.

16. M. C. Tun, "Five Fiery Days," *FEER* 88.26 (27 June 1975): 20; *Forward* 13.10 (1 July 1975): 3; *Times*, 25 March 1976, 8; 2 September 1976, 5.

17. *Times*, 2 December 1981, 8; Wiant, "Tradition in the Service of Revolution," 64.

18. *Times*, 21 July 1976, 6; Rodney Tasker, "The Power Game," *FEER* (7 July 1983): 31; M. C. Tun, "Purge Points to a Power Struggle," *FEER* 98.51 (23 December 1977): 24–25.

19. *Times*, 22 February 1977, 7; 28 February 1977, 6; 30 March 1977, 9; Tasker, "The Power Game," 31; Tun, "Purge Points to a Power Struggle," 24.

20. *Times*, 16 November 1977, 13; 18 January 1978, 7; 4 March 1978, 4; 10 November 1981, 7.

21. *Times*, 29 June 1983, 5; Neil Kelly, "London Spree Leads to Burma Purge," *Times*, 19 July 1983, 7; Neil Kelly, "Burmese Tipped to Succeed Ne Win is Jailed for Life," *Times*, 15 November 1983, 5.

22. *Times*, 10 October 1983, 1; 11 October 1983, 5; 12 October 1983, 15; Kelly, "Burmese Tipped to Succeed Ne Win is Jailed for Life," 5; Neil Kelly, "Burma Cuts Links With N. Korea," *Times*, 5 November 1983, 5.

23. *Times*, 3 December 1981, 9; RHS, 8 October 1982, BBCSWB.

24. RHS, 8 October 1982, BBCSWB.

25. Bertil Lintner, "Loss and Exile," *FEER* 158.9 (2 March 1995): 23; Smith, *Burma: Insurgency and the Politics of Ethnicity*, 280, 284, 298–299; *Times*, 13 February 1964, 13; 14 March 1964, 7.

26. *Nation* (Bangkok), 14 July 1986, BBCSWB; *Times*, 2 June 1976, 5; Paisal Sricharatchanya, "Choosing Losing Sides," *FEER* 134.50 (11 December 1986): 33; Smith, *Burma: Insurgency and the Politics of Ethnicity*, 280.

27. Martin Smith, "Karen War Strikes an Impasse," GUK, 18 June 1986; Neil Kelly, "Key Rebel Base Falls to Burma," *Times*, 9 May 1986.

28. Kelly, "Thais Put Price on Head of Drugs Chief," 5; Neil Kelly, "Drive Against Narcotics," *Times*, 13 August 1981, 5; Neil Kelly, "Thais Tame Warlord's Town," *Times*, 8 February 1982, 6; Neil Kelly, "Warlord's Heroin Base Seized," *Times*, 24 August 1983, 4; *Times*, 6 August 1984, 5; Smith, *Burma: Insurgency and the Politics of Ethnicity*, 315, 343.

29. *Times*, 13 September 1976, 15; 17 March 1977, 7; 21 October 1980, 5; *Forward* 26.3 (1 December 1987): 1; 25.11 (1 August 1987): 1.

30. *FEER* 131.1 (2 January 1986): 9; Paisal Sricharatchanya, "Isolation Patient," *FEER* 132.16 (17 April 1986): 114, 115, 118; *Times*, 7 November 1985, 8; Alan Hamilton, "When Money Turns into Confetti," *Times*, 19 November 1985, 36.

31. Anatol Lieven, "Economic Ills Fuel Riots," *Times*, 25 June 1988; Chit Tun, "Burma Property Curbs," *FT*, 19 March 1987, 4; RHS, 1 September 1987, BBCSWB.

32. RHS, 5 September 1987, 9 October 1987, 19 October 1987, 28 October 1987, 2 February 1988, BBCSWB; Kuala Lumpur Radio, 6 September 1987, BBC-SWB; Lieven, "Economic Ills Fuel Riots."

33. *Xinhua* (English), 14 March 1988, BBCSWB.

34. RHS, 27 March 1988, 20 April 1988, 24 May 1988, 3 July 1988, BBCSWB; Dennis Barker, "Top Gun Fuels Burma Riots," GUK, 12 August 1988, 2.

8 TOWARD DEMOCRACY, 1988–1990

1. Maung Maung, *The 1988 Uprising in Burma*, 1.

2. Bertil Lintner, *Outrage: Burma's Struggle for Democracy* (London: White Lotus, 1990): 1–7; RHS, 14, 15, 17 March 1988, BBCSWB; Chit Tun, "Burmese Shortages Spark Surge of Discontent," *FT*, 14 July 1988, 3.

3. *Times*, 20 July 1988; Chit Tun, "Burmese Minister Quits Over Police Van Deaths," *FT*, 21 July 1988, 4; RHS, 19 March 1988, BBCSWB; Chit Tun, "Burmese Shortages Spark Surge of Discontent," 3.

4. Lintner, *Outrage*, 75–77; Agence France-Presse, 16 June 1988, BBCSWB; *Xinhua* (English), 16 June and 18 June 1988, BBCSWB; Nick Cumming-Bruce, "Burma Puts City Under Martial Law," GUK, 23 July 1988; Chit Tun, "Burmese Shortages Spark Surge of Discontent," *FT*, 14 July 1988, 3; RHS, 20, 21 and 22 June 1988, BBCSWB; *FT*, 24 June 1988, 1.

5. Chit Tun, "Burmese Shortages Spark Surge of Discontent," 3; Anatol Lieven, "Economic Ills Fuel Riots," *Times*, 25 June 1988.

6. RHS, 7, 9, 13, 22, 23, 24 July 1988, BBCSWB; John Miller, "Ne Win Offers to Step Down," *Times*, 24 July 1988.

7. RHS, 24 July 1988, BBCSWB.

8. RHS, 23 July 1988, BBCSWB; Miller, "Ne Win Offers to Step Down."

9. RHS, 23, 25, 26 July 1988, BBCSWB.

10. RHS, 26 July 1988, BBCSWB; Barker, "Top Gun Fuels Burma Riots"; *Times*, 28 July 1988.

11. RHS, 1, 3 August 1988, BBCSWB; Neil Kelly and Anatol Lieven, "Martial Law Declared," *Times*, 4 August 1988; Nick Cumming-Bruce, "Burma's New Leader Imposes Martial Law," *GUK*, 4 August 1988.

12. RHS, 23, 25 July 1988, BBCSWB.

13. Neil Kelly, "Warning Shots Fired," *Times*, 5 August 1988; Various, 8 August 1988, BBCSWB; Neil Kelly, "Burma Rioters Killed," *Times*, 8 August 1988; Various, 9 August 1988, BBCSWB; RHS, 8, 9 August 1988, BBCSWB; Nicholas Cumming-Bruce, "At Least 36 Die," GUK, 10 August 1988.

14. Richard Gourlay, "Burmese Protestors Open Fire on Troops," *FT*, 11 August 1988; RHS, 7, 9, 10, 12, 13 August 1988, BBCSWB; Neil Kelly, "1,000 Die," *Times*, 12 August 1988; Richard Gourlay, "Troops Killed 3,000 in Rangoon Rioting," *FT*, 18 August 1988.

15. RHS, 19 August 1988, BBCSWB.
16. Neil Kelly, "Dr. Maung Maung Elected President of Burma," *Times*, 20 August 1988; Richard Gourlay, "Dismay Greets General Ne Win Surrogate," *FT*, 20 August 1988, 3; RHS, 19 August 1988, 22 August 1988, BBCSWB.
17. RHS, 23, 24 August 1988, BBCSWB; Richard Gourlay, "Burmese Reject Slow Change," *FT*, 26 August 1988, 16.
18. Roger Matthews, "The Monday Interview: An Inheritance by Election," *FT*, 24 October 1988; Nicholas Cumming-Bruce, "Burmese Hero's Daughter Puts Democracy Plan," GUK, 18 August 1988; Karan Thapar, "People's Heroine Spells Out Objectives," *Times*, 29 August 1988.
19. Nicholas Cumming-Bruce, "Burma Party Faces Strike Ultimatum," GUK, 6 September 1988; RHS, 7, 8 September 1988, BBCSWB; Neil Kelly, "Vigilantes Lynch Rangoon Looters; Savage Lawlessness Could Help Rangoon Regime," *Times*, 7 September 1988; Richard Gourlay, "Burma in Confusion as Neither Side Ready to Yield," *FT*, 8 September 1988, 3.
20. RHS, 10, 11 September 1988, BBCSWB.
21. RHS, 1, 10 September 1988, BBCSWB.
22. RHS, 10 September 1988, BBCSWB.
23. RHS, 10 September 1988, BBCSWB.
24. Maung Maung, *The 1988 Uprising in Burma*, 117.
25. RHS, 10 September 1988, BBCSWB.
26. *Times*, 30 July 1980, 7.
27. RHS, 17 November, 29 December 1989, BBCSWB; Martin Smith, "Move to Democracy in Burma 'Unstoppable'," GUK, 5 September 1988; the quote from Nu is take from Anatol Lieven, "Opposition in Burma Sets Up 'Government'," *Times*, 10 September 1988; Jon Swain, "Burmese Students Win Their Fight for a General Election," *Times*, 11 September 1988.
28. RHS, 13 September 1988, BBCSWB; Nick Cumming-Bruce, "Burma Opposition Rejects Regime Offer of Elections," GUK, 13 September 1988; Neil Kelly, "Opposition Unmoved by Burmese Election Offer," *Times*, 12 September 1988.
29. RHS, 16 September 1988, BBCSWB.
30. Lintner, *Outrage*, 128; *Times*, 18 September 1988.
31. *Times*, 10 September 1988; 18 September 1988.
32. Mya Maung, "The Burma Road From the Union of Burma to Myanmar," *Asian Survey* 30.6 (June 1990): 617; RHS, 18, 19 September 1988, BBCSWB.
33. RHS, 18, 19, 20, 21 September 1988, BBCSWB.
34. RHS, 26 September 1988, BBCSWB.
35. These four tasks are taken verbatim from Saw Maung's speech to the Institute for the Development of National Groups recorded in RHS, 1 March 1989, BBCSWB; see also Mya Maung, "The Burma Road From the Union of Burma to Myanmar," 618.
36. Sein Win, "Troops Shoot 12 in Rangoon," *Independent*, 5 October 1988; RHS, 19 October, 9, 11 November 1988, BBCSWB; Mya Maung, "The Burma Road From the Union of Burma to Myanmar," 617.

37. RHS, 11 November 1988, BBCSWB.
38. RHS, 27 September, 20 October 1988, 3, 14, 16 November, 7 December 1988, 18, 19 January 1989, 23 February 1989, BBCSWB; Neil Kelly, "Intelligence Chief Emerging as Burma's Leader," *Times*, 23 January 1989; Mya Maung, "The Burma Road From the Union of Burma to Myanmar," 617–618.
39. AFP, 3 October 1988, BBCSWB; RHS, 3 November 1988, BBCSWB; Neil Kelly, "Rebels Train Students for a Burma Offensive," *Times*, 1 October 1988; *Bangkok Post*, 10 October 1988; 6 November 1988.
40. RHS, 17, 24 October 1988, 3 February 1989, BBCSWB; Terry McCarthy, "Rangoon Pressed on Fate of Students," *Independent*, 7 January 1989.
41. RHS, 20 January 1989, BBCSWB.
42. RHS, 16, 17 February, 7 November 1989, BBCSWB; GUK, 2 March 1989.
43. RHS, 20 January, 9 February, 1 March 1989, BBCSWB.
44. RHS, 26 September, 11, 14 October 1988, BBCSWB; Donald M. Seekins, *Historical Dictionary of Burma (Myanmar)* (Oxford: The Scarecrow Press, 2006): 128, 326.
45. Bertil Lintner, *Burma in Revolt: Opium and Insurgency since 1948* (Boulder, CO: Westview Press, 1994): 283.
46. *Xinhua*, 27 September 1988 and RHS, 12, 28 September 1988, BBCSWB; Roger Matthews, "Opposition in Burma Set up Political Party," *FT*, 28 September 1988; *Times*, 10 September 1988.
47. RHS, 10 August, 16 December 1989, BBCSWB; Japan Broadcasting Corporation (NHK), 1 September 1988, BBCSWB; *Loktha Pyithu Nezin*, 16 March 1989, BBCSWB.
48. GUK, 25 January 1989; 2 March 1989; Terry McCarthy, "Burmese Dissident Cheats Death," *Independent*, 13 April 1989; Terry McCarthy, "Aung San Suu Kyi Appeals to Burmese Army," *Independent*, 19 April 1989.
49. Jon Swain, "General Jailed," *Times*, 24 December 1989; RHS, 21 July, 5, 18 August 1989, BBCSWB; *NYT*, 13 August 1989; *Independent*, 29 July 1989; Martin Smith, "Suu Kyi Ends Protest Fast," *GUK*, 15 August 1989.
50. RHS, 11 January, 18 July 1989, BBCSWB.
51. RHS, 18 August, 16 November 1989, BBCSWB; *FT*, 9 January 1990; Chit Tun, "Burma's Suu Kyi Wins Poll Ruling," *FT*, 16 January 1990; Terry McCarthy, "Rangoon Bars Opposition Leader," *Independent*, 30 January 1990.
52. Chit Tun, "Burma Outlaws Privileges for Ousted Military Men," *FT*, 11 October 1989; RHS, 26 May 1990, BBCSWB; *NYT*, 10 May 1990.
53. Khin Kyaw Han, "1990 Multi-Party Democracy General Elections"; Robin Pauley, "Burma's Army Leaders Seek to Keep Election Victor from Power," *FT*, 16 June 1990; *Independent*, 25 May 1990; AFP, 16 May 1990, BBCSWB; RHS, 30 May 1990, BBCSWB.

9 PERPETUAL DELAY, 1990 TO THE PRESENT

1. RHS, 19 October 1988, BBCSWB.
2. *Times*, 3 June 1989; RHS, 26 May, 18 June 1989, BBCSWB.

3. RHS, 18 June 1989, BBCSWB.
4. RHS, 29 April, 30 May, 18 June 1990, BBCSWB.
5. Roger Matthews, "Burma's Rulers Show Their Hand," *FT*, 21 June 1990; RHS, 8, 10 August 1990, BBCSWB; *NYT*, 9 August 1990.
6. Matthews, "Burma's Rulers Show Their Hand"; RHS, 13 July, 27 July 1990, BBCSWB; *Independent*, 28 July 1990.
7. RHS, 13 July 1990, 27 August 1990, BBCSWB.
8. David I. Steinberg, "Myanmar in 1992: Plus Ça Change . . . ?," *Asian Survey* 33.2 (1993): 178–179; VOM, 2, 6, 8, and 25 January, 2 and 13 February 1992, BBCSWB.
9. Steinberg, "Myanmar in 1992," 178–179.
10. VOM, 27 January 1992, BBCSWB.
11. VOM, 28 January 1992, BBCSWB.
12. Bertil Lintner and Rodney Tasker, "General Malaise," *FEER* 155.6 (13 February 1992): 15; Steinberg, "Myanmar in 1992," 176; Jon Swain, "General Jailed," *Times*, 24 December 1989; Abby Tan, "Lecturers Among Thousands Sacked," *Times*, 10 April 1992.
13. Lintner and Tasker, "General Malaise," 15.
14. RHS, 23 March 1992, BBCSWB; Steinberg, "Myanmar in 1992," 176; Bertil Lintner, "Army Divisions," FEER (23 April 1992): 16; Steinberg, "Myanmar in 1992," 176; Bertil Lintner, "Flanking Movement," FEER 155.41 (15 October 1992): 20.
15. Steinberg, "Myanmar in 1992," 176–177.
16. *VOM*, 27 January 1992, BBCSWB; Abby Tan, "Lecturers Among Thousands Sacked"; Steinberg, "Myanmar in 1992," 176–177.
17. Bertil Lintner, "The Secret Mover," FEER 155.18 (7 May 1992): 20; Steinberg, "Myanmar in 1992," 176–178.
18. Mary P. Callahan, *Making Enemies: War and State Building in Burma* (Singapore: Singapore University Press, 2004): 217; Mary P. Callahan, "Cracks in the Edifice? Military–Society Relations in Burma Since 1988," in Robert H. Taylor (ed.), *Burma: Political Economy Under Military Rule* (London: Hurst & Co., 2001): 39; GUK, 22 November 2001.
19. BBCN, 10 March 2002; 12 March 2002; 15 September 2002; GUK, 27 September 2002.
20. Larry Jagan, "Behind Burma's Non-Coup," BBCN, 18 March 2002; DVB, 22 September 2002.
21. Jonathan Head, "Burma Promises Free Elections," BBCN, 30 August 2003; Larry Jagan, "Cabinet Reshuffle in Burma," BBCN, 25 August 2003; BBCN, 15 August 2003.
22. DVB, 25 October 2004; Tony Cheng, "Burma Crackdown on Luxury Cars," BBCN, 11 November 2004.
23. *NYT*, 20 October 2004; BBCN, 22 October 2004; DVB, 21 October 2004; 23 October 2004; 24 October 2004; 26 October 2004; 5 November 2004; 8 November 2004; 11 November 2004.

24. BBCN, 18 November 2004; DVB, 23 October 2004; 9 February 2005; 10 February 2005; 11 February 2005; 12 July 2005; 22 July 2005.

25. Robin Pauley, "US Senate Takes Lead," *FT*, 25 May 1990, 6; Ian Rodger, "Japan Recognizes Burmese Regime," *FT*, 18 February 1989, 3; *Times*, 5 November 1988; Martin Smith, "Bonn Ties Burma Aid to Reform," GUK, 2 November 1988.

26. RHS, 31 October, 30 November 1988, BBCSWB.

27. Roger Matthews, "Burmese Regime to Start Opening Schools," *FT*, 10 May 1989, 4; Chit Tun, "US Companies in Burma Deals," *FT*, 27 September 1989, 7; Pauley, "US Senate Takes Lead," 6; Ian Rodger, "Japan Recognizes Burmese Regime," *FT*, 18 February 1989, 3; *NYT*, 2 April 1996; 26 April 1996; 11 July 1996; *IHT*, 16 July 1996.

28. Terry McCarthy, "Aung San Appeals to Burmese Army," *Independent*, 19 April 1989, 12; *Independent*, 2 June 1989; *NYT*, 2 April 1995; 26 April 1996; 11 July 1996; Michael Richardson, "Is it Possible to Pressure Burma?," *IHT*, 16 July 1996.

29. Michael Richardson, "ASEAN Weighs Moves Against Abuses in Burma," *IHT*, 31 March 1992; S. Kamaluddin, "The Arakan Exodus," *FEER* 155.12 (26 March 1992): 25.

30. Rodney Tasker, "Drive Against Karen Rebels," *FEER* 155.13 (2 April 1992): 11.

31. Richardson, "ASEAN Weighs Moves Against Abuses in Burma"; Michael Vatikiotis and Paul Handley, "Anxious Neighbors," *FEER* 155.12 (26 March 1992): 27–28.

32. Michael Richardson, "A Green Light for Burma to Join ASEAN's Ranks," *IHT*, 25 January 1997; Brian Knowlton, "Albright says Regime Continues Repression," *IHT*, 23 April 1997; Executive Order 13047 of May 20, 1997, *Federal Register* 62.99 (22 May 1997); *NYT*, 23 April 1997.

33. BBCN, 29 July 2003; Larry Jagan, "US Sanctions hit Burma Hard," BBCN, 3 October 2003; *Irrawaddy*, 2 August 1006.

34. Larry Jagan, "Indian and Burmese Forces Bond Afresh," BBCN, 7 December 2001.

35. BBCN, 11 December 2001; *Irrawaddy*, 4 August 2006.

36. BBCN, 10 February 2001; 11 December 2001; 21 January 2002; 16 May 2002; Larry Jagan, "Burma Announces Nuclear Plans," BBCN, 11 January 2002.

37. Josef Silverstein, "For Burma's Minorities, a Reckoning," *IHT*, 25 December 1993; Smith, *Burma: Insurgency and the Politics of Ethnicity*, 440.

38. *NYT*, 28 January 1995; *The Independent*, 30 January 1995; Bertil Lintner, "Loss and Exile," *FEER* 158.9 (2 March 1995): 23.

39. *NYT*, 15 July 1994; 5 March 1996; *The Independent*, 25 August 1995; Bertil Lintner, "The Noose Tightens," *FEER* 158.42 (19 October 1995): 30; Bertil Lintner, "Dangerous Play," *FEER* 158.10 (9 March 1995): 26; *NYT*, 5 March 1996; Smith, *Burma: Insurgency and the Politics of Ethnicity*, 440, 447. Additional helpful comments were provided by one of the anonymous referees.

40. Silverstein, "Minority Problems in Burma Since 1962," 51; Callahan, *Making Enemies*, 224–225.
41. Larry Jagan, "Burma's Military: Purges and Coups Prevent Progress Toward Democracy," in Trevor Wilson (ed.), *Myanmar's Long Road to National Reconciliation* (Singapore: ISEAS, 2006): 35.
42. DVB, 1 February 2002; 3 July 2003; Steinberg, *Burma: The State of Myanmar*, 110.
43. Steinberg, *Burma: The State of Myanmar*, 110; DVB, 3 July 2003.
44. DVB, 20 April 2005; 24 May 2005; 17 October 2005; 27 October 2005; 4 November 2005.
45. Aung Lwin Oo, "Report Spotlights USDA's Political Ambitions," *Irrawaddy*, 30 May 2006.
46. Myanmar State Television, 10 November 2005, BBCSWB.
47. *NYT*, 21 March 1990; Roger Matthews, "Burmese Announce Plans for a Super City," *FT*, 25 April 1990; RHS, 23 October 1988, 11 January 1989, 29 April 1990, BBCSWB.
48. RHS, 2 April 1990, BBCSWB; Matthews, "Burmese Announce Plans for a Super City"; Donald M. Seekins, *Burma and Japan Since 1940: From "Co-Prosperity" to "Quiet Dialogue"* (Copenhagen: NIAS, 2007): 117.
49. DVB, 15 June 2005; BBCN, 6 November 2005.
50. BBCN, 17 February 2005; 6 November 2005; 7 November 2005; DVB, 6 November 2005; 7 November 2005; Jan McGirk, "Burma's Rulers Take the Road to Mandalay," *The Independent*, 8 November 2005.
51. Seth Mydans, "Myanmar Constitution Guidelines Ensure Military Power," *NYT*, 4 September 2007; *Xinhua News Service* (English), 3 December 2007; Katerina Ossenova, "Myanmar Constitution to be drafted solely by government-appointed panel," *Jurist*, 3 December 2007.
52. Jonathan Head, "The Hardship that Sparked Burma's Unrest," *BBCN*, 2 October 2007.
53. Callahan, "Cracks in the Edifice?" 47.
54. Seth Mydans, "What Makes a Monk Mad," *NYT*, 30 September 2007; Seth Mydans, "Myanmar Monks' Protest Contained by Junta's Forces," *NYT*, 28 September 2007; "Myanmar Quashes Fuel Ration Cut Rumors," GUK, 1 January 2008; "Timeline – A Timeline Charting Myanmar's Fuel Protests," *Reuters*, 31 August 2007; Head, "The Hardship that Sparked Burma's Unrest."
55. Patrick Pranke, "Religion and Politics in Burma: The Use of Buddhist Symbolism in the Burmese Democracy Movement," Center for Asian Democracy Speaker Series, University of Louisville, 15 November 2007; Mydans, "What Makes a Monk Mad."
56. Michael W. Charney, "Burma: The History Behind the Protests," *New Statesman* (online), 26 September 2007.
57. Pranke, "Religion and Politics in Burma"; Mydans, "Myanmar Monks' Protest Contained by Junta's Forces"; Seth Mydans, "Myanmar Raids Monasteries Before Dawn," NYT, 27 September 2007.

58. Michael W. Charney, "Buddha's Irresistible Maroon Army," *Times*, 14 December 2007.

59. Pranke, "Religion and Politics in Burma"; Chris McGreal, "Spies, Suspicion and Empty Monasteries – Burma Today," GUK, 15 December 2007; Aung Hla Tun, "Myanmar Monks March Again, U.N. Envoy Due Back," *Reuters*, 31 October 2007; Personal communications from informants living in Burma who must remain anonymous.

60. Charney, "Burma: The History Behind the Protests"; "The Saffron Revolution," *The Economist*, 27 September 2007.

CONCLUSION

1. Tin Maung Maung Than, "The Essential Tension: Democratization and the Unitary State in Myanmar (Burma)," *South East Asia Research* 12.2 (July 2004): 188–189.

2. Despite the arbitrary nature of the division of highland Burma into "states" as opposed to lowland "divisions," they nonetheless contributed to the notion of these areas as "nation-states." Rachel M. Safman, "Minorities and State-building in Mainland Southeast Asia," in N. Ganesan and Kyaw Yin Hlaing (eds.), *Myanmar: State, Society and Ethnicity* (Singapore: ISEAS, 2007): 55.

3. Seekins, *Burma and Japan Since 1940: From "Co-Prosperity" to "Quiet Dialogue"* (Copenhagen: NIAS, 2007): 25.

4. Kyaw Yin Hlaing, "Reconsidering the Failure of the Burma Socialist Program Party Government to Eradicate Internal Economic Impediments," *South East Asia Research* 11.1 (March 2003): 5–58.

Readings

Although Burma is often referred to as being understudied, there is actually a substantial body of literature available for the interested reader. Good general works that cover the breadth of modern Burmese history are the old standard John F. Cady, *A History of Modern Burma* (Ithaca, NY: Cornell University Press, 1958) and the more recent Thant Myint-U, *The River of Lost Footsteps: Histories of Burma* (New York: Farrar, Straus and Giroux, 2006). The standard study of the Burmese state throughout most of the period examined in the present volume remains Robert H. Taylor, *The State in Burma* (Honolulu, HI: University of Hawaii Press, 1987). For the ethnic insurgencies, the two main works are Martin Smith, *Burma: Insurgency and the Politics of Ethnicity*, 2nd edition (London: Zed Books, 1999) and Bertil Lintner, *Burma in Revolt: Opium and Insurgency since 1948* (Boulder, CO: Westview Press, 1994). A good reference work complementing the aforementioned books is Donald M. Seekins, *Historical Dictionary of Burma (Myanmar)* (Oxford: The Scarecrow Press, 2006).

Works (including some fiction) more circumspect in their periodization are listed below according to the most appropriate chapter and topic. In a limited list such as this it is not possible to include anything but a small representative sample.

BURMA UNDER COLONIAL RULE

Adas, Michael, *The Burma Delta: Economic Development and Social Change on an Asian Rice Frontier, 1852–1941* (Madison, WI: University of Wisconsin Press, 1974).

Brown, Ian, *A Colonial Economy in Crisis: Burma's Rice Cultivators and the World Depression of the 1930s* (London: RoutledgeCurzon, 2005).

Cheng Siok-Hwa, *The Rice Industry of Burma, 1852–1940* (Kuala Lumpur: University of Malaya Press, 1968).

Ghosh, Parimal, *Brave Men of the Hills: Resistance and Rebellion in Burma, 1825–1932* (Honolulu, HI: University of Hawaii Press, 2000).

Richell, Judith L., *Disease and Demography in Colonial Burma* (Copenhagen: NIAS Press, 2006).

Scott, James C., *The Moral Economy of the Peasant: Rebellion and Subsistence in Southeast Asia* (New Haven, CT: Yale University Press, 1976).

THE COLONIAL CENTRE

Bhattacharya, [Chakraborti], Swapna, *India–Myanmar Relations, 1886–1948* (Kolkata: K P Bagchi & Co., 2007).

Christian, John LeRoy, *Modern Burma* (New York: Institute of Pacific Relations, 1942).

Furnivall, J. S., *Colonial Policy and Practice: A Comparative Study of Burma and Netherlands India* (Cambridge: Cambridge University Press, 1948).

Larkin, Emma, "The Self-Conscious Censor: Censorship Under the British, 1900–1939," *Journal of Burma Studies* 8 (2003): 64–101.

Orwell, George, *Burmese Days* (San Diego, CA: Harcourt Brace, n.d.).

Pearn, B. R., *History of Rangoon* (Rangoon: American Baptist Mission Press, 1939).

Pham, Julie, "Ghost Hunting in Colonial Burma: Nostalgia, Paternalism and the Thoughts of J. S. Furnivall," *South East Asia Research* 12.2 (July 2004): 237–268.

SELF-GOVERNMENT WITHOUT INDEPENDENCE, 1937–1947

Ba Maw, *Breakthrough in Burma: Memoirs of a Revolution* (New Haven, CT: Yale University Press, 1968).

Bayly, Christopher and Tim Harper, *Forgotten Armies: The Fall of British Asia 1941–1945* (London: Allen Lane, 2004).

Kratoska, Paul H. (ed.), *The Thailand–Burma Railway, 1942–1946*, 6 vols. (New York: Routledge, 2006).

McEnery, John H., *Epilogue in Burma 1945–1948* (Bangkok: White Lotus, 2000).

Nemoto, Kei (ed.), *Reconsidering the Japanese Military Occupation in Burma (1942–45)* (Tokyo: Tokyo University of Foreign Studies, Research Institute for Languages and Cultures of Asia and Africa, 2007).

Singh, Balwant, *Independence & Democracy in Burma, 1945–1952: The Turbulent Years* (Ann Arbor, MI: University of Michigan Centers for South and Southeast Asian Studies, 1993).

Tamayama, Kazuo, *Railwaymen in the War: Tales by Japanese Railway Soldiers in Burma and Thailand 1941–47* (Houndmills: Palgrave Macmillan, 2005).

Tarling, Nicholas, *A Sudden Rampage: The Japanese Occupation of Southeast Asia, 1941–1945* (London: Hurst & Co., 2001).

THE DEMOCRATIC EXPERIMENT, 1948–1958 & DRESS REHEARSALS, 1958–1962

Butwell, Richard, *U Nu of Burma* (Stanford, CA: Stanford University Press, 1968).

Callahan, Mary, *Making Enemies: War and State Building in Burma* (Singapore: Singapore University Press, 2004).

Mendelson, E. Michael, *Sangha and State in Burma: A Study of Monastic Sectarianism and Leadership* (Ithaca, NY: Cornell University Press, 1975).

U Nu, *U Nu Saturday's Son*, translated by U Law Yone (New Haven, CT: Yale University Press, 1975).

U Sein Win, *The Split Story: An Account of Recent Political Upheaval in Burma* (Rangoon: The Guardian Press, 1959).

Tinker, Hugh, *The Union of Burma* (London: Oxford University Press, 1957).

Walinsky, Louis, *Economic Development in Burma 1951–1960* (New York: Twentieth Century Fund, 1962).

THE REVOLUTIONARY COUNCIL

Cady, John F., *The United States and Burma* (Cambridge, MA: Harvard University Press, 1976).

Maung Maung, *Burma and General Ne Win* (London: Asia Publishing House, 1969).

Seekins, Donald M., *The Disorder of Order: The Army-State in Burma Since 1962* (Bangkok: White Lotus, 2002).

Smith, Donald Eugene, *Religion and Politics in Burma* (Princeton, NJ: Princeton University Press, 1965).

Steinberg, David I., *Burma's Road to Development: Growth and Ideology Under Military Rule* (Boulder, CO: Westview Press, 1981).

U Thaung, *A Journalist, a General and an Army in Burma* (Bangkok: White Lotus, 1995).

THE BSPP YEARS

Kyaw Yin Hlaing, "Reconsidering the Failure of the Burma Socialist Program Party Government to Eradicate Internal Economic Impediments," *South East Asia Research* 11.1 (March 2003): 5–58.

Lehman, F. K. (ed.), *Military Rule in Burma Since 1962* (Singapore: Maruzen Asia, 1981).

Smith, Charles B., *The Burmese Communist Party in the 1980s* (Singapore: Institute of Southeast Asian Studies, Regional Strategic Studies Programme, 1984).

Steinberg, David I., *Burma: A Socialist Nation of Southeast Asia* (Boulder, CO: Westview Press, 1982).

TOWARD DEMOCRACY, 1988–1990

Aung San Suu Kyi, *Freedom from Fear and Other Writings* (London: Penguin Books, 1991).

Lintner, Bertil, *Outrage: Burma's Struggle for Democracy* (Bangkok: White Lotus, 1990).

—, *The Rise and Fall of the Communist Party of Burma (CPB)* (Ithaca, NY: Cornell University Southeast Asia Program, 1990).

Maung Maung, *The 1988 Uprising in Burma* (New Haven, CT: Yale University Southeast Asia Studies, 1999).

PERPETUAL DELAY, 1990 TO THE PRESENT

Carey, Peter (ed.), *Burma: The Challenge of Change in a Divided Society*, foreword by Aung San Suu Kyi (Houndmills: Macmillan, 1997).

Fink, Christina, *Living Silence: Burma under Military Rule* (Bangkok: White Lotus, 2001).

Rotberg, Robert I. (ed.), *Burma: Prospects for a Democratic Future* (Washington, DC: Brookings Institution Press, 1998).

Seekins, Donald M., *Burma and Japan Since 1940: From 'Co-Prosperity' to 'Quiet Dialogue'* (Copenhagen: NIAS, 2007).

Selth, Andrew, *Burma's Armed Forces: Power Without Glory* (Norwalk, CT: East-Bridge, 2002).

Skidmore, Monique (ed.), *Burma: At the Turn of the 21st Century* (Honolulu, HI: University of Hawaii Press, 2005).

South, Ashley, *Mon Nationalism and Civil War in Burma: The Golden Sheldrake* (London: RoutledgeCurzon, 2003).

Steinberg, David I., *Burma: The State of Myanmar* (Washington, DC: Georgetown University Press, 2001).

Taylor, Robert H. (ed.), *Burma: Political Economy Under Military Rule* (London: Hurst & Co., 2001).

Tucker, Shelby, *Burma: The Curse of Independence* (London: Pluto Press, 2001).

Index

234